Settele
Tutoring

When it comes to your scores,
don't settle for less…

Settele for more!

W9-AGY-523

SAT® Reading & Writing Packets

Practice Materials and Study Guide for the
SAT Evidence-Based Reading and Writing Sections

By Mike Settele

Los Angeles, CA

www.setteletutoring.com

2020 Edition

Settele
Tutoring

Published by Settele Tutoring
For permissions and other inquiries, contact by email at mike@setteletutoring.com

The SAT® is a trademark registered by the College Board, which is not affiliated with, and does not endorse, this product.

Note: All Khan Academy content is available for free at (www.khanacademy.org). Khan Academy is not affiliated with, and does not endorse, this product.

This publication is designed to help students improve on the SAT. However, nothing in this publication should be construed as a guarantee of score improvement.

ISBN-13: 978-1697714203

Thank you for purchasing!

I strongly believe that everyone should be able to achieve their best scores, and the cost of test prep should not limit any student's potential. I'm grateful that you've chosen Settele Tutoring to help you reach your goals.

If you received this copy of the SAT Reading & Writing Packets from a friend or other source, please consider purchasing your own copy at:

www.setteletutoring.com

Purchasing this book supports a small business and helps me produce more practice materials. Creating these packets required a lot of effort, but my goal is to keep the price low so that more students can benefit from using them. At the same time, I have plenty of free test prep resources available on my website and social media. Subscribe and follow for more!

YouTube.com/SetteleTutoring

Instagram @SetteleTutoring

Twitter @SetteleTutoring

Facebook @SetteleTutoring

Email mike@setteletutoring.com

Author's Note

Dear Hardworking Student,

Thanks for buying my book! I hope it helps you improve your scores, not only by teaching you the topics tested on the SAT, but also by boosting your confidence in yourself.

I've been an SAT and ACT tutor since 2006, and I consistently find that students tend to be overwhelmed and intimidated by the standardized testing process. The scope of the exams is massive, and the pressure to succeed is intense. Maybe it's the stress, maybe it's the wording of the questions, but something about the SAT makes students doubt themselves. They feel like there's just too much that they don't know. But let me be clear — **you're smarter than you think you are**.

In fact, this book wasn't designed to teach you anything new. Instead, it's meant to remind you of what you already know. Still, I've included several test-taking strategies to help you apply your knowledge to the weird world of the SAT. This test is absolutely trying to trick you. But once you learn to see through their traps and disguises, you'll be able to solve and answer with confidence.

I also recommend purchasing *The Official SAT Study Guide* and registering for free SAT prep on the Khan Academy website. Both are great resources, but they can be just as overwhelming and intimidating as the SAT itself if you don't know where to start. This book will help you sort through it all, and you can get even more practice and advice by connecting with me on social media. I post an SAT or ACT question on Instagram every day, and my YouTube channel has free, comprehensive lessons. As much as possible, test prep should be affordable and accessible. By purchasing this book, you're supporting my efforts to create more free content. I also offer a limited amount of private online tutoring for students who need help with particular packets or want a personalized program for all subjects on the SAT or ACT. Please visit my website to book sessions.

Once again, thank you for purchasing this book. I wish you the best of luck in your studying and on the test!

Sincerely,

Mike Settele
Settele Tutoring
mike@setteletutoring.com
www.setteletutoring.com

Table of Contents

Introduction

This study guide is a little different than other practice materials, so don't just dive into the lessons. Take a few minutes to read this introduction so that you know what you're getting into. It's better to have a plan!

What are "Packets"?

introduction

The Basics

Think of this book as a collection of tiny "packets" of SAT Reading & Writing information. Each packet is designed to be a miniature lesson on one very specific topic. Here's how you should work on each packet:

1. Read **The Basics** to learn the most essential information that you'll need for that topic.

2. Work on the basic **Examples**, which will help you practice that topic with relatively straightforward questions.

3. Read **The Twists** to learn how the SAT makes that topic more difficult.

4. Work on the twisted **Examples**, which will help you practice avoiding the SAT's tricks and traps.

5. Compare the basic and twisted Examples to find the **patterns** for that topic. What makes the questions similar? How did the SAT try to disguise the topic so that you'd be more confused? How did you "untwist" the hard questions to get back to basics?

6. Use the **Exercise** to continue practicing. Keep looking for patterns that make the questions similar, even when they seem very different.

Narrow Your Focus

The whole point of these packets is to help you NARROW YOUR FOCUS as much as possible. Each packet lets you see several questions of the same type in a row, which means that you can practice one topic without interruption. You're much more likely to learn a pattern for a topic when you're not distracted by everything else on the SAT.

In general, NARROW YOUR FOCUS is an important idea on the SAT. If studying is stressing you out, NARROW YOUR FOCUS to one packet at a time. If a question is confusing you, NARROW YOUR FOCUS to the most important information.

The Twists

In some ways, the packets in this book are similar to the chapters that you'd find in any other test prep guide — they break the test down into more manageable pieces. However, there are two key differences between this book and most others:

1. **Much Less Reading** — Most test prep guides have a lot of text, which can be overwhelming. My packets only have a few sentences of guidance before the Examples. That's because you need to get in the habit of trusting yourself. You're smarter than you think you are! Through English class in school, you've already learned pretty much everything you need for the SAT, so use the Examples to see how much you remember. These are just practice questions, so don't be afraid to try something and fail. When you've found an answer, go to the **detailed Lesson in the back of the book** to see if you're right and to learn the best way to solve the question. Many students struggle with the SAT because they have a bad habit of giving up on questions without really trying them. My packets are designed to help you form the good habit of trying something — anything! — on questions that seem confusing.

2. **Much Less Grammar** — Most study guides just repeat the same-old, complicated, grammatical explanations that you've already heard from your teachers. They use too many technical terms that make the rules hard to understand. In fact, the SAT doesn't even test all of the rules and terms that other guides think you should know. **This guide tries to avoid grammar terms unless they're absolutely necessary for understanding a rule.** And since the SAT doesn't test every single grammar rule you've learned in school, the packets will give you the situations that are most likely to appear on the test so that you can NARROW YOUR FOCUS to the ideas that matter most.

Reading Packets

POE	**LR**	line reference
	noLR	no line reference
	WP	whole passage
	both	both passages
evidence	**evU**	unpaired evidence
	ev1	evidence pairs (part 1)
	ev2	evidence pairs (part 2)
quick	**Rvoc**	reading vocab
	Rfig	reading figures

Reading Passages

According to the College Board, the SAT Reading section consists of 5 passages:

- 1 literature (classic or contemporary)
- 1 Great Global Conversations (founding document or speech)
- 1 social sciences (psychology, economics, sociology, etc.)
- 2 natural sciences (biology, chemistry, physics, Earth science, etc.)

Some tutors put a lot of emphasis on the differences between the passages. However, the questions for each passage are basically the same. **Notice that the Packets are focused on different types of questions, not the types of passages.**

Some students will decide to tweak their Reading strategy, depending on the type of passage. But the division that really matters has less to do with the subject matter and more to do with the year that the piece was written:

- **1 or 2 "old-timey" passages**
  - typically written before 1900
  - literature and/or Great Global Conversations
- **3 or 4 "modern" passages**
  - typically from journals or magazines from the past 20 years
  - science passages

Typical SAT Reading Section

No two SATs will be exactly the same, but there are still general trends. The chart below represents the average breakdown of the 52 questions on the Reading section of the SAT.

There is tremendous variability on the questions and passages, which is why the Reading section tends to be the most inconsistent from test to test. In other words, there's a good chance that you get a passage on your actual SAT that surprises you. The best way to manage the variability is to study the strategies — they work for every conceivable passage! For this reason, the Reading questions are <u>not</u> grouped by topic or passage type. They are organized by strategy.

Reading	LR	LR	LR	LR
noLR	noLR	noLR	LR	LR	LR
noLR	noLR	WP	WP	WP	WP
ev1	ev1	ev1	both	both	both
ev1	ev1	ev2	ev2	ev2	evU
ev1	ev1	ev2	ev2	ev2	evU
ev1	ev1	ev2	ev2	ev2	Rfig
Rvoc	Rvoc	Rvoc	Rvoc	Rfig	Rfig
Rvoc	Rvoc	Rvoc	Rvoc	Rfig	Rfig

Writing Packets

ideas	**goal**	accomplish the goal
	AD	add or delete
	trans	transitions
	comb	combine sentences
	place	sentence placement
	Wfig	writing figures
punctuation	**comma**	general comma rules
	apstv	appositives
	list	lists & examples
	apost	apostrophes
	punc+	advanced punctuation
	FRO	fragments & run-ons
consistency	**pron**	pronouns
	verb	verb agreement
	sym	symmetry
	mod	modifiers
style	**conc**	concision
	Wvoc	writing vocab
	dict	diction
	FCW	frequently confused words

Writing Passages

The College Board says that the topics of the SAT Writing section passages are:

- careers
- history
- social studies
- humanities
- science

But it could not matter less! The topics of the passages are irrelevant. Focus on the individual questions. If they're about grammar, the topic of the passage will not affect your answer. If they're about the Ideas in the passage, the question itself will tell you what to care about.

Typical SAT Writing Section

No two SATs will be exactly the same, but there are still general trends. The chart below represents the average breakdown of the 44 questions on the Writing section of the SAT.

As you can see, some packets are more important than others. Still, each question is worth about 5 points, so even the minor grammar rules can add up to significant improvement. For example, if you study Pronouns so that you get those questions right every time, you're essentially guaranteeing yourself 10 points on every SAT. Since grammar rules don't really change, the Writing section tends to be the most consistent section from one SAT to the next. In fact, Writing can be even more formulaic than Math.

Writing				goal	goal
goal	goal	goal	goal	goal	goal
AD	AD	trans	trans	trans	comb
comma	Wfig	Wfig	place	place	comb
apstv	punc+	pron	pron	conc	conc
list	punc+	verb	verb	Wvoc	Wvoc
apost	punc+	sym	sym	Wvoc	FCW
FRO	FRO	sym	mod	dict	dict

Practice Tests

introduction

The Basics

These packets are comprehensive, but they're not meant to be the only study tool that you use. I strongly recommend that you purchase *The Official SAT Study Guide*. It contains 8 practice tests made by the same people who make the real SAT. Most of the 8 tests are also available for free on The College Board and Khan Academy websites (plus an additional 2 tests), but you should print them out if you can. The real SAT is a pencil-and-paper exam, and you should take practice tests the same way so that you can show your work and cross off answers.

But don't just dive into the practice tests without a plan. They are a limited resource, so use them sparingly! Use my packets to learn and practice specific topics, and save the official exams to diagnose weaknesses and to practice enduring a 4-hour test. Here's my recommendation:

The 2 to 3 Plan

- Start practicing 2-3 months before test day.

- Take a practice test every 2-3 weeks.

- Practice for an additional 2-3 hours per week.

It's important that you create a test prep schedule and stick to it. I know that full-length practice tests are long and boring, but you have to do them. You have to build your endurance. Every 2 to 3 weeks, you need to set aside several hours to take a practice test in one sitting, just like the real SAT. To make it easier, I've made a timer video that will proctor the test for you. It will announce the time remaining in the sections and give you breaks so that you can focus on taking the test. Subscribe to my YouTube channel or visit my website for the timers:

www.setteletutoring.com/SATtimer

www.youtube.com/SetteleTutoring

The Twists

After you take a practice test, you need to make sure that you're learning from your mistakes. You can use Khan Academy or the College Board's SAT phone app to easily score the tests and get feedback. But you should also use these packets! Here's how:

Start your prep with a full-length practice test. Don't worry about the scores. Think of it like the PSAT — it's just to see where you're starting from. Compare your answers to the charts on the next page, which give the packet category for every question on the 8 official practice tests. Choose the 5 topics that you had the most difficulty with and work on the corresponding packets. Don't try to do too much. NARROW YOUR FOCUS and you're more likely to learn from your mistakes.

Take another full-length practice test 2 to 3 weeks later. Review your answers the same way. Compare your answers to the charts, and work on the 5 packets that you had the most difficulty with. Repeat this process right up until the real test. If you need more practice with a packet that you've already completed, use the Khan Academy website.

Notes on the Test Numbers

As of October 2019, the College Board has released 10 official practice exams. However, they are not all found in the same places. Here's where to find each test, as of October 2019:

Test #	Official SAT Study Guide		Online	
	2018 edition	2020 edition	CB website	Khan Academy
1	✔	✔	✔	✔
2	✔		✔	✔
3	✔	✔	✔	✔
4	✔		✔	✔
5	✔	✔	✔	✔
6	✔	✔	✔	✔
7	✔	✔	✔	✔
8	✔	✔	✔	✔
9		✔	✔	✔
10		✔	✔	✔

Scoring Your Test

Unfortunately, the College Board does not make scoring tests easy. They want you to use their *Daily Practice for the New SAT* app. I do recommend downloading the app on your phone since it works pretty well. You can take pictures of your practice test answer forms, and the app will automatically score the test for you. However, there are a lot of reasons you might want to score your practice tests manually. For one, the app can be glitchy, and it might not accept the pictures if they're not great quality. But also, many students like to ask, "what if?" You might check over a Writing section and notice that you made 5 careless mistakes. What if you had gotten those five questions right? The app doesn't let you easily understand how your mistakes can improve your score. For comprehensive scoring tables, visit:

https://collegereadiness.collegeboard.org/sat/practice/full-length-practice-tests

Pacing

One of the most important reasons to take practice tests is so you can get used to the correct pacing for the Reading and Writing sections. Some students have no problem reading all five Reading passages and answering all of the questions. But many students have to rush through the final passage, and others never even get to it.

On your first practice test, make a note of how many questions you didn't get to because you ran out of time. **If you only left 1-5 questions blank, you should have no problem finishing the Reading section by the time you get to the real exam.** The strategies in this study guide will help you move faster, especially the No Reading strategy. Just keep practicing, and don't be afraid to "guess and go" when you hit a hard question.

If you're leaving more than 5 questions blank, you might have a bigger problem. The strategies will definitely speed you up, but you might also be a naturally slow reader. **On the SAT, you cannot afford to read and reread and reread again.** You need to keep moving.

Perfectionists lose a lot of time because they can't let go. They feel like they need to thoroughly answer every question. This is a bad habit! Even I don't do this! With the strategies and rules, you can get better at picking out wrong answers. But occasionally, you'll get down to two choices that look almost identical. **Sometimes you just need to guess.** It's better to risk getting that one question wrong than to waste 5 minutes trying to get it right. If you run out of time and leave questions blank, then you've lost more points than the question was worth.

If you're running out of time with two or more passages left to go, then you might have a problem that goes well beyond the SAT. The College Board does offer extra time accommodations to some students. You need a lot of documentation from your school and from doctors, but it might be worth pursuing. Talk to your school counselor about getting tested for extra time. This process takes many months, so do not procrastinate.

SAT Practice Test 1

Sect. 1	#	Sect. 2	Sect. 1	#	Sect. 2
WP	1	Wvoc	LR	27	trans
WP	2	goal	Rfig	28	AD
Rvoc	3	apost	Rfig	29	Wfig
ev1	4	list	Rfig	30	verb
ev2	5	place	Rfig	31	place
noLR	6	AD	WP	32	punc+
LR	7	dict	WP	33	Wvoc
Rvoc	8	sym	WP	34	trans
ev1	9	trans	noLR	35	conc
ev2	10	Wvoc	ev1	36	sym
LR	11	FRO	ev2	37	goal
Rvoc	12	Wfig	ev1	38	trans
ev1	13	comb	ev2	39	comb
ev2	14	trans	LR	40	verb
LR	15	apstv	LR	41	apost
ev1	16	FRO	LR	42	AD
ev2	17	FRO	ev1	43	FRO
Rvoc	18	sym	ev2	44	pron
LR	19	pron	Rvoc	45	
Rfig	20	goal	LR	46	
Rfig	21	conc	WP	47	
LR	22	place	Rvoc	48	
evU	23	conc	both	49	
LR	24	mod	ev1	50	
noLR	25	dict	ev2	51	
LR	26	list	both	52	

SAT Practice Test 2

Sect. 1	#	Sect. 2	Sect. 1	#	Sect. 2
WP	1	FCW	noLR	27	comma
LR	2	trans	LR	28	Wvoc
LR	3	verb	both	29	pron
LR	4	AD	both	30	pron
noLR	5	conc	both	31	place
ev1	6	sym	evU	32	dict
ev2	7	comb	WP	33	apstv
LR	8	FRO	LR	34	dict
ev1	9	goal	ev1	35	punc+
ev2	10	Wvoc	ev2	36	Wvoc
WP	11	goal	Rvoc	37	goal
ev1	12	trans	LR	38	FCW
ev2	13	apstv	Rvoc	39	FRO
Rvoc	14	punc+	ev1	40	trans
LR	15	AD	ev2	41	dict
Rvoc	16	FRO	LR	42	place
evU	17	goal	LR	43	AD
LR	18	comb	Rvoc	44	trans
Rfig	19	goal	ev1	45	
Rfig	20	apost	ev2	46	
Rfig	21	mod	Rvoc	47	
ev1	22	place	ev1	48	
ev2	23	FRO	ev2	49	
noLR	24	Wfig	Rfig	50	
Rvoc	25	trans	Rfig	51	
noLR	26	AD	Rfig	52	

Number Wrong Per Reading Passage

1	modern literature	#1-10	_____ ✗
2	modern science	#11-21	_____ ✗
3	modern science	#22-31	_____ ✗
4	old-timey GGC	#32-41	_____ ✗
5	modern science double	#42-52	_____ ✗

Number Wrong Per Reading Passage

1	old-timey literature	#1-10	_____ ✗
2	modern science	#11-21	_____ ✗
3	modern science double	#22-32	_____ ✗
4	old-timey GGC	#33-42	_____ ✗
5	modern science	#43-52	_____ ✗

Note on Tests 1-4: These were the first four tests released by the College Board ahead of the new SAT in 2016. In my opinion, they are not as perfectly polished as Tests 5-10. Test 4, in particular, has a lot of quirky questions and a highly unusual emphasis on Exponential Models for Math. **If you want to practice taking sections without timing yourself, I recommend using Tests 1-4.**

SAT Practice Test 3

Sect. 1	#	Sect. 2	Sect. 1	#	Sect. 2
WP	1	sym	noLR	27	FRO
Rvoc	2	goal	Rvoc	28	sym
ev1	3	AD	ev1	29	punc+
ev2	4	apost	ev2	30	place
LR	5	verb	Rvoc	31	Wfig
Rvoc	6	goal	ev1	32	Wfig
noLR	7	comb	ev2	33	goal
noLR	8	conc	noLR	34	FRO
ev1	9	trans	Rvoc	35	punc+
ev2	10	FRO	ev1	36	verb
LR	11	dict	ev2	37	goal
ev1	12	pron	both	38	sym
ev2	13	goal	both	39	place
ev1	14	punc+	both	40	Wvoc
ev2	15	verb	both	41	apstv
Rvoc	16	Wvoc	LR	42	goal
Rvoc	17	AD	ev1	43	AD
evU	18	conc	ev2	44	Wvoc
Rfig	19	FRO	ev1	45	
Rfig	20	goal	ev2	46	
WP	21	punc+	Rvoc	47	
Rvoc	22	AD	LR	48	
ev1	23	comb	noLR	49	
ev2	24	FRO	Rfig	50	
LR	25	Wvoc	Rfig	51	
LR	26	pron	Rfig	52	

SAT Practice Test 4

Sect. 1	#	Sect. 2	Sect. 1	#	Sect. 2
ev1	1	FRO	ev1	27	place
ev2	2	trans	ev2	28	verb
Rvoc	3	punc+	LR	29	punc+
LR	4	goal	LR	30	FCW
ev1	5	Wvoc	LR	31	Wfig
ev2	6	sym	WP	32	FCW
noLR	7	pron	Rvoc	33	goal
LR	8	comb	Rvoc	34	sym
Rvoc	9	sym	noLR	35	punc+
Rvoc	10	goal	ev1	36	punc+
LR	11	AD	ev2	37	AD
noLR	12	sym	ev1	38	goal
Rvoc	13	FRO	ev2	39	trans
ev1	14	conc	both	40	pron
ev2	15	trans	both	41	conc
ev1	16	Wvoc	WP	42	Wvoc
ev2	17	trans	ev1	43	mod
Rvoc	18	AD	ev2	44	place
Rfig	19	verb	LR	45	
Rfig	20	goal	ev1	46	
Rfig	21	verb	ev2	47	
WP	22	list	LR	48	
noLR	23	goal	evU	49	
Rvoc	24	FRO	Rfig	50	
ev1	25	goal	Rfig	51	
ev2	26	conc	Rfig	52	

Number Wrong Per Reading Passage

1	old-timey literature	#1-10	___ ✗
2	modern science	#11-20	___ ✗
3	modern science	#21-30	___ ✗
4	old-timey GGC double	#31-41	___ ✗
5	modern science	#42-52	___ ✗

Number Wrong Per Reading Passage

1	old-timey literature	#1-10	___ ✗
2	modern science	#11-21	___ ✗
3	modern science	#22-31	___ ✗
4	old-timey GGC double	#32-41	___ ✗
5	modern science	#42-52	___ ✗

GGC = Great Global Conversations

SAT Practice Test 5

Sect. 1	#	Sect. 2		Sect. 1	#	Sect. 2
WP	1	AD		ev2	27	AD
LR	2	Wvoc		LR	28	trans
LR	3	AD		Rvoc	29	FRO
ev1	4	FRO		Rfig	30	pron
ev2	5	dict		Rfig	31	pron
noLR	6	pron		WP	32	place
LR	7	place		ev1	33	Wfig
LR	8	trans		ev2	34	place
evU	9	verb		evU	35	apost
Rvoc	10	comb		noLR	36	dict
ev1	11	pron		Rvoc	37	conc
ev2	12	trans		Rvoc	38	AD
WP	13	comb		Rfig	39	Wvoc
Rvoc	14	FRO		Rfig	40	goal
Rvoc	15	comma		Rfig	41	goal
WP	16	AD		ev1	42	list
ev1	17	comma		ev2	43	trans
ev2	18	conc		Rvoc	44	mod
both	19	goal		ev1	45	
both	20	FCW		ev2	46	
both	21	sym		Rvoc	47	
Rvoc	22	Wvoc		LR	48	
noLR	23	pron		noLR	49	
ev1	24	comb		ev1	50	
ev2	25	trans		ev2	51	
ev1	26	comma		LR	52	

SAT Practice Test 6

Sect. 1	#	Sect. 2		Sect. 1	#	Sect. 2
LR	1	FRO		ev1	27	pron
Rvoc	2	comma		ev2	28	list
LR	3	comb		LR	29	punc+
evU	4	punc+		LR	30	sym
LR	5	goal		ev1	31	trans
LR	6	conc		ev2	32	Wfig
ev1	7	verb		ev1	33	FCW
ev2	8	Wvoc		ev2	34	comb
noLR	9	trans		Rvoc	35	Wvoc
noLR	10	goal		LR	36	comma
WP	11	goal		Rvoc	37	goal
ev1	12	apost		ev1	38	goal
ev2	13	trans		ev2	39	punc+
Rvoc	14	FRO		both	40	goal
LR	15	Wvoc		both	41	sym
ev1	16	AD		both	42	apost
ev2	17	comma		WP	43	trans
Rvoc	18	goal		Rvoc	44	sym
Rfig	19	FRO		ev1	45	
Rfig	20	conc		ev2	46	
Rfig	21	dict		ev1	47	
WP	22	place		ev2	48	
WP	23	goal		Rvoc	49	
noLR	24	Wvoc		LR	50	
noLR	25	Wvoc		Rfig	51	
Rvoc	26	AD		Rfig	52	

Number Wrong Per Reading Passage

1	modern literature	#1-10	_____ ✗
2	old-timey GGC double	#11-21	_____ ✗
3	modern science	#22-31	_____ ✗
4	modern science	#32-41	_____ ✗
5	modern science	#42-52	_____ ✗

Number Wrong Per Reading Passage

1	modern literature	#1-10	_____ ✗
2	modern science	#11-21	_____ ✗
3	modern science	#22-32	_____ ✗
4	old-timey GGC double	#33-42	_____ ✗
5	modern science	#43-52	_____ ✗

Note on Tests 5-8: These four tests were added to *The Official SAT Study Guide* in 2018. They are actual SAT exams that were given to real students just like you. Those students took these exams under proctored conditions, got official scores, sent those scores to colleges, and received acceptances based on those scores. For that reason, I trust Tests 5-8 more than Tests 1-4. **Save Tests 5-8 for when you need to take full exams under proctored conditions to receive reliable practice scores.**

SAT Practice Test 7

Sect. 1	#	Sect. 2		Sect. 1	#	Sect. 2
WP	1	conc		ev1	27	comma
noLR	2	FCW		ev2	28	goal
noLR	3	sym		LR	29	pron
LR	4	list		LR	30	conc
ev1	5	goal		Rvoc	31	Wvoc
ev2	6	Wvoc		Rvoc	32	punc+
LR	7	verb		ev1	33	trans
ev1	8	sym		ev2	34	comma
ev2	9	place		Rvoc	35	goal
Rvoc	10	AD		ev1	36	dict
WP	11	trans		ev2	37	dict
ev1	12	conc		both	38	trans
ev2	13	punc+		both	39	comb
LR	14	trans		both	40	goal
Rvoc	15	goal		both	41	FCW
ev1	16	comma		WP	42	place
ev2	17	conc		LR	43	FRO
Rvoc	18	Wvoc		ev1	44	goal
Rfig	19	verb		ev2	45	
Rfig	20	trans		ev1	46	
Rfig	21	Wfig		ev2	47	
WP	22	punc+		LR	48	
LR	23	trans		Rvoc	49	
ev1	24	punc+		Rfig	50	
ev2	25	AD		Rfig	51	
LR	26	sym		Rfig	52	

Number Wrong Per Reading Passage

1	old-timey literature	#1-10	_____ ✗
2	modern science	#11-21	_____ ✗
3	modern science	#22-31	_____ ✗
4	old-timey GGC double	#32-41	_____ ✗
5	modern science	#42-52	_____ ✗

SAT Practice Test 8

Sect. 1	#	Sect. 2		Sect. 1	#	Sect. 2
WP	1	trans		Rvoc	27	pron
LR	2	Wvoc		ev1	28	place
ev1	3	sym		ev2	29	comb
ev2	4	punc+		Rfig	30	FRO
ev1	5	Wfig		Rfig	31	trans
ev2	6	Wfig		LR	32	conc
noLR	7	FCW		ev1	33	goal
Rvoc	8	verb		ev2	34	trans
LR	9	Wvoc		Rvoc	35	mod
noLR	10	goal		ev1	36	goal
WP	11	FCW		ev2	37	verb
Rvoc	12	comb		Rvoc	38	conc
Rvoc	13	comma		both	39	goal
ev1	14	goal		both	40	apstv
ev2	15	goal		both	41	AD
ev1	16	FRO		WP	42	sym
ev2	17	sym		ev1	43	goal
LR	18	goal		ev2	44	comma
Rfig	19	place		LR	45	
Rfig	20	pron		LR	46	
evU	21	mod		noLR	47	
WP	22	conc		noLR	48	
WP	23	Wvoc		Rvoc	49	
evU	24	list		ev1	50	
Rvoc	25	Wfig		ev2	51	
noLR	26	dict		noLR	52	

Number Wrong Per Reading Passage

1	modern literature	#1-10	_____ ✗
2	modern science	#11-21	_____ ✗
3	modern science	#22-31	_____ ✗
4	old-timey GGC double	#32-41	_____ ✗
5	modern science	#42-52	_____ ✗

GGC = Great Global Conversations

SAT Practice Test 9

Sect. 1	#	Sect. 2	Sect. 1	#	Sect. 2
WP	1	conc	ev1	27	trans
WP	2	place	ev2	28	goal
WP	3	trans	Rfig	29	trans
ev1	4	pron	Rfig	30	punc+
ev2	5	sym	Rfig	31	sym
noLR	6	punc+	WP	32	conc
ev1	7	goal	WP	33	goal
ev2	8	comb	WP	34	AD
Rvoc	9	sym	LR	35	verb
Rvoc	10	apost	ev1	36	conc
WP	11	AD	ev2	37	trans
evU	12	FRO	noLR	38	punc+
noLR	13	comb	LR	39	sym
noLR	14	FRO	Rvoc	40	FRO
Rvoc	15	pron	ev1	41	goal
ev1	16	goal	ev2	42	Wvoc
ev2	17	FRO	LR	43	pron
Rvoc	18	Wvoc	ev1	44	goal
Rfig	19	Wfig	ev2	45	
Rfig	20	Wfig	noLR	46	
LR	21	sym	Rvoc	47	
LR	22	goal	LR	48	
evU	23	pron	both	49	
LR	24	place	both	50	
Rvoc	25	AD	ev1	51	
noLR	26	pron	ev2	52	

SAT Practice Test 10

Sect. 1	#	Sect. 2	Sect. 1	#	Sect. 2
WP	1	sym	ev2	27	Wfig
noLR	2	goal	LR	28	list
ev1	3	apstv	noLR	29	Wfig
ev2	4	comb	LR	30	goal
LR	5	goal	noLR	31	goal
noLR	6	trans	noLR	32	FCW
LR	7	mod	noLR	33	goal
noLR	8	conc	LR	34	goal
ev1	9	verb	Rvoc	35	goal
ev2	10	punc+	ev1	36	apost
WP	11	goal	ev2	37	FRO
evU	12	sym	Rvoc	38	comb
Rvoc	13	goal	both	39	punc+
LR	14	apost	both	40	apstv
ev1	15	conc	ev1	41	Wvoc
ev2	16	goal	ev2	42	conc
noLR	17	FCW	noLR	43	dict
Rvoc	18	Wvoc	LR	44	place
Rfig	19	comma	Rvoc	45	
Rfig	20	sym	evU	46	
Rfig	21	goal	ev1	47	
ev1	22	goal	ev2	48	
ev2	23	dict	Rvoc	49	
Rvoc	24	conc	Rfig	50	
Rvoc	25	punc+	Rfig	51	
ev1	26	dict	Rfig	52	

Number Wrong Per Reading Passage

1	modern literature	#1-10	_____ ✗
2	modern science	#11-20	_____ ✗
3	modern science	#21-31	_____ ✗
4	old-timey GGC	#32-42	_____ ✗
5	modern science double	#43-52	_____ ✗

Number Wrong Per Reading Passage

1	modern literature	#1-10	_____ ✗
2	modern science	#11-21	_____ ✗
3	modern science	#22-32	_____ ✗
4	old-timey GGC double	#33-42	_____ ✗
5	modern science	#43-52	_____ ✗

Note on Tests 9-10: Like Tests 5-8, these tests were official exams given to students just like you. Since they are the most recent official tests, I believe they are the most representative of the content and difficulty that you're likely to see on your own SAT. **Since I trust Tests 9-10 the most, I recommend saving them for big moments in your test prep schedule, like the halfway point and your final practice test before the real SAT.**

Additional Practice

Khan Academy

The Basics

Khan Academy is a great free resource for more practice. You can sync your PSAT and practice test scores with your account, and the website will tell you which topics to practice. The exercises will get easier or harder, depending on your skill level.

The Twists

Unfortunately, *Khan Academy's* topic categories aren't great. They mix a lot of different kinds of questions together, so it's harder to NARROW YOUR FOCUS to very specific ideas. Also, the questions don't always capture the style of SAT questions. They don't involve as many twists or tricks.

Still, *Khan Academy* is very useful if you need more practice with The Basics. Sometimes you just need to practice simple things like pronoun agreement and vocabulary. What follows is a list of the packets from this book and the *Khan Academy* categories that include similar questions.

Khan Academy Categories

- <u>Reading</u>
  - Unfortunately, *Khan Academy* only groups Reading practice by passage type, which is not helpful if you need to practice one of the question-specific strategies.
- <u>Writing Ideas</u>
  - Most **Ideas questions** are tested in the Writing and Language practice section, which separates passages by type: Argument, Informative, Narrative.
  - Additionally, these other quizzes can help:
    - **accomplish the goal**
      - style and tone
    - **transitions**
      - subordination and coordination
    - **combine sentences**
      - syntax

- <u>Punctuation</u>
  - **general comma rules**
    - within-sentence punctuation
    - sentence boundaries
  - **appositives**
    - nonrestrictive and parenthetical elements
  - **lists & examples**
    - within-sentence punctuation
    - items in a series
  - **apostrophes**
    - possessive pronouns
  - **advanced punctuation**
    - end of sentence punctuation
    - within-sentence punctuation
    - nonrestrictive and parenthetical elements
  - **fragments & run-ons**
    - sentence boundaries
- <u>Consistency</u>
  - **pronouns**
    - pronoun clarity
    - pronoun agreement
    - possessive determiners
    - noun agreement
  - **verb agreement**
    - shifts in verb, tense, and mood
    - subject-verb agreement
  - **symmetry**
    - parallel structure
    - shifts in verb, tense, and mood
    - logical comparison
  - **modifiers**
    - modifier placement
- <u>Style</u>
  - **concision**
    - precision and concision
  - **writing vocab**
    - precision and concision
  - **diction**
    - conventional expression
  - **frequently confused words**
    - frequently confused words

Social Media

The Basics

So many students start their SAT prep with high ambitions — "I'll practice everyday!" But life gets in the way, and SAT studying tends to fall to the bottom of the to-do list. Suddenly, two weeks before test day, you remember that you should probably do some practice tests or something. **The problem is that you cannot cram for the SAT**. That's why I recommend that you start consistently practicing 2 to 3 months before test day. Set a schedule and stick to it.

But without a structured prep course or regular tutoring sessions, it can be difficult to know what to do. And it's hard to get motivated on your own. That's why **I post a Daily Test Prep question or strategy every single day.** One question a day isn't much, but it's enough to remind you to do a little more on your own. And if you have trouble with that day's topic, you can use this book to seek out more practice. So use the links below to follow me!

YouTube.com/SetteleTutoring

Instagram @SetteleTutoring

Twitter @SetteleTutoring

Facebook @SetteleTutoring

Daily Test Prep Schedule
Mondays — *short FAQ videos*
Tuesdays — *Reading questions*
Wednesdays — *Writing questions*
Thursdays — *Math questions*
Fridays — *ACT-only questions*
Saturdays — *Reading vocabulary words*
Sundays — *Math vocabulary words*

The Twists

One of the benefits of social media is that it's social! If you have questions, you have lots of ways to reach out to me. My Minute Movie Monday videos are meant to concisely answer the most common SAT and ACT questions. But if you have another, ask it. Who knows? Maybe I'll turn the answer into my next video!

I also love feedback. I only have so much time to make new materials, and I want to spend it making things that you find useful. So if there's a topic you want more practice with, let me know! If there's a resource that you think is missing from the test prep world, let me know!

I've already made a video series that can help you with a few of the math topics from *SAT Math Packets Study Guide*. Many of the overall ideas apply to the Reading and Writing sections as well. Subscribe to my YouTube channel to get those five free lessons. The playlist is titled "**5 Test Prep Problems**". You'll also be notified when I make lessons for the Reading and Writing packets in this study guide.

Frequently Asked Questions

introduction

Is there a Guessing Penalty?

No. You do not lose points for wrong answers on the SAT. That's why **you should never leave an SAT question blank.**

For grammar questions on the Writing section, your best bet is to guess the shortest answer choice when you're unsure. When this rule doesn't apply or when you're in the Reading section, simply guess choice B.

Are the Questions in Order of Difficulty?

Unlike the SAT Math sections, the Reading and Writing sections are <u>not</u> in order of difficulty. **Easy and hard questions are scattered throughout each passage.** That said, the Reading passages sometimes get harder as you go. However, some students find the literature passage, which is always first, to be more difficult. Additionally, a hard passage might not have hard questions if you're careful and stick to the line references. In the case of Writing, the hardest questions usually test Consistency rules, but if you know the rules, these can actually be easy points.

Essentially, don't worry about difficulty. One of the most important strategies for the Reading and Writing sections is to **keep moving and keep trying.** If something is hard, don't get fixated on it. Eliminate what you can, and take an educated guess. There might be easier questions later that are a better use of your time. You also might understand the passage better than you think you do. Often, students feel like they're guessing on a lot of questions, but they end up getting most of their guesses right. That's because your brain is pretty good at sensing right and wrong, especially as you get better at using Process of Elimination and incorporating the SAT's rules.

Are These Real SAT Passages?

Yes and no. Most of the old-timey Reading passages in this guide are taken from classic novels or important historical documents. The SAT does the exact same thing. The science passages in this book were written by me to reflect the SAT passage style and to test the kinds of things that are asked in the SAT questions. **However, in most cases, the actual science facts are not true!** I made up whatever was necessary to test the important skills for the SAT. Do not cite these passages for any papers or essays. The SAT will always use real articles from science journals and magazines. I chose to write my own passages so that I could put all of our attention on the questions themselves. You bought this book to practice SAT questions, not to learn about science!

What's the SAT's Format?

The SAT Reading section is 65 minutes long and contains 52 questions. The questions are divided among five passages, including one double passage.

The SAT Writing and Language section is 35 minutes long and contains 44 questions. The questions are divided among four passages.

If you have more questions, just go online and look them up. It's super easy to find information about the SAT! My YouTube channel has short FAQ videos, and *The Official SAT Study Guide* will answer all of your formatting questions. You didn't buy this book to learn SAT trivia. You bought it to practice the SAT Reading and Writing. Get to work!

SAT-Specific Strategies

The Evidence-Based Reading and Writing isn't as simple as just reading passages and answering questions. This chapter provides an overview of the strategies and question types that are unique to the SAT Reading and SAT Writing and Language sections.

SAT Reading

SAT-specific strategies

The Basics

Many people think that they should read the questions first so that they know what to look for in the passage. **Reading the questions first isn't necessary.** In fact, most of the questions either give you a line reference or ask about the passage as a whole. Here's a sample set of questions from an SAT passage:

#	Question	Type
1	Over the course of the passage, the main focus shifts from a…	Whole Passage
2	The main purpose of the first paragraph is to…	Line Reference
3	It can reasonably be inferred from the description of John Reed in lines 1-7 that…	Line Reference
4	The narrator most strongly implies that John Reed is not currently at school because he…	Evidence Pair (Part 1)
5	Which choice provides the best evidence for the answer to the previous question?	Evidence Pair (Part 2)
6	The narrator indicates that she cannot prevent John from bullying because…	No Line Reference
7	As used in line 41, "retired" most nearly means…	Reading Vocab
8	It can reasonably be inferred from the passage that the main reason John Reed feels justified in his abuse of the narrator is because…	Evidence Pair (Part 1)
9	Which choice provides the best evidence for the answer to the previous question?	Evidence Pair (Part 2)
10	As used in line 72, "succeeded" most nearly means…	Reading Vocab

The Twists

So then you should read the passage first? Maybe. Everyone reads differently, and for some people, it might be advantageous to skip the passage entirely and go directly to the questions — **The No Reading Strategy**. That's what I do! Advice is below, but you may need to experiment until you find the strategy that works best for you.

Read if…	Don't read if…
average to fast reader	slow reader
good vocabulary	skipping lots of words
context = comfort	context = confusion
plenty of time	run out of time
straightforward passage	old-timey passage
whole passage or double passage question	evidence, line reference, vocab, or figure question

Narrow Your Focus

Reading passages can feel overwhelming because you have to read, understand, and recall a lot of information in a relatively short amount of time. Whether you read the passage or not, try to NARROW YOUR FOCUS as much as possible.

- Keep the main idea in mind, but stick close to line references.

- Don't bring in your own opinions or a lot of outside information.

- Base your answers on the passage.

The "No Reading" Strategy

This exercise is meant to show you what it would feel like to skip reading the passage and go directly to the questions. The questions, line references, and answer choices have been "cut out" and rearranged to force you to follow the "No Reading" strategy. Even if you decide that you prefer to read the passages, the other strategies in this section will help you adjust to the unique way the SAT asks questions.

Read the Blurb

Even though you are not reading the passage, you must **always read the blurb!** Sometimes, you get vital information about the characters or the setting. You'll often be given the relationship between the double passages. Even the title of the article can reveal something important about the main idea. Here's the blurb for this passage:

> This passage is adapted from Charlotte Bronte, *Jane Eyre*. Originally published in 1847.

It's not much to work with, but at least you have an idea who the main character might be.

Whole Passage

The first question will almost always look like this:

> **1**
>
> Over the course of the passage, the main focus shifts from a

Since you didn't read the passage, you aren't really qualified to answer this. It's okay. You'll come back to this question later, after you've answered the others. By then, you'll have read enough line references to have a much better chance of getting this right.

Even if you decide that you prefer to read the passages, you should still **save Whole Passage questions for last.** Answering the other questions will force you to reread large sections of the passage. Essentially, you'll be reading the passage a second time, making it twice as likely that you'll understand the main idea.

Line Reference

Most questions refer to a few lines in the passage. You should always work through Line Reference questions in this order:

1. **Question**
2. **Line Reference**
3. **Choices**

The **QLC Method** forces you to NARROW YOUR FOCUS to the lines the question cares about. Try it!

1. **Question** — read it and understand it

> **2**
>
> The main purpose of the first paragraph is to

2. **Line Reference** — go back to it, read it, and try to understand the gist of it

> *first paragraph*
>
> John Reed was a schoolboy of fourteen years old; four years older than I, for I was but ten: large and stout for his age, with a dingy and unwholesome skin; thick lineaments in a spacious visage, heavy limbs and large extremities. He gorged himself habitually at table, which made him bilious, and gave him a dim and bleared eye and flabby cheeks. He ought now to have been at school; but his mama had taken him home for a month or two, "on account of his delicate health." Mr. Miles, the master, affirmed that he would do very well if he had fewer cakes and sweetmeats sent him from home; but the mother's heart turned from an opinion so harsh, and inclined rather to the more refined idea that John's sallowness was owing to over-application and, perhaps, to pining after home.

3. **Choices** — read them and eliminate the wrong answers

> A) introduce a character.
> B) provide historical context.
> C) discuss the merits of education.
> D) recount a past event.

POE

You probably used some form of Process of Elimination (POE) to get your answer. But on the SAT, it's important to remember that POE is a process. In this case, Choice A probably "felt" right. But harder questions might have multiple answers that seem right. When done correctly, POE forces you to think about answer choices in a new way:

Stop treating answer choices like they're either completely right or completely wrong:

A)	introduce a character.	✔
B)	provide historical context.	✗
C)	discuss the merits of education.	✗
D)	recount a past event.	✗

Start treating answer choices like they're composed of smaller choices that could be individually right or wrong:

A)	introduce a character.		
		✔	✔
B)	provide historical context.		
			✗
C)	discuss the merits of education.		
		✗	✔
D)	recount a past event.		
		✔	✗

If you NARROW YOUR FOCUS down to individual words and phrases, you're more likely to notice when something isn't quite right. In fact, the SAT is remarkably good at disguising wrong answers so that they "feel" right. **Sometimes an answer choice will be 90% correct, but the 10% that's wrong makes the entire choice wrong.** One wrong word is all it takes! POE is all about finding that one wrong word.

You <u>must</u> use POE on the SAT Reading. **Change your strategy, change your score!**

Show Your Work

By the time you select an answer, your choices should look like this:

2

The main <u>purpose</u> of the first paragraph is to

(A) introduce a character.

~~B)~~ provide <u>historical context</u>.

~~C)~~ discuss the <u>merits</u> of education.

D) recount a past <u>event</u>.

This is mandatory! When you don't show your work in Math, you make careless mistakes. Reading is no different. As the questions get more complex, it's also helpful to underline key words in the question itself so that you know what you're looking for in the line references and choices. Use POE and show your work on this harder question:

3

It can reasonably be inferred from the description of John Reed in lines 1-7 that

---

Lines 1-7

John Reed was a schoolboy of fourteen years old; four years older than I, for I was but ten: large and stout for his age, with a dingy and unwholesome skin; thick lineaments in a spacious visage, heavy limbs and large extremities. He gorged himself habitually at table, which made him bilious, and gave him a dim and bleared eye and flabby cheeks.

+1 sentence

He ought now to have been at school; but his mama had taken him home for a month or two, "on account of his delicate health."

A) children should not consume unhealthy foods in large quantities.

B) the narrator is only concerned with John Reed's physical attributes.

C) the narrator has repeatedly witnessed the behavior she describes.

D) John Reed suffers from a chronic illness that affects his appearance.

Strong Words

One of the benefits of using POE to break choices into smaller pieces is that you start to notice words that you previously ignored. On difficult questions, the most common reason to eliminate a choice is that it includes a small yet powerful word. Recall choice B from the last question:

> B) the narrator is <u>only</u> concerned with John Reed's physical attributes.

Is the narrator concerned with John Reed's physical attributes? **Yes**. He's fat and ugly.

Is the narrator <u>only</u> concerned with John Reed's physical attributes? **No**. She talks about his age.

Which is stronger?

1. <u>most</u> / <u>some</u> scientists believe the theory

2. <u>many</u> / <u>all</u> of the leaders were present

3. the ship will sink <u>if</u> / <u>only if</u> the pump fails

4. the data <u>confirms</u> / <u>supports</u> the hypothesis

5. the article <u>examines whether</u> / <u>argues that</u> Ned is the killer

+1 Sentence Rule

Even though the line reference was only 1-7, you should read an extra sentence to increase your chances of reading important information. In general, **read 1 sentence before and after any line reference mentioned in the question.** (In this case, there was no sentence before because it was the beginning of the passage.) If the line reference is in the answer choices, stick to just the reference.

Line reference in question:
+1 sentence before and after

Line reference in answer choices:
read line reference only

Evidence Pairs

If a question doesn't have a line reference, skip to the next question before you try to answer:

4

The narrator most strongly implies that John Reed is not currently at school because he

---

5

Which choice provides the best evidence for the answer to the previous question?

A) Lines 1-2 ("John … ten")

B) Lines 8-10 ("He … health")

C) Lines 10-16 ("Mr. Miles … after home")

D) Lines 20-22 (every nerve … near")

This is an Evidence Pair, but it doesn't really change anything. You still use the **QLC Method**:

1. **Question (from Part 1)**
2. **Line References (from Part 2)**
3. **Choices (from Part 1)**

1. **Question** — read it and understand it

2. **Line References** — go back to <u>all of them</u>, read <u>only</u> the indicated lines, and eliminate any choices that do not relate to the question

---

A) Lines 1-2
John Reed was a schoolboy of fourteen years old; four years older than I, for I was but ten

B) Lines 8-10
He ought now to have been at school; but his mama had taken him home for a month or two, "on account of his delicate health."

C) Lines 10-16
Mr. Miles, the master, affirmed that he would do very well if he had fewer cakes and sweetmeats sent him from home; but the mother's heart turned from an opinion so harsh, and inclined rather to the more refined idea that John's sallowness was owing to over-application and, perhaps, to pining after home.

D) Lines 20-22
every nerve I had feared him, and every morsel of flesh in my bones shrank when he came near.

The goal of Step 2 is to eliminate line references that are completely irrelevant to the question. **You do not need to decide on one answer at this point.** In fact, you'll almost always have two or three line references left. It's okay to have a favorite that you think will be correct, but be flexible. Step 3 might reveal new information that makes you change your mind:

3. **Choices** — read them, compare them to the remaining line references, and use POE to eliminate any choices that do not relate to the question or the evidence. Remember that you are looking for a <u>pair</u> of correct answers!

4

The narrator most strongly implies that <u>John Reed is not currently at school because</u> he

A) was too old to enroll in classes.

B) requires constant medical attention.

C) is spoiled by his mother.

D) bullied the other students.

5

Which choice provides the best evidence for the answer to the previous question?

A̶) Lines 1-2 ("John … ten")

B) Lines 8-10 ("He … health")

C) Lines 10-16 ("Mr. Miles … after home")

D̶) Lines 20-22 (every nerve … near")

B) Lines 8-10
He ought now to have been at school; but his mama had taken him home for a month or two, "on account of his delicate health."

C) Lines 10-16
Mr. Miles, the master, affirmed that he would do very well if he had fewer cakes and sweetmeats sent him from home; but the mother's heart turned from an opinion so harsh, and inclined rather to the more refined idea that John's sallowness was owing to over-application and, perhaps, to pining after home.

Evidence Pairs take practice, so don't worry if you struggled with this question. Just remember that you answer the pair in the same order as any other question by using the **QLC Method.**

No Line Reference

Here's another question without a line reference. Remember to check the next question to see if it's an Evidence Pair:

6

The narrator indicates that she cannot prevent John from bullying her because

A) she is too preoccupied with reading to learn self-defense.

B) the adults in the household were unwilling to discipline him.

C) she believes it is immoral to engage in violence.

D) her injuries have made her too weak to fight back.

7

As used in line 41, "retired" most nearly means

This is a true No Line Reference question. These can be difficult because you haven't read the passage. **Should you skip it and come back? NO!** A No Line Reference question is not the same as a Whole Passage question. Even though they didn't give you a line reference, there is still a specific line in the passage that contains the answer. So how do you find the line?

1. Focus on names, places, or unusual phrases that would be easy to skim for.

2. Estimate a line reference using surrounding questions and the Chronology Rule.

Chronology Rule

In general, the line references and questions are in chronological order. You can NARROW YOUR FOCUS on **No Line Reference** questions by reading between the previous line reference and the next line reference. This is also true with **Evidence Pairs:** line references from much earlier or much later in the passage, relative to the surrounding questions, are unlikely to be correct.

However, the Chronology Rule is occasionally broken (maybe once or twice per SAT), so be flexible. If you're sure the answer is out of order, then break the rule.

Using the **Chronology Rule**, you know:

Questions 4 & 5 Lines 10-16
Question 6   Lines ??? (probably 16-41)
Question 7   Line 41

Since line 17 begins a new paragraph and line 42 ends another, you can probably stick to these two full paragraphs. It's still a long line reference, but it's easier than skimming the entire passage. Remember to **underline key words from the question so that you're reading with purpose**. You don't need to understand everything that you read. You only need to find the answer to this particular question.

6

The narrator indicates that she cannot prevent John from bullying her because

---

Lines 17-42

John had not much affection for his mother and sisters, and an antipathy to me. He bullied and punished me; not two or three times in the week, nor once or twice in the day, but continually: every nerve I had feared him, and every morsel of flesh in my bones shrank when he came near. There were moments when I was bewildered by the terror he inspired, because I had no appeal whatever against either his menaces or his inflictions; the servants did not like to offend their young master by taking my part against him, and Mrs. Reed was blind and deaf on the subject: she never saw him strike or heard him abuse me, though he did both now and then in her very presence, more frequently, however, behind her back.

Habitually obedient to John, I came up to his chair: he spent some three minutes in thrusting out his tongue at me as far as he could without damaging the roots: I knew he would soon strike, and while dreading the blow, I mused on the disgusting and ugly appearance of him who would presently deal it. I wonder if he read that notion in my face; for, all at once, without speaking, he struck suddenly and strongly. I tottered, and on regaining my equilibrium retired back a step or two from his chair.

A) she is too preoccupied with reading to learn self-defense.

B) the adults in the household were unwilling to discipline him.

C) she believes it is immoral to engage in violence.

D) her injuries have made her too weak to fight back.

Reading Vocab

Gone are the days of memorizing hundreds of obscure vocabulary words for the SAT! Or so the College Board says. At the least, the Reading Vocabulary questions now test common words that have multiple meanings, depending on the context. Answer them the same way as any other question:

1. **Question** — find the word they care about

7

As used in line 41, "retired" most nearly means

---

2. **Line Reference** — read the sentence that contains the word, but replace the word with a blank and come up with your own guess

---

Lines 40-42
I tottered, and on regaining my equilibrium _____ back a step or two from his chair.

your guess

It's extremely important that you read the line reference before the choices. **The SAT is trying to lure you into a trap.** They ask about words that you know, but they use the words in unusual ways. If you look at the choices first, you're going to be biased in favor of the definition you're used to.

Your guess is meant to keep you unbiased. You're not looking to guess the actual answer. You're looking for a placeholder word that captures the definition. Your guess doesn't need to be well-written or sophisticated. Use clues in the sentence to better understand the meaning of the "blank".

3. **Choices** — compare your guess to the choices, and eliminate anything that doesn't match

---

A) resigned.

B) preserved.

C) retreated.

D) slept.

Finish Up

Use the **QLC Method** to answer the remaining questions.

8

It can reasonably be inferred from the passage that the main reason John Reed feels justified in his abuse of the narrator is because

A) Mrs. Reed ordered him to punish the narrator.

B) the narrator has insulted him on numerous occasions.

C) he considers himself the rightful master of the estate.

D) the narrator stole valuable items that belonged to him.

9

Which choice provides the best evidence for the answer to the previous question?

A) Lines 55-58 ("you are … like us")

B) Lines 60-62 ("Now … years")

C) Lines 76-77 ("1 had … Caligula, etc.")

D) Lines 99-102 ("Then … upstairs")

A) Lines 55-58

you are a dependent, mama says; you have no money; your father left you none; you ought to beg, and not to live here with gentlemen's children like us

B) Lines 60-62

Now, I'll teach you to rummage my bookshelves: for they *are* mine; all the house belongs to me, or will do in a few years.

C) Lines 76-77

I had read Goldsmith's History of Rome, and had formed my opinion of Nero, Caligula, etc.

D) Lines 99-102

Then Mrs. Reed subjoined—
"Take her away to the red-room, and lock her in there."
Four hands were immediately laid upon me, and I was bourne upstairs.

HINT: You might have more than one pair that seems correct. Normally, you'd be able to read more of the passage to better understand the context. But can you use the **Chronology Rule** instead?

10

As used in line 72, "succeeded" most nearly means

Lines 70-72

The cut bled, the pain was sharp: my terror had passed its climax; other feelings _____.

your guess

A) ensued.

B) conquered.

C) abandoned.

D) accomplished.

Whole Passage, 2nd Try

When you get to the end of a passage, don't forget to return to any Whole Passage questions that you skipped.

1

Over the course of the passage, the main focus shifts from a

You may still feel like you don't know enough about the passage to answer this question. There were a lot of big words and confusing sentences. Are you really qualified to discuss the main focus of a passage that you **barely understood?** Some tutors will tell you to summarize each paragraph and the whole passage before you answer the questions, but **summarizing is not necessary**. If you insist on summarizing, use a **"dumb summary"** to boil the passage down to its simplest possible form:

Dumb Summary — Jane does not like John

Another concern: are you really qualified to discuss the main focus of a passage that you **barely read?** The main idea is not going to be hidden away in some obscure line reference. Main ideas are repeated again and again. **How much of this passage did you read?**

Questions 1-10 are based on the following passage.

This passage is adapted from Charlotte Bronte, *Jane Eyre*. Originally published in 1847.

John Reed was a schoolboy of fourteen years old; four years older than I, for I was but ten: large and stout for his age, with a dingy and unwholesome
Line skin; thick lineaments in a spacious visage, heavy
5 limbs and large extremities. He gorged himself habitually at table, which made him bilious, and gave him a dim and bleared eye and flabby cheeks. He ought now to have been at school; but his mama had taken him home for a month or two, "on account
10 of his delicate health." Mr. Miles, the master, affirmed that he would do very well if he had fewer cakes and sweetmeats sent him from home; but the mother's heart turned from an opinion so harsh, and inclined rather to the more refined idea that John's
15 sallowness was owing to over-application and, perhaps, to pining after home.

John had not much affection for his mother and sisters, and an antipathy to me. He bullied and punished me; not two or three times in the week, nor
20 once or twice in the day, but continually: every nerve I had feared him, and every morsel of flesh in my bones shrank when he came near. There were moments when I was bewildered by the terror he inspired, because I had no appeal whatever against
25 either his menaces or his inflictions; the servants did not like to offend their young master by taking my part against him, and Mrs. Reed was blind and deaf on the subject: she never saw him strike or heard him abuse me, though he did both now and then in
30 her very presence, more frequently, however, behind her back.

Habitually obedient to John, I came up to his chair: he spent some three minutes in thrusting out his tongue at me as far as he could without
35 damaging the roots: I knew he would soon strike, and while dreading the blow, I mused on the disgusting and ugly appearance of him who would presently deal it. I wonder if he read that notion in my face; for, all at once, without speaking, he struck
40 suddenly and strongly. I tottered, and on regaining my equilibrium retired back a step or two from his chair.

"That is for your impudence in answering mama awhile since," said he, "and for your sneaking way
45 of getting behind curtains, and for the look you had in your eyes two minutes since, you rat!"

Accustomed to John Reed's abuse, I never had an idea of replying to it; my care was how to endure the blow which would certainly follow the insult.

50 "What were you doing behind the curtain?" he asked.

"I was reading."

"Show the book."

I returned to the window and fetched it thence.

55 "You have no business to take our books; you are a dependent, mama says; you have no money; your father left you none; you ought to beg, and not to live here with gentlemen's children like us, and eat the same meals we do, and wear clothes at our
60 mama's expense. Now, I'll teach you to rummage my bookshelves: for they *are* mine; all the house belongs to me, or will do in a few years. Go and stand by the door, out of the way of the mirror and the windows."

65 I did so, not at first aware what was his intention; but when I saw him lift and poise the book and stand in act to hurl it, I instinctively started aside with a cry of alarm: not soon enough, however; the volume was flung, it hit me, and I fell, striking my head
70 against the door and cutting it. The cut bled, the pain was sharp: my terror had passed its climax; other feelings succeeded.

"Wicked and cruel boy!" I said. "You are like a murderer—you are like a slave-driver—you are like
75 the Roman emperors!"

I had read *Goldsmith's History of Rome*, and had formed my opinion of Nero, Caligula, etc. Also I had drawn parallels in silence, which I never thought thus to have declared aloud.

80 "What! what!" he cried. "Did she say that to me? Did you hear her, Eliza and Georgiana? Won't I tell mama? but first—"

He ran headlong at me: I felt him grasp my hair and my shoulder: he had closed with a desperate
85 thing. I really saw in him a tyrant, a murderer. I felt a drop or two of blood from my head trickle down my neck, and was sensible of somewhat pungent suffering: these sensations for the time predominated over fear, and I received him in frantic sort. I don't
90 very well know what I did with my hands, but he called me "Rat! Rat!" and bellowed aloud. Aid was near him: Eliza and Georgiana had run for Mrs. Reed, who was gone upstairs: she now came upon the scene, followed by Bessie and her maid Abbot.
95 We were parted: I heard the words—

"Dear! dear! What a fury to fly at Master John!"

"Did ever anybody see such a picture of passion!"

Then Mrs. Reed subjoined—
100 "Take her away to the red-room, and lock her in there." Four hands were immediately laid upon me, and I was bourne upstairs.

*Highlighted lines were read for questions 2-10

The 50% Rule

It looks like you ended up reading about half of the passage. Is that enough? Let's see.

1

Over the course of the passage, the main focus shifts from a

A) detailed depiction of the narrator's past to a preview of another character's future.

B) general discussion of educational habits to a satisfying exchange of ideas between two characters.

C) statement of the main character's inner thoughts to observations made by the other characters.

D) description of a character to a recounting of an altercation between that character and the narrator.

This is still a hard question, but it's doable, even without reading the entire passage. Plus, did you actually understand 100% of the 50% you read? There's an important lesson here:

Do <u>not</u> try to understand everything.

For one, **if you try, you will likely fail**. Every passage has hard words and confusing sentences. You can't prepare for everything. If your goal is to truly understand the entire passage, then you will waste a lot of time reading and re-reading line references.

It's also **unnecessary**. The vast majority of Reading questions have line references, which automatically NARROW YOUR FOCUS. And significant portions of some passages won't be relevant to any of the questions. Even the line references will contain blindspots that you might not understand, but the context will usually be enough to allow you to confidently answer the question using POE.

Finally, reading everything can be **counterproductive**. It wastes time and clutters your brain with unhelpful lines and information. Read lines 83-89 and take another look at question #6. If we had read the whole passage to start, Choice D might have been much more tempting!

Reading Strategy Summary

General Strategies

- Figure out if reading the passage helps you understand or slows you down and confuses you.

- Always read the blurb.

- Use the **QLC** method:
    1. Question
    2. Line Reference(s)
    3. Choices

- **Show your work**, just like in Math.

- **Use POE** — Treat choices like they're composed of many little pieces. All it takes is for one word to be wrong.

- Be careful of **Strong Words**.

- **+1 Sentence Rule**
    - Line reference in question — read a sentence before and after
    - Line reference in answer — read the line reference only

- Answers and line references generally follow the **Chronology Rule**.

- **50% Rule** - Don't worry if you don't understand everything. It's okay to feel lost and confused. You probably understand more than you think you do.

Question Types

- Save **Whole Passage** questions for the end.

- Treat **Evidence Pairs** as one question with two parts using the **QLC Method**:
    1. Question (from Part 1)
    2. Line References (from Part 2)
    3. Choices (from Part 1)

- For **No Line Reference** questions, use surrounding line references to estimate where to read using the **Chronology Rule**.

- For **Reading Vocab** questions, guess the meaning of the word before you look at the choices. Compare your guess to the choices and eliminate anything that doesn't fit.

Exercise: Reading Passage

Questions 11-22 are based on the following passage and supplementary material.

This passage is adapted from Mike Settele, *Bending the Brain: How We Think About How We Think.* ©2017 by Mike Settele.

In January 2007, Jasper Burnberry, a neuroscientist at the Ohio College of Science, wanted to know if the mice used in the university's
Line experiments might be anatomically different from
5   mice of the same species living in the wild. He examined the brains of twenty laboratory mice and twenty wild mice with matching ages. What he found surprised him—the wild mice, which had spent a lifetime braving the elements and struggling for food,
10 showed signs of healthier brains than the mice that had spent their entire lives being pampered in the lab. One brain region in particular, the dentate gyrus, was 9 percent larger in the wild mice. Burnberry concluded that the challenges that come with living in
15 the wild had changed the physical structure of the mice's brains. The older the mouse, the larger its dentate gyrus.

The dentate gyrus is part of the hippocampus, the area of the brain associated with memory and
20 navigation. The scientific consensus had long been that, while different species could have smaller or larger brain structures to reflect evolutionary development, the differences within a single species were more or less negligible. Burnberry's study
25 provided evidence that would upend the old orthodoxy.

Looking to further explain the reasons behind his unexpected discovery, Burnberry sought the help of Wendell Strong and Felicity Hoskins, authors of a
30 paper on spatial memory. Together, they devised a study to test whether laboratory mice could develop the same enlarged dentate gyrus as the wild mice. They wanted to know if the larger structure required a lifetime of certain behaviors or if it could develop
35 with training just like a muscle.

The team implanted brain scanners onto two groups of mice. The experimental group was given large, complex cages to live in. A control group continued living like laboratory mice with simple,
40 rectangular cages and regular feeding schedules. The experimental group, however, was forced to forage like mice in the wild. Food was scattered throughout the cage, typically in the same locations but at times that did not perfectly conform to a regular schedule.

45 The mice had to remember which areas were more likely to bear fruit and how often. In addition, the food in each location was frequently trapped inside of a puzzle to simulate the work required to open a seed pod or crack a nut, so the mice had to remember how
50 to solve the puzzle for each type of food.

After years of "training" the mice's brains, the team still found no difference in the sizes of the dentate gyrus, or any other structures, between the experimental group and the control. Furthermore,
55 when each group was tested in a maze meant to measure cognitive ability, both groups performed equally. The only difference was that the brains of the experimental mice showed increased activity in the dentate gyrus region. It was as if the two groups'
60 brains were taking entirely different paths to get to the same destination.

The brain scanners showed that the control mice were utilizing a region known as the striatum, which is associated with motor skills and, interestingly, the
65 perception of rewards. The dentate gyrus was silent. For the experimental mice, the dentate gyrus lit up like fireworks, as if they were back in their cages foraging for food. Burnberry's team was surprised by this result. Why would two groups of anatomically
70 identical mice think about the same maze in completely different ways? What did the simulated wild mice see as they moved through this new space?

Burnberry and his team performed one final experiment with the two groups. They put the mice
75 back into the maze to see if they navigated through it any faster. Even though both groups improved their times, the experimental group was significantly faster than the control. This suggested that the simulated wild mice had previously treated the new maze like
80 an extension of their environment that needed to be mapped for future use. Years of practice using their dentate gyrus to form spatial memories had paid off in the maze. Perhaps the brains of true wild mice behave the same way. A wild mouse's environment is
85 probably magnitudes more complex than the cages set up for the experimental mice. Over time, a mouse's brain might grow and change to better navigate its world.

Note: This passage is deliberately harder than usual because it's meant to show off some of the ways the SAT pushes the limits of its own rules. In other words, these questions are quirky. Still, you should try out the **No Reading Strategy** and use **Process of Elimination** to help you sort through the answer choices. You'll also notice that this passage features the two remaining question types — Unpaired Evidence and Reading Figures.

Average Time to Complete Maze

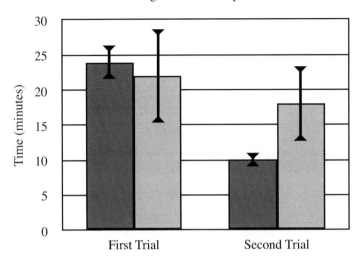

Experimental Group   □ Control

First Trial: both groups of mice completed a new maze, and the individual times were recorded

Second Trial: both groups of mice completed the same maze as in the first trial, and the individual times were recorded

The bars show the average completion time for each group. The triangles show the maximum and minimum completion time for each group.

11

Over the course of the passage, the main focus shifts from

A) a list of the shortcomings of a current theory to a revision of that theory to accommodate new data.

B) a description of the results of an experiment to an analysis of the practical applications of those results.

C) the implications of an unexpected finding to a series of experiments designed to explore that finding.

D) the explanation of a new method to an experiment designed to test the limits of that method.

12

The passage most strongly suggests that wild mice have healthier brains because they

A) have to overcome difficult environmental circumstances.

B) create maps using visual landmarks so they can find food more easily.

C) train their brains by regularly working on puzzles and running through mazes.

D) age more slowly than mice raised in laboratories.

13

Which choice provides the best evidence for the answer to the previous question?

A) Lines 7-11 ("What … lab")

B) Lines 12-13 ("One … mice")

C) Lines 13-16 ("Burnberry … brains")

D) Lines 16-17 ("The older … gyrus")

14

As used in line 22, "reflect" most nearly means

A) consider.

B) demonstrate.

C) echo.

D) reverse.

15

Which question was Burnberry, Strong, and Hoskins' study primarily intended to answer?

A) Do wild mice exhibit unique anatomical structures that are not present in laboratory mice?

B) Are genetic mutations responsible for the physical differences between wild mice and those used in laboratory experiments?

C) How does the dentate gyrus allow the brain to form a mental map of the environment?

D) Are differences in brain structure the result of long term behavioral patterns or short term exposure to new environments?

16

Which choice provides the best evidence for the answer to the previous question?

A) Lines 1-5 ("In … wild")

B) Lines 24-26 ("Burnberry's … orthodoxy")

C) Lines 30-32 ("Together … wild mice")

D) Lines 33-35 ("They … muscle")

17

As used in line 40, "regular" most nearly means

A) cyclic.

B) common.

C) symmetrical.

D) genuine.

18

According to the passage, when compared to the control group, the simulated wild mice in Burnberry's second study

A) exhibited more neural connections in the dentate gyrus region.

B) registered activity in a different part of the brain.

C) displayed larger brain structures in areas associated with navigation.

D) were less similar to actual wild mice.

19

The questions in lines 69-72 primarily serve to

A) speculate about the reasons for a result.

B) indicate skepticism about the accuracy of a study.

C) elaborate on an unexpected finding.

D) explain the basis of an experiment.

20

Which choice best supports the claim that the skills developed by the experimental group could be put to use outside of the mice's cages?

A) Lines 73-75 ("Burnberry … groups")

B) Lines 76-78 ("Even … control")

C) Lines 81-83 ("Years … maze")

D) Lines 84-86 ("A wild … mice")

21

According to the graph, control mice in the second trial had an average completion time of

A) 10 minutes.

B) 13 minutes.

C) 18 minutes.

D) 22 minutes.

22

Which of the following statements is supported by the graph?

A) At least one mouse in the control group took more time than every mouse in the experimental group to complete the first trial.

B) At least one mouse in the experimental group took less time than every mouse in the control group to complete the first trial.

C) In both trials, the mice in the experimental group had a wider range of completion times than the mice in the control group.

D) In the second trial, the mice in the experimental group made fewer wrong turns than did the mice in the control group.

Reading Figures

Don't be fooled — most graph and chart questions have very little to do with the passage. Just make sure you understand the data. **Read the title, the axis labels, and any other text that accompanies the figure.** If you're running out of time on the Reading section, these questions can be answered quickly for easy points.

Unpaired Evidence

Sometimes, they combine both Evidence parts into one. The process is the same:

1. **Question** — pay close attention to what they're asking for; it's filled with clues that will make it easier to sort through the lines

2. **Line References** — stick to just the given lines, like any other evidence question

3. **Choices** — the line references are the choices!

SAT Writing and Language

SAT-specific strategies

The Basics

You don't need to read every word of the passage. While the Writing section is easier to finish than the Reading, you still don't want to waste time on lines that don't matter. **Typically, you only need to read the sentence that contains the underlined words.** That said, don't cut corners. Read the full sentence, especially if it continues onto the next page. If you think you need to read extra sentences, then read them.

The Twists

The College Board divides the SAT Writing into two kinds of questions:

- Expression of Ideas
- Standard English Conventions

For once, these are actually fairly useful categories, but this study guide will amend them slightly:

- Ideas
- Grammar
- Style

Most questions will test formulaic grammar rules or word choice, but the **Ideas** questions are more like Reading questions. The question will give you a goal or objective, and you need to follow the instructions. **Sometimes you'll be instructed to read:**

Which choice most effectively sets up the examples in the following sentences?

Which choice adds the most relevant supporting information to the paragraph?

Which choice offers an accurate interpretation of the data in the graph?

For the sake of the logic and cohesion of the paragraph, sentence 3 should be placed…

Ideas Questions

If the question instructs you to read something, read it. Don't be lazy!

The War of 1812 was fought, in part, to defend American honor, **1** but there were other causes as well. Despite being vastly outnumbered by the British Royal Navy, the Americans were able to secure several important victories. In 1813, the Battle of Lake Erie gave the Americans control of the lake for the remainder of the war, which allowed troops to be transported throughout the region unimpeded. Additionally, the successful defense of the port of Baltimore was subsequently enshrined in the American national anthem. **2** In England, the War of 1812 was derogatorily referred to as "Mr. Madison's War."

Example 1

Which choice best establishes the main idea of the paragraph?

A) NO CHANGE

B) which had been damaged by a number of embarrassing incidents in the decade before.

C) yet historians do not agree on why the British decided to engage in battle.

D) and the fledgling American Navy proved to be up to the task.

Example 2

At this point, the writer wants to add a supporting detail to indicate that the American Navy also suffered defeats during the war. Which choice best accomplishes this goal?

A) NO CHANGE

B) Today, the American Navy continues to defend the port of Baltimore.

C) Still, the powerful Royal Navy blockaded the coast, allowing the British to strike American merchants at will.

D) Just a day earlier, the American Navy had defeated the British at Plattsburgh, halting their attempts to attack across the Canadian border.

Grammar Questions

You probably learned English grammar at some point in your early years of school, but it isn't covered as much (or at all) once you get to high school. So you might be a bit rusty. Do you remember the relevant rules?

Example 3

In 1807, Britain passed laws that made it more <u>difficult for the United States to trade with France;</u> the country that Britain was then fighting in the Napoleonic Wars.

A) NO CHANGE

B) difficult, for the United States to trade with France

C) difficult for the United States, to trade with France

D) difficult for the United States to trade with France,

Example 4

While the United States argued that immigrants serving on its ships were Americans, the British believed these sailors were still subjects of the Crown, <u>this</u> made them targets for impressment.

A) NO CHANGE

B) that

C) which

D) it

The bigger problem with the SAT is that they deliberately test rules that defy your expectations. They know which errors you make in your daily life, and they purposely test those rules. If you always pick the answer choice that sounds best, you will get a lot of questions wrong. **Sometimes the wrong answers sound right and the right answer sounds wrong.**

Example 5

Britain frequently reclaimed <u>they're</u> sailors by boarding American ships and capturing anyone suspected of being a British subject.

A) NO CHANGE

B) their

C) its

D) it's

Example 6

While impressment was the primary problem in the eyes of Atlantic merchants, the issue of American sovereignty over the Mississippi River and its tributaries <u>was getting</u> increased attention in the West.

A) NO CHANGE

B) were getting

C) are getting

D) gets

Style

While some questions try to trick you with complex rules, others obey stylistic rules that are easy to follow once you know them.

Example 7

Americans on the frontier accused the British of supporting Indian raids on small settlements and places where people lived.

A) NO CHANGE

B) settlements, communities, and towns.

C) settlements, which were not very large.

D) settlements.

Example 8

Westerners believed that conquering Canada would end these conflicts because the British would be unable to give weapons and armaments to those who were raiding.

A) NO CHANGE

B) supply the raiders with munitions.

C) kick in the supplies that were needed by the raiders throughout the region.

D) continue to provide the raiders with supplies in terms of the materials they needed to fight.

It's also important that you don't overcompensate for the potential traps by doubting yourself on every question. Sometimes your instincts will be correct.

Example 9

Domestically, the enfeeblement of the Federalist Party meant that there were fewer voices in Congress opposing war with Britain.

A) NO CHANGE

B) diminution

C) decline

D) lessening

Example 10

In the Northeast, there was such little support for the war that some Federalists even discussed the possibility of secession.

A) NO CHANGE

B) as little to

C) as little

D) little for

Predict the Question

The Writing section can be intimidating because it feels like there are too many things to think about. With practice, you can get good at figuring out what each question is testing based on the answer choices. NARROW YOUR FOCUS.

Big picture, you at least want to be able to distinguish between the three question types — Ideas, Grammar, and Style. Each type has its own thought-process. You need to know when you can trust your instincts and when you need to doubt them.

Ideas — follow instructions

> Which choice best establishes the main idea of the paragraph?

> At this point, the writer wants to add a supporting detail to indicate that the American Navy also suffered defeats during the war. Which choice best accomplishes this goal?

Grammar — follow the rules

A) NO CHANGE
B) difficult, for the United States to trade with France
C) difficult for the United States, to trade with France
D) difficult for the United States to trade with France,

A) NO CHANGE
B) their
C) its
D) it's

Style — follow your gut

A) NO CHANGE
B) settlements, communities, and towns.
C) settlements, which were not very large.
D) settlements.

A) NO CHANGE
B) diminution
C) decline
D) lessening

Writing Strategy Summary

There are more grammar rules to learn, but here is the Writing section strategy in a nutshell:

- **Don't read** the passage unless you have to.

- Try to **predict the question** based on the answer choices.

  - **Ideas**

    - accomplish the goal in the question

    - read what the question tells you to

    - look for problem words in the choices

  - **Grammar**

    - be careful of fragments and run-ons

    - follow punctuation rules

    - pronouns and verbs must be consistent with their subjects

  - **Style**
    - avoid redundancy
    - be concise
    - use the most appropriate word for the context
    - trust your instincts

Exercise: Writing Questions

Note: In the following exercise, try to identify whether the question is about Ideas, Grammar, or Style before you answer it.

Questions 1-26 are based on the following passage.

The Great Compromiser

In recounting the major events that shaped American **[1]** moments in history, most people skip directly from the Founding **[2]** Father's, Washington, Jefferson, Franklin— to the Civil War and Lincoln's emancipation of Southern slaves. **[3]** In between, America's second generation of leaders worked to preserve the legacy of freedom enshrined in the Declaration of Independence and Constitution, but they also struggled to live up to the promises of those documents. Before the devastation of the Civil War, political conflicts nearly divided the United States several times. Henry **[4]** Clay; a largely forgotten statesman, helped forge three great compromises that kept the Union together during his 50 years of public service in the first half of the 19th century.

---

1 Ideas Grammar Style

A) NO CHANGE

B) historical moments,

C) history of the past,

D) history,

---

2 Ideas Grammar Style

A) NO CHANGE

B) Fathers,

C) Fathers—

D) Fathers'—

---

3 Ideas Grammar Style

At this point, the writer is considering adding the following sentence.

> Lincoln gave the Gettysburg Address, in part, to defend the Emancipation Proclamation, which he had signed a few months earlier.

Should the writer make this addition here?

A) Yes, because it gives more information about Lincoln's decisions during the Civil War.

B) Yes, because it provides context for the legacy of freedom mentioned in the next sentence.

C) No, because it blurs the focus of the paragraph by introducing irrelevant information.

D) No, because it undermines the main claim of the paragraph.

---

4 Ideas Grammar Style

A) NO CHANGE

B) Clay a largely, forgotten statesman, helped

C) Clay, a largely forgotten statesman, helped

D) Clay, a largely forgotten statesman helped,

---

[1] Clay rose to **5** top billing at a time when the nation was moving to the West. [2] While Speaker of the House and leader of the "War Hawks," Clay spoke in favor of war with Britain as a way to **6** push America's independence, which was still precarious even 30 years after the end of the Revolution. [3] As a Senator and Congressman from Kentucky, he was one of the most influential voices representing this growing region. [4] The War of 1812 could be considered a failure for several **7** reasons: the British burned the Capitol, Americans failed to capture Canada, and the practice of impressment continued. [5] **8** Moreover, a few key battles helped give the American people and Clay an important symbolic victory—the young nation had held **9** their own against the world's most powerful empire. **10**

5 | Ideas | Grammar | Style

A) NO CHANGE
B) celebrity
C) prominence
D) priority

6 | Ideas | Grammar | Style

A) NO CHANGE
B) assert
C) insist
D) argue

7 | Ideas | Grammar | Style

A) NO CHANGE
B) reasons;
C) reasons,
D) reasons, and

8 | Ideas | Grammar | Style

A) NO CHANGE
B) However,
C) Therefore,
D) Thus,

9 | Ideas | Grammar | Style

A) NO CHANGE
B) they're
C) its
D) it's

10 | Ideas | Grammar | Style

To make this paragraph most logical, sentence 3 should be placed

A) where it is now.
B) before sentence 1.
C) after sentence 1.
D) after sentence 5.

After the war, Clay continued his leadership in national politics. His first great compromise came in 1820, when Missouri [11] petitioned, to enter the Union as a slave state. Even though Clay was a slaveholder, he understood that Missouri threatened to upset the balance of free and slave states [12] that than existed in the Senate. Clay devised a compromise that let Maine join the Union as a free state, [13] which prevented one side from gaining an advantage. [14] By limiting the expansion of slavery, he hoped to create conditions that would eventually cause it to disappear entirely.

11   Ideas   Grammar   Style

A) NO CHANGE
B) petitioned to enter, the Union
C) petitioned to enter the Union,
D) petitioned to enter the Union

12   Ideas   Grammar   Style

A) NO CHANGE
B) that then
C) who than
D) who then

13   Ideas   Grammar   Style

A) NO CHANGE
B) this
C) that
D) so

14   Ideas   Grammar   Style

At this point, the writer is considering adding the following sentence.

> To prevent this problem from reappearing, Clay also proposed that slavery be prohibited north of the 36°30' latitude line.

Should the writer make this addition here?

A) Yes, because it defines a term that is necessary to understand the argument that follows.
B) Yes, because it sets up the next sentence by describing another part of the compromise.
C) No, because it interrupts the paragraph's discussion with irrelevant information.
D) No, because it repeats information that is provided earlier in the passage.

The Missouri Compromise became as fundamentally important to the country as the Constitution, but restricting slavery in the territories did not have the [15] intended effect. Only 12 years later, Clay was again called upon to find a solution to a sectional crisis. When South Carolina threatened to [16] nullify or veto a federal tariff, President, Andrew Jackson responded with a threat of his own. He made it clear that the state's disobedience would be stopped by the U.S. Army. [17] Clay's compromise ended the potential for violence. This potential was ended by a lowering of the tariff to a rate that was acceptable to South Carolina.

15   Ideas   Grammar   Style

A) NO CHANGE

B) intended affect.

C) intending affects.

D) intending effects.

16   Ideas   Grammar   Style

A) NO CHANGE

B) nullify, or veto, a federal tariff, President

C) nullify or veto, a federal tariff President

D) nullify, or veto a federal tariff, President

17   Ideas   Grammar   Style

Which choice most effectively combines the underlined sentences?

A) Clay's compromise ended the potential for violence by lowering the tariff to a rate that was acceptable to South Carolina.

B) Clay's compromise, by lowering the tariff, ended the potential for violence with a rate that was acceptable to South Carolina.

C) In lowering the tariff, Clay's compromise ended the potential for violence to a rate that was acceptable to South Carolina.

D) The potential for violence was lowered by Clay's compromise, and their rate was acceptable to South Carolina.

[1] The Nullification Crisis **18** <u>fastened</u> Clay's reputation as the "The Great Compromiser" and is a major reason why he was called upon **19** <u>with</u> one last compromise in 1850. [2] Weak and dying of tuberculosis, Clay still managed to persuade the Senate to pass several bills that solved problems created by the new territories acquired after the Mexican-American War. [3] Once again, the issue was slavery. [4] The compromise was not particularly popular, since both slave and free states had to make concessions **20** <u>they</u> did not like. [5] **21** <u>By and by,</u> the country was relieved that yet another sectional crisis had been averted without bloodshed and civil war. **22**

---

18 Ideas Grammar Style

A) NO CHANGE

B) welded

C) cemented

D) cohered

---

19 Ideas Grammar Style

A) NO CHANGE

B) for

C) to

D) by

---

20 Ideas Grammar Style

A) NO CHANGE

B) it

C) he or she

D) these

---

21 Ideas Grammar Style

A) NO CHANGE

B) Nevertheless,

C) For example,

D) Furthermore,

---

22 Ideas Grammar Style

To make this paragraph most logical, sentence 3 should be placed

A) where it is now.

B) before sentence 1.

C) after sentence 4.

D) after sentence 5.

[23] Other Americans, including Daniel Webster, favored compromise as well. Some historians believe that Clay could have found yet another compromise to prevent the Civil War if he had been alive in 1860. Others feel that [24] Clay's achievement's merely postponed the inevitable conflict over slavery. In fact, Clay's reputation as one of early America's most heroic figures [25] were dimmed over time, perhaps outshone by Lincoln's refusal to compromise with the rebelling South. While it's important to study the great Americans who prevailed during times of war, it's also necessary to [26] protest wars that are waged unjustly. Henry Clay did not get a nickname because he helped to start the War of 1812. He became The Great Compromiser because he fought to prevent a war that could destroy the Union. For this, he became one of the 19th century's most celebrated Americans.

23   Ideas   Grammar   Style

Which choice most effectively introduces the main idea of the paragraph?

A) NO CHANGE

B) The Civil War was the most deadly conflict in American history.

C) Scholars use a variety of primary sources to learn about Clay's life.

D) Clay died only two years later, respected by his friends and enemies alike.

24   Ideas   Grammar   Style

A) NO CHANGE

B) Clay's achievements'

C) Clay's achievements

D) Clay achievements

25   Ideas   Grammar   Style

A) NO CHANGE

B) have dimmed

C) has dimmed

D) dimming

26   Ideas   Grammar   Style

Which choice is most consistent with the previous example in the sentence?

A) NO CHANGE

B) examine the lives of those who led in times of peace.

C) interview the veterans who were wounded or captured in battle.

D) understand the tactics that other nations use to fight.

SAT Essay
SAT-specific strategies

The Basics

Here's the deal: the Essay barely matters. Only a handful of schools either require or recommend it. But you really should take it because it's hard to know if you'll end up needing it. If you're a junior, you might change your mind about the schools you want to apply to by the time you're sending your applications. You don't want to be stuck retaking the entire SAT in the fall of your senior year just because you need the Essay.

Luckily, the format should be very similar to the kinds of essays you write for school. You'll be given a two page article, and the task is to analyze the author's argument. You're not supposed to say whether you agree with the author. **Instead, analyze the techniques that the author uses to persuade the audience.** You should follow the 5-paragraph structure that you probably use in school:

1. **Introduction**
   - short, 2 or 3 sentences
   - restate author's thesis (given in the question)
   - state your thesis (topics of your body paragraphs)

2. **Body Paragraph**
   - a technique the author uses
   - examples of the author using the technique
   - why the technique would persuade readers

3. **Body Paragraph**
   - a second technique the author uses
   - examples of the author using the technique
   - why the technique would persuade readers

4. **Body Paragraph**
   - a third technique the author uses
   - examples of the author using the technique
   - why the technique would persuade readers

5. **Conclusion**
   - rephrase your introduction

The Twists

The Essay is a separate score that does not affect your score out of 1600. Two readers will grade your essay based on these three criteria:

Reading — out of 8

Start by jumping to the box at the end of the passage. They'll explicitly tell you the author's thesis, so you won't need to guess it. You can even copy the phrasing word-for-word into your introduction if you want. Beyond that, you shouldn't worry too much about summarizing the passage. You'll do this naturally as you analyze. But as you read the article, **outline by writing in the margins**. Make note of any persuasive techniques that the author uses as you go. Organize your thoughts before you start writing, and your essay will come out much better.

Analysis — out of 8

This is the hardest part of the task. It's not enough to point out persuasive techniques. You also need to talk about why they are persuasive. **How do the author's rhetorical techniques function in the article as a whole?** People often complain that some articles don't have enough techniques to write about, but that's nonsense. You just need to know what to look for. The next page has some examples.

Writing — out of 8

You are allowed to make a few spelling and grammar mistakes, but try to keep them to a minimum. Also, handwriting isn't supposed to count against you, but it can. A reader can't give you credit for words she can't unscramble. **Try to vary your vocabulary and sentence structure**, but don't overdo it by misusing words or creating run-on sentences. Outlining will help you avoid the "word vomit" that comes out when you haven't planned.

Total Score — out of 24

The truth is that you don't need to be amazing. A score of 6/6/6 is good enough. You just want to show that you're a competent writer.

Persuasive Techniques

Citations and Statistics

They say:
- 243 million Americans…
- 50% less energy…
- Centers for Disease Control…
- NASA scientist John Mulready…

You say:
- By citing an authority, the author shows that others share his view.
- Including this data gives the author credibility.

Anecdote and Descriptive Language

They say:
- When I was a boy…
- Imagine the vast African grasslands…

You say:
- The anecdote engages the reader and makes the author more relatable.
- The descriptive story transports the reader to the grasslands…

Word Choice and Tone

They say:
- Ignoring the problem has created a crisis that threatens to spiral out of control.
- We must take action or our children will be stuck cleaning up our mess.

You say:
- The author chooses words that emphasize the severity of the problem, such as "crisis" and "out of control."
- By repeatedly using "we," the author can include the reader in the problem and the solution.

Counterargument

They say:
- Some claim that savings won't be as high as projected, but actually…

You say:
- The author anticipates an objection to his argument, but quickly refutes it, which further persuades the reader that the author is right.

Write Better

This packet is short because, unfortunately, there isn't much I can teach you. Your writing habits are strong, and they'll be hard to change just for this Essay. Improving your writing ability takes a long time and many hours of practice. It's a low priority for the SAT. That said, here are a few common mistakes:

Instead of "uses"…

The author uses evidence, word choice, and reasoning.

… be active and specific:

The author cites numerous authorities, chooses words that appeal to emotion, and describes the consequences of a failure to act.

Instead of long citations followed by analysis…

Jones describes the nature preserve as a "vast and remarkably pristine wilderness, with herds of impala and water buffalo traversing the grasslands, newly flooded from the torrential storms that mark the beginning of the rainy season." This makes the audience create a mental image of the nature preserve.

… integrate quotes into your analysis:

In describing the refuge as a "pristine wilderness" with "herds of impala and water buffalo" crossing "flooded" plains, Jones helps the reader create a mental image of the place he wants to protect.

Instead of repeating yourself…

Jones uses data when he says that the preserve only contains "1 to 2 percent" of the world's lithium. He uses this data to show that there is not much benefit to mining there, and the benefits can be gotten in other ways, such as "instituting recycling programs."

… use complex sentences and fewer words:

Jones argues that the preserve would only supply "1 to 2 percent" of the world's lithium, an amount that could instead be saved through investments in "recycling programs."

Reading Packets

I usually recommend that you take a practice test and pick the packets that correspond to questions you got wrong. But the Reading packets also follow a logical progression from the easiest question types to the hardest, so you could just start with the POE chapter, and then continue into the Evidence chapter after you've improved your POE skills. Practice the Quick questions at any point.

Process of Elimination

The Basics

Process of Elimination (POE) is the most powerful weapon in your SAT arsenal. It works on every question type in this chapter, as well as the Evidence Pairs, most of the Reading Figure questions, and many of the Ideas questions in Writing. Essentially, POE is about NARROWING YOUR FOCUS to the individual words that make up the answer choices and "testing" them against the passage. In many cases, it's easier to find the wrong answers than the right ones. The right answers won't always feel right because the SAT is very good at disguising them.

The Twists

The SAT Reading section looks similar to other standardized reading tests, but it also has its own set of rules that most people don't know when they first start practicing. If you don't learn these rules and integrate them into your process, you won't improve your score.

For Line Reference questions, you need to follow the **+1 Sentence Rule** so that you read the context surrounding the lines the question directs you to. For No Line Reference questions, you need to follow the **Chronology Rule** so that you know where to find the answer in the passage. The Whole Passage questions are always the first questions for each passage because the SAT is trying to trick you into answering them too quickly. Follow the rules and **save Whole Passage questions for last**.

When you use POE to sort through the answer choices, you'll need to look out for traps. Remember that it only take one word to make a choice wrong. Don't pick an answer just because it copies memorable words and phrases from the passage. Pay attention to the ideas that the phrases represent. Be very careful of **Strong Words** that take the ideas too far. Many Strong Words deal with quantities (most, majority, consensus, widely held) or with intention (want, desire, wish, hope, argue). Always base your answers on the passage. If the lines don't say or suggest it, then it's probably not correct.

Packets

- line reference
- no line reference
- whole passage
- both passages

approximately 19 questions per test

worth approximately 100 points total

Reading	LR	LR	LR	LR
noLR	noLR	noLR	LR	LR	LR
noLR	noLR	WP	WP	WP	WP
ev1	ev1	ev1	both	both	both
ev1	ev1	ev2	ev2	ev2	evU
ev1	ev1	ev2	ev2	ev2	evU
ev1	ev1	ev2	ev2	ev2	Rfig
Rvoc	Rvoc	Rvoc	Rvoc	Rfig	Rfig
Rvoc	Rvoc	Rvoc	Rvoc	Rfig	Rfig

Important Ideas

Process of Elimination (POE)

Change your strategy, change your score.

Shift your focus from the passages to the questions and choices. Instead of picking the choice that feels the most right, try to eliminate choices that you know are wrong.

Start thinking of each answer choice as if it's composed of several smaller choices. An answer choice can be 90% correct, but if it's 10% wrong, then it's totally wrong. Sometimes it only takes one word to make an answer choice incorrect.

Show Your Work

Underline key words in the questions.

Underline words and phrases that make each choice wrong, especially **Strong Words**.

Benefits:
- prevents careless mistakes
- keeps your mind and body active
- trains you to pay attention to words you would normally ignore

QLC Method

Answer questions in this order:
1. Question
2. Line Reference
3. Choices

Start by reading the question carefully. Underline key words so that you're reading the line reference with purpose.

Read the line reference, and try to understand it as best you can. Do not re-read it multiple times. Use a **dumb summary** of 1-5 words to capture the most basic ideas.

Use POE to sort through the choices. Eliminate answers that are obviously wrong. Use yes/no questions to match ideas from the line reference.

Whole Passage

Save Whole Passage questions for last (regardless of whether you use the No Reading strategy).

Always read the blurb. Titles sometimes give away the main idea.

Remember the **50% Rule**. Main ideas are not hidden in an obscure line reference. They are repeated throughout the passage. If you read and understood 50% of the passage, you probably know the main ideas.

Line Reference

Use the **+1 Sentence Rule** to gain context. The answer is often just outside where the question tells you to read.

No Line Reference

Use the **Chronology Rule** to estimate a line reference. The Reading questions are almost always in the order in which the answers appear in the passage. You can also use distinctive phrases from the question to skim the passage for the answer.

No Line Reference questions are typically more straightforward than other questions. When you find the answer in the passage, the correct answer choice will usually be fairly obvious.

Both Passages

Always read the blurb. Titles and descriptions sometimes give away the relationship between the two passages.

Use **dumb summaries** to determine whether the passages agree or disagree.

You can treat the Double Passage as if it's two separate passages:
- read and answer Passage 1 questions
- read and answer Passage 2 questions
- answer Both Passage questions

Line Reference

process of elimination

The Basics

The **No Reading Strategy** works best when you have a lot of Line Reference questions. The question itself will tell you how to NARROW YOUR FOCUS by telling you not only where to read but also what to look for in the lines. Remember to follow the **QLC Method**:

1. **Question** — read it and understand it

2. **Line Reference** — go back to it, read it, and try to understand the gist of it

3. **Choices** — read them and use Process of Elimination to find the wrong answers

Example 1

Fish species that are long-lived and high on the food chain, such as tuna and swordfish, are great candidates for research on how pollutants can spread
Line throughout an ecosystem. These predators may live
5 far from runoff that seeps into coastal waters, but they prey on smaller species that do inhabit these areas and absorb harmful chemicals, like mercury. Over a lifetime, the concentration of pollutants can build up to dangerous levels in these top predators. "We may
10 be reaping what we sow," says Harold Armstrong, a marine biologist at New Jersey University. "After all, humans are at the very top of the food chain."

— — — — — — — — — — — — — — — — — —

The first paragraph mainly serves to

A) explain why certain types of fish were chosen as the basis of a study.

B) demonstrate the importance of conservation efforts in coastal waters.

C) discuss the origins of an emerging area of scientific inquiry.

D) illustrate how food chains function in marine environments.

The Twists

Unfortunately, you won't always understand the line references. Difficult vocabulary words and confusing sentences can leave you feeling like you need to read and re-read and re-read again... And even then, you might be unable to summarize what the lines say. There are a few things you can do to maximize the chances you still get the question right:

- **the +1 Sentence Rule** — Line Reference questions will often ask for the purpose of certain lines. Reading one sentence before and after the stated line reference will give you the context. Ideas usually flow from one sentence to the next, so if you don't understand the ideas in the line reference, you might be able to guess based on the surrounding ideas.

- **ask "yes or no" questions** — Which question is easier to answer:
    1. What is this line reference about?
    2. Is this line reference about the researchers' methods?

Example 2

In line 10, Armstrong uses the phrase "reaping what we sow" to imply that

A) researchers have devised new methods of measuring chemical concentrations in fish.

B) pollutants are entering the environment at an increasing rate due to human activity.

C) humans could be susceptible to the same negative consequences as the species the author mentions.

D) scientists blame most of the ocean pollution the author describes on agricultural runoff.

Exercise: Line Reference

Note: These are excerpts from larger passages. For each question, the line reference is included, as well as an extra sentence before and after so you can follow the +1 Sentence Rule.

1

… Neurologists specializing in the study of language
15 have found that human beings can read words in which the middle letters have been jumbled, as long as the first and last letters remain. Why doesn't the brain respond the same way when it has to read a five or six character string of numbers?
20 Two speech language pathologists, Brian Van Owen and Marcia Underdown, devised an experiment to answer that very question. …

——————————————————

The question in the third paragraph (lines 17-19) primarily serves to

A) suggest the researchers are skeptical about a solution proposed in the passage.

B) emphasize the need to solve a problem that will be explained in the passage.

C) imply that a research method mentioned in the passage is unlikely to succeed.

D) highlight an area of study that will be discussed in the passage.

2

25 Bosworth and Yang developed a novel way of comparing living standards that emphasizes the day-to-day experiences of average citizens. It starts with Gross Domestic Product—the standard measurement of economic activity in a country—and refines the
30 number using the prices of essential purchases, such as bread and cellular telephone services. They call their value the Citizens Product. …

——————————————————

The primary purpose of lines 28-29 ("the standard … country") is to

A) describe a formula.

B) emphasize a contrast.

C) explain a term.

D) suggest a remedy.

3

It is not the critic who counts; not the man who points out how the strong man stumbles, or where the
35 doer of deeds could have done them better. The credit belongs to the man who is actually in the arena, whose face is marred by dust and sweat and blood; who strives valiantly; who errs, who comes short again and again, because there is no effort without error and
40 shortcoming; but who does actually strive to do the deeds; who knows great enthusiasms, the great devotions; who spends himself in a worthy cause; who at the best knows in the end the triumph of high achievement, and who at the worst, if he fails, at least
45 fails while daring greatly, so that his place shall never be with those cold and timid souls who neither know victory nor defeat.

——————————————————

In context, what is the main of effect of Roosevelt's use of the word "deeds" in lines 35 and 41?

A) It illustrates the need for careful planning.

B) It demonstrates a controversial benefit of declaring war.

C) It emphasizes the importance of action.

D) It references a specific action that Roosevelt finds commendable.

4

"Sources of fresh water are shrinking at an alarming rate, and it's only going to get worse as climate change causes long periods of drought and
Line urban population growth strains rivers and reservoirs,"
5 says climatologist Nancy Flenderson of Bartlett College.
Flenderson is leading a team that recently demonstrated a new, energy efficient way of converting salt water into drinkable fresh water. …

——————————————————

The first paragraph of the passage primarily serves to

A) introduce a theory that is undermined by the evidence presented in the passage.

B) present a problem that the policies advocated for in the passage may alleviate.

C) identify a consensus that is directly challenged by the experiment discussed in the passage.

D) state a hypothesis that is supported and refined throughout the passage.

... Theories that assumed that living fur behaves like a stationary symmetrical lattice predicted that animals
10 stay warm by trapping bubbles of air, but the movement of the individual hairs as animals walk, crawl, and swim makes the actual bubbles far more varied than those produced by uniform networks. "The geometry gets pretty complicated underneath all
15 that fur," said Marvin Klipperman, a thermoregulation biologist at the Mount Hamilton School at the University of Nevada in Oakdale, where the experiment was conducted. ...

———————————————————

The author includes the quotation from Marvin Klipperman (lines 14-15) to

A) emphasize that the bubbles created by actual fur differ from those found in theoretical models.

B) explain that the structure of an animal's fur is composed of repeating units.

C) analyze the mathematical formulas used to calculate fur thickness and thermal efficiency.

D) describe how locomotion affects the size of bubbles trapped by animals hairs.

6

... They have already drafted a new experiment that
75 will investigate how learning new information about stress can impact a person's perception of his or her own stress levels, and whether that perception has further impacts on the body's stress response.
    "Their research has done a lot to advance the field,
80 but this is just the beginning," says Alfred Blackburn, a cardiologist at the College of East Hampton's Covington Hospital, who specializes in stress-induced conditions. No matter what, he says, "the modern world is changing the human body in ways we had
85 never imagined."

———————————————————

What is the main idea of the final paragraph (lines 79-85)?

A) Studying for exams can cause an increase in stress.

B) People have a responsibility to learn about the ways in which stress affects the body.

C) More research will give scientists a better understanding of the body's stress response.

D) Stress-induced conditions pose the primary threat to human health in the modern world.

... Two-hundred years later, a good number of these books still appear on shelves all over the world.
25   Yet for many people, reading the classics is anything but enjoyable—a tedious struggle through boring stories and archaic language. In many cases, their frustration is valid. Novels from the nineteenth century often feature scenarios that do not resonate
30 with modern audiences. The day-to-day lives of the characters look nothing like the experiences of today's readers. While some may point to the jostling, cramped carriage rides in Dickensian England as the equivalent of an early morning subway commute in
35 twenty-first century New York City, most people will have trouble seeing the similarity through unfamiliar language that describes a long-outdated mode of transportation. With so many other options available, who wouldn't pick up a modern novel set in a world
40 with smart phones, social media, and air travel? That kind of setting doesn't require much effort to understand.
    There are ways to make the classics easier to digest. ...

———————————————————

What function does the fourth paragraph (lines 25-42) serve in the passage as a whole?

A) It provides a more detailed version of the argument introduced in the previous paragraph.

B) It admits that cultural cornerstones valued by the author of the passage can reasonably be seen as flawed.

C) It describes a problem that literary professionals mentioned in the passage have failed to address.

D) It undermines an educational policy that the passage as a whole supports with concrete data.

Exercise: LR Short Passage

Questions 1-4 are based on the following passage.

This passage is adapted from George Washington's *Farewell Address*, first published in 1796. Washington was the first president of the United States of America from 1789 to 1797.

    Friends and Fellow Citizens:
    The period for a new election of a citizen to administer the executive government of the United
Line States being not far distant, and the time actually
5 arrived when your thoughts must be employed in designating the person who is to be clothed with that important trust, it appears to me proper, especially as it may conduce to a more distinct expression of the public voice, that I should now apprise you of the
10 resolution I have formed, to decline being considered among the number of those out of whom a choice is to be made.
    I beg you, at the same time, to do me the justice to be assured that this resolution has not been taken
15 without a strict regard to all the considerations appertaining to the relation which binds a dutiful citizen to his country; and that in withdrawing the tender of service, which silence in my situation might imply, I am influenced by no diminution of zeal for
20 your future interest, no deficiency of grateful respect for your past kindness, but am supported by a full conviction that the step is compatible with both.
    The acceptance of, and continuance hitherto in, the office to which your suffrages have twice called me
25 have been a uniform sacrifice of inclination to the opinion of duty and to a deference for what appeared to be your desire. I constantly hoped that it would have been much earlier in my power, consistently with motives which I was not at liberty to disregard, to
30 return to that retirement from which I had been reluctantly drawn. The strength of my inclination to do this, previous to the last election, had even led to the preparation of an address to declare it to you; but mature reflection on the then perplexed and critical
35 posture of our affairs with foreign nations, and the unanimous advice of persons entitled to my confidence, impelled me to abandon the idea.
    I rejoice that the state of your concerns, external as well as internal, no longer renders the pursuit of
40 inclination incompatible with the sentiment of duty or propriety, and am persuaded, whatever partiality may be retained for my services, that, in the present circumstances of our country, you will not disapprove my determination to retire.

1

The sentence in lines 2-12 ("The period ... made") suggests that Washington decided to address the American public because

A) he was prohibited from seeking reelection.

B) the people did not want him to run for another term.

C) the date for the next presidential election was approaching.

D) he wanted to assure the people that they could trust the executive branch.

2

In describing his reasons for declining a third term, Washington indicates that this "step" (line 22)

A) was undertaken for the nation's future benefit.

B) lacked respect for the nation's past kindness.

C) did not reflect his personal desire.

D) was met with wide praise.

3

In context, what is the main effect of Washington's use of the word "inclination" in lines 25 and 31?

A) It illustrates his preference for democracy.

B) It explains his political philosophy.

C) It emphasizes his hesitance to serve as president.

D) It identifies his reason for seeking reelection.

4

Which choice best summarizes the final paragraph?

A) Washington introduces a controversial viewpoint and asks for agreement.

B) Washington analyzes a counterargument and dismisses it with a relatable anecdote.

C) Washington makes a proposal and proposes steps to achieve it.

D) Washington acknowledges a change in circumstances and hopes for sympathy.

No Line Reference

The Basics

No Line Reference Questions present a major hurdle to the **No Reading Strategy**. How can you find an answer if you don't know where to look? Some students save No Line Reference questions for last (just like Whole Passage questions). But smart students **remember the Chronology Rule**:

Example 1

Without seeing the passage, where should you expect to find the answers to the following questions?

1

The main purpose of the first paragraph (lines 1-12) is to

2

The narrator indicates that the train is

3

As used in line 19, "figure" most nearly means

4

According to the passage, the narrator is flustered because

5

As used in line 27, "right" most nearly means

6

In the third paragraph, the narrator most likely uses the words "crept" (line 31) and "lurked" (line 42) in order to

7

The interaction between the narrator and Florence serves mainly to

The Twists

Whole Passage and Evidence questions complicate things. But mastering the Chronology Rule will definitely save you a few points.

Example 2

Without seeing the passage, where should you expect to find the answers to the following questions? Which questions should be saved until the end?

8

The main purpose of the passage is to

9

Based on the passage, which of the following would be considered a habit loop?

10

In context, the author's analogy of the burn reflex mainly serves to

11

As used in line 23, "portrait" most nearly means

12

The discussion of the experiments suggests that people form habit loops in response to

13

Which choice provides the best evidence for the answer to the previous question?

14

In lines 47-48, Martinez uses the phrase "more bark than bite" to suggest that

Exercise: No Line Reference

Note: It can be a bit difficult to tell the difference between Whole Passage and No Line Reference questions. But you should try to distinguish them because they're not solved the same way. Whole Passage questions ask about repeated ideas and should be saved for last. No Line Reference questions may seem like they're about the entire passage, but they actually refer to a specific line, so they should be answered in order, according to the Chronology Rule. **Which questions in this passage are true No Line Reference questions?**

Questions 1-11 are based on the following passage.

This passage is adapted from Mike Settele, *Discovering the Narwhal: The Search for the Truth about the Whale's Famous Tooth.* ©2019 by Mike Settele.

Scientists at the Arctic College of Norway in Svalbard have undertaken one of the most extensive marine mammal studies to date, hoping to finally put
Line to rest the question of why narwhals have their unique
5 tusk. By comparing narwhals to other toothed whales across 19 different characteristics, the researchers were able to cast doubt on a number of theories regarding the evolutionary origin of the narwhal's most distinctive feature.
10 The most popular theory was that male narwhals use their tusk to assert dominance against rival males, similar to how terrestrial mammals use horns to compete for alpha status. This hypothesis was supported by researchers who had witnessed tusk
15 rubbing behavior in the wild and corroborated by Arctic peoples who have hunted narwhals for generations. Furthermore, narwhals are sexually dimorphic, in that only males typically have the singular tusk. (It should be noted, however, that
20 approximately 15 percent of female narwhals grow a tusk, albeit smaller than that of males.)
"We didn't have much to go on," said lead researcher Emilie Jacobsen. "Narwhals aren't called the 'unicorns of the sea' just because of the lone tusk
25 jutting out of their heads. They're extremely elusive. Spotting one in the wild can feel like you've stumbled upon a mythical creature."
Knowing that data on narwhals would be limited, Jacobsen decided to design a comparative study that
30 could use various metrics to alert the team to any major discrepancies between the narwhal and similar species, especially its closest living relative, the beluga. Very quickly, it became clear that the tusk is not primarily used to settle male rivalries. Other

35 toothed whales do not exhibit this kind of competitive behavior, and the tusk rubbing that researchers had seen firsthand never took on the overtly aggressive tone that typically accompanies horn and antler duels in land mammals.
40 The researchers found that narwhals differed most from their whale relatives with respect to diet. "Belugas are opportunists. They'll eat pretty much anything," according to Barry Hawkins, a professor of marine biology at New Jersey University, who was not
45 involved in the study. "Narwhals, however, are picky eaters. They prey upon just a few species of cod, squid, and shrimp."
Like other whales, narwhals hunt using echolocation, a type of animal sonar that uses sound
50 waves to detect prey and map the environment, but they are much less vocal than belugas. In fact, Jacobsen's team found that there was a high correlation between a whale's "talkativeness" and the diversity of its diet. She speculated that the tusk
55 served as an antenna of sorts that enhances or replaces echolocation.
Belugas emit clicks and whistles, which bounce off a school of fish, alerting the whales that there is food ahead. However, the belugas will not know the type of
60 prey that they are hunting until they are within close proximity. Perhaps the tusk allows narwhals to identify their prey from a much larger distance so that they do not waste valuable energy pursuing something that they are unable to digest. If they did have this
65 ability, then they would not have to rely as much on echolocation, which explains why they do not "chatter" as much as belugas and other whales.
While Jacobsen's study was unable to confirm this new theory, subsequent research has found that
70 narwhal tusks contain highly sensitive nerve endings that are capable of detecting chemical changes in the water. Some narwhals were even shown to respond to changes in salinity when scientists poured water samples of varying salt content over their tusks. It is
75 not unreasonable to believe that narwhals might also be able to detect chemical markers that fish leave behind. If so, the tusk rubbing behavior, Jacobsen believes, could be a way for males to share information about where they have been, transferring
80 chemical signatures that have become ingrained in the tusk's fibers. Whatever the case, there's one thing that's clear: the narwhal is a truly amazing creature that is only beginning to share its secrets.

According to the passage, the scientists' study was unique because of the

A) diversity of the research team.

B) extreme environment in which it was conducted.

C) instruments used to collect data.

D) wide scope of its subject matter.

As used in line 7, "cast" most nearly means

A) choose.

B) mold.

C) shed.

D) place.

According to the passage, scientists believed that narwhal tusks were used to assert dominance because

A) narwhals are closely related to animals with horns.

B) people had observed tusk rubbing behavior.

C) narwhals are sexually dimorphic.

D) the tusks contain highly sensitive nerve endings.

Based on the information in the passage, which of the following would be an example of sexual dimorphism?

A) Both dolphins and bats use echolocation to hunt for food.

B) Adult mountain goats have short black horns, but newborn mountain goats do not have horns.

C) Male turkeys have brightly colored feathers, but female turkeys have drab, brown feathers.

D) Polar bears have white fur, but grizzly bears have brown fur.

The parenthetical statement in lines 19-21 ("It should … males") serves mainly to

A) analyze a method.

B) question a hypothesis.

C) define a term.

D) identify an exception.

The author of the passage implies that an advantage of the method used by Jacobsen's team was that it

A) managed to overcome a difficulty associated with studying narwhals.

B) interviewed local fishermen who had directly encountered narwhals in the wild.

C) identified the factors that have the greatest impact on narwhal diet.

D) used sonar to locate narwhals in areas that had not been included in past studies.

7

Which choice provides the best evidence for the answer to the previous question?

A) Lines 1-5 ("Scientists … tusk")

B) Lines 13-17 ("This … generations")

C) Lines 28-33 ("Knowing … beluga")

D) Lines 48-51 ("Like … belugas")

8

As used in line 41, "with respect to" most nearly means

A) in reference to.

B) with esteem for.

C) as tribute to.

D) in admiration of.

9

Which finding, if accurate, would undermine Jacobsen's theory?

A) Belugas are found to prefer eating squid over cod when both types of prey are available in similar quantities.

B) Narwhals are shown to use echolocation while hunting at rates comparable to those of other whales.

C) The population of narwhals in the Arctic is discovered to be significantly larger than previously believed.

D) Other animals with tusks do not exhibit a physical response to changes in salinity when water is poured over their tusks.

10

Which choice best supports the idea that belugas possess some ability to identify their prey?

A) Lines 42-43 ("Belugas … anything")

B) Lines 51-54 ("In fact … diet")

C) Lines 59-61 ("However … proximity")

D) Lines 74-77 ("It is … behind")

11

Based on the passage, Jacobsen would most likely agree with which statement about communication between narwhals?

A) It is conducted primarily through tusk rubbing behavior.

B) There is evidence it includes information about their past experiences.

C) It is less complex than researchers previously believed.

D) Narwhals' level of talkativeness is linked to the distance to their prey.

Whole Passage
process of elimination

The Basics

Most Whole Passage questions won't have line references, but they'll look a little different from the true No Line Reference questions. You'll see words like "main idea" and "central claim". Plus, they'll always be the first question or two immediately after the passage. Whole Passage questions are a great reminder of several parts of the SAT Reading strategy:

1. **Save Whole Passage questions for last.**
   Regardless of whether you read the passage or not, you should always answer Whole Passage questions after you've answered every other question in the passage. If you used the **No Reading Strategy**, then you'll need to answer the other questions first so that you know what the passage is about. But even if you read the passage, saving Whole Passage questions for the end gives you twice as much information about the passage because you'll be re-reading large parts of it for the other questions.

2. **Always read the blurb.**
   The blurb will include the title of the passage. Sometimes, the title will give away the main idea, especially for the science passages.

Example 1

This passage is adapted from "Growing Up: How Did the Giraffe Get Its Long Neck?" ©2015 by Science Plus News Magazine, Inc.

The main purpose of the passage is to

A) question the empirical basis of a widely held belief about giraffe anatomy.

B) describe the findings of a study examining the origins of an evolutionary trait.

C) argue that extinct species with long necks are much more common than previously thought.

D) analyze how different mammals adapted to environmental conditions in Africa.

The Twists

Some people just don't like deciding on the main idea without having read the full passage. What if you skipped an important line? That's very unlikely. **Main ideas aren't buried in some obscure corner of the passage — they're repeated throughout the passage so you won't miss them.** See if you can answer this Whole Passage example where a third of the words have been blacked out! The main ideas should still peek through…

Example 2

This passage is adapted from "Typhoon" ©1903 by Joseph Conrad. Jukes is the first mate of a ship at sea in the Pacific Ocean.

The ship, ▮ a pause ▮ comparative steadiness, ▮ upon a ▮ of rolls, ▮ worse than ▮ other, and ▮ a time ▮, preserving his ▮, was too ▮ to open ▮ mouth. As ▮ as the swinging had ▮ down somewhat, ▮ said: "This ▮ a bit ▮ much of ▮ good thing. ▮ anything is ▮ or not ▮ think she ▮ to be ▮ head on that swell. ▮ old man ▮ just gone ▮ to lie ▮. Hang me ▮ I don't ▮ to him."
▮ when he ▮ the door ▮ the chart-room ▮ saw his ▮ reading a ▮. Captain MacWhirr ▮ not lying ▮: he was ▮ up with hand grasping ▮ edge of ▮ bookshelf and ▮ other holding ▮ before his ▮ a thick ▮. The lamp ▮ in the ▮, the loosened ▮ toppled from ▮ to side ▮ the shelf, ▮ long barometer ▮ in jerky ▮, the table ▮ its slant ▮ moment. In ▮ midst of ▮ this stir ▮ movement Captain ▮, holding on, ▮ his eyes ▮ the upper ▮, and asked, "▮ the matter?"

Which choice best summarizes the passage?

A) A character's concern over a dangerous situation contrasts with another character's relative calm.

B) A character has an unexpected encounter with a friend who does not want to be disturbed.

C) Two characters disagree about the best way to solve a problem.

D) A character engages in risky behavior for the sake of accomplishing a lifelong goal.

Exercise: Whole Passage

Note: It can be a bit difficult to tell the difference between Whole Passage and No Line Reference questions. But you should try to distinguish them because they're not solved the same way. Whole Passage ask about repeated and ideas and should be saved for last. No Line Reference questions may seem like they're about the entire passage, but they actually refer to a specific line, so they should be answered in order, according to the Chronology Rule. **Which questions in this passage are about the Whole Passage?**

Questions 1-10 are based on the following passage.

This passage is adapted from Willa Cather, *My Ántonia*, originally published in 1918.

Winter comes down savagely over a little town on the prairie. The wind that sweeps in from the open country strips away all the leafy screens that hide one
Line yard from another in summer, and the houses seem to
5 draw closer together. The roofs, that looked so far away across the green tree-tops, now stare you in the face, and they are so much uglier than when their angles were softened by vines and shrubs.

In the morning, when I was fighting my way to
10 school against the wind, I couldn't see anything but the road in front of me; but in the late afternoon, when I was coming home, the town looked bleak and desolate to me. The pale, cold light of the winter sunset did not beautify—it was like the light of truth
15 itself. When the smoky clouds hung low in the west and the red sun went down behind them, leaving a pink flush on the snowy roofs and the blue drifts, then the wind sprang up afresh, with a kind of bitter song, as if it said: "This is reality, whether you like it or not.
20 All those frivolities of summer, the light and shadow, the living mask of green that trembled over everything, they were lies, and this is what was underneath. This is the truth." It was as if we were being punished for loving the loveliness of summer.
25 If I loitered on the playground after school, or went to the post-office for the mail and lingered to hear the gossip about the cigar-stand, it would be growing dark by the time I came home. The sun was gone; the frozen streets stretched long and blue before me; the
30 lights were shining pale in kitchen windows, and I could smell the suppers cooking as I passed. Few people were abroad, and each one of them was hurrying toward a fire. The glowing stoves in the houses were like magnets. When one passed an old
35 man, one could see nothing of his face but a red nose sticking out between a frosted beard and a long plush cap. The young men capered along with their hands in their pockets, and sometimes tried a slide on the icy sidewalk. The children, in their bright hoods and
40 comforters, never walked, but always ran from the moment they left their door, beating their mittens against their sides. When I got as far as the Methodist Church, I was about halfway home. I can remember how glad I was when there happened to be a light in
45 the church, and the painted glass window shone out at us as we came along the frozen street. In the winter bleakness a hunger for color came over people, like the Laplander's craving for fats and sugar. Without knowing why, we used to linger on the sidewalk
50 outside the church when the lamps were lighted early for choir practice or prayer-meeting, shivering and talking until our feet were like lumps of ice. The crude reds and greens and blues of that colored glass held us there.
55 On winter nights, the lights in the Harlings' windows drew me like the painted glass. Inside that warm, roomy house there was color, too. After supper I used to catch up my cap, stick my hands in my pockets, and dive through the willow hedge as if
60 witches were after me. Of course, if Mr. Harling was at home, if his shadow stood out on the blind of the west room, I did not go in, but turned and walked home by the long way, through the street, wondering what book I should read as I sat down with the two
65 old people.

Such disappointments only gave greater zest to the nights when we acted charades, or had a costume ball in the back parlor, with Sally always dressed like a boy. Frances taught us to dance that winter, and she
70 said, from the first lesson, that Ántonia would make the best dancer among us. On Saturday nights, Mrs. Harling used to play the old operas for us,—"Martha," "Norma," "Rigoletto,"—telling us the story while she played. Every Saturday night was like a party. The
75 parlor, the back parlor, and the dining-room were warm and brightly lighted, with comfortable chairs and sofas, and gay pictures on the walls. One always felt at ease there. Ántonia brought her sewing and sat with us—she was already beginning to make pretty
80 clothes for herself. After the long winter evenings on the prairie, with Ambrosch's sullen silences and her mother's complaints, the Harlings' house seemed, as she said, "like Heaven" to her. She was never too tired to make taffy or chocolate cookies for us. If Sally
85 whispered in her ear, or Charley gave her three winks, Tony would rush into the kitchen and build a fire in the range on which she had already cooked three meals that day.

1

Which choice best summarizes the passage?

A) The narrator recalls the day when a winter storm disrupted life in the town where he grew up.

B) The narrator explains how a town's residents coped with harsh weather conditions.

C) The narrator describes a period during his childhood that was filled with poignant memories.

D) The narrator provides details about another character's weekend routine.

2

Over the course of the passage, the narrator's use of "light" shifts from being a

A) symbol of loneliness to a potential source of entertainment.

B) reminder of the bleakness of winter to a means of escaping that bleakness.

C) sensory detail to a metaphor for newfound knowledge.

D) representation of hope to a warning that false hope can make a situation worse.

Throughout the passage, the narrator frequently

A) uses figurative language to convey his understanding of the world.

B) gives precise locations so that readers have a mental map of his hometown.

C) introduces characters who taught him valuable lessons when he was a child.

D) provides historical context so that readers learn about the events that shaped his adolescence.

In the passage, winter is mainly presented as a

A) reality that is usually obscured.

B) cozy contrast to the heat of summer.

C) temporary condition that most citizens endure.

D) hazard in the morning that reveals beauty throughout the day.

The quotation in lines 19-22 ("This ... truth") serves mainly to

A) personify the cycle of life and death in nature.

B) disclose Ántonia's true feelings about the frivolities of summer.

C) suggest that the narrator does not believe that winter is as harsh as others claim.

D) emphasize the narrator's resentment of his current environment.

It can reasonably be inferred from the passage that people's tolerance for the cold

A) fades as they get hungrier.

B) increases when they encounter an isolated pocket of color.

C) is unexplainable because they act against their own best interest.

D) is faked so that they can appear tougher.

7

Which choice provides the best evidence for the answer to the previous question?

A) Lines 31-33 ("Few … fire")

B) Lines 39-42 ("The … sides")

C) Lines 48-52 ("Without … ice")

D) Lines 52-54 ("The crude … there")

8

As used in line 56, "drew" most nearly means

A) attracted

B) tied

C) composed.

D) lengthened.

9

According to the passage, the narrator would be most disappointed when

A) the lights were on inside the Methodist Church.

B) Mr. Harling was not out of town.

C) Ambrosch and his mother would complain.

D) Mrs. Harling would sing opera.

10

As used in line 70, "make" most nearly means

A) create.

B) manufacture.

C) become.

D) appoint.

Both Passages

process of elimination

The Basics

The double passage is annoying, but it isn't inherently harder than the other passages. Most questions will be normal Reading questions. About 4 will technically be about <u>both</u> passages, but even these are more like traditional Reading questions. Follow the same rules:

Whole Passage and Line Reference
- Use POE.
- Make Dumb Summaries.
- Obey the +1 Sentence Rule.

No Line Reference and Evidence Pairs
- Use POE.
- Make Dumb Summaries.
- **The Chronology Rule might not work!** The questions that are only about one of the passages will still be in order, but the chronology "resets" with the comparative/ double questions. Essentially, be flexible on the double passage. Since they're making you jump between two passages, it can be hard to tell what the chronology is anyway.

Also, don't forget to **read the blurb** before the passages. As always, it will include helpful information about the passages. Sometimes, you can even figure out the relationship between them:

Example 1

Use only the blurb to make a dumb summary for the relationship question (choices omitted):

These passages are adapted from the Webster-Hayne debate. Passage 1 is from a speech by Senator Robert Y. Hayne of South Carolina. Passage 2 is from a speech by Senator Daniel Webster of Massachusetts. Hayne and Webster engaged in a debate on the Senate floor over several days in January 1830.

Which choice best states the relationship between the two passages?

The Twists

The worst thing about the double passage is that it's frequently the old-timey Great Global Conversations passage. It's already difficult to juggle two passages, but when they're written in 1800s vocabulary, it's even more annoying. Three pieces of advice:

First, **dumb summaries** are your best friend. Remember the **50% Rule**. You don't need to understand every nuance of the author's point. Are they in favor of something or against something? Do they like government or hate it? Connotations can usually help you eliminate half of the wrong answers, which at least allows you to guess more intelligently.

Second, **base all of your answers on the passage**. It's tempting to use your own history knowledge, but you're not supposed to. You may remember that Lincoln freed the slaves, but that does <u>not</u> mean that he was always in favor of abolition. In fact, you will often encounter old-timey passages that argue something we would find offensive today. You <u>must</u> answer based on the passage, not your own morals. Some authors will argue in favor of slavery or against women's rights.

Third, if you insist on reading the passages before you answer the questions, break the passages up so that you only have to focus on one at a time:

1. **read passage 1**
   - write a dumb summary
2. **answer passage 1 questions**
   - usually 3 questions
3. **read passage 2**
   - write a dumb summary, and note how it relates to passage 1
4. **answer passage 2 questions**
   - usually 3 questions
5. **answer Both Passages questions**
   - usually 4 questions
   - refer back to your dumb summaries

Exercise: Both Passages

Questions 1-11 are based on the following passage.

These passages are adapted from the Webster-Hayne debate. Passage 1 is from a speech by Senator Robert Y. Hayne of South Carolina. Passage 2 is from a speech by Senator Daniel Webster of Massachusetts. Hayne and Webster engaged in a debate on the Senate floor over several days in January 1830.

Passage 1

Sir, as to the doctrine that the Federal Government is the exclusive judge of the extent as well as the limitations of its powers, it seems to be utterly
Line subversive of the sovereignty and independence of the
5 States. It makes but little difference, in my estimation, whether Congress or the Supreme Court, are invested with this power. If the Federal Government, in all or any of its departments, are to prescribe the limits of its own authority; and the States are bound to submit to
10 the decision, and are not to be allowed to examine and decide for themselves, when the barriers of the Constitution shall be overleaped, this is practically "a Government without limitation of powers;" the States are at once reduced to mere petty corporations, and
15 the people are entirely at your mercy.

I have but one word more to add. In all the efforts that have been made by South Carolina to resist the unconstitutional laws which Congress has extended over them, she has kept steadily in view the
20 preservation of the Union, by the only means by which she believes it can be long preserved—a firm, manly, and steady resistance against usurpation. The measures of the Federal Government have, it is true, prostrated her interests, and will soon involve the
25 whole South in irretrievable ruin. But this evil, great as it is, is not the chief ground of our complaints. It is the principle involved in the contest, a principle which, substituting the discretion of Congress for the limitations of the Constitution, brings the States and
30 the people to the feet of the Federal Government, and leaves them nothing they can call their own.

Sir, if the measures of the Federal Government were less oppressive, we should still strive against this usurpation. The South is acting on a principle she has
35 always held sound—resistance to unauthorized taxation. These, Sir, are the principles which induced the immortal Hampden[1] to resist the payment of a tax of twenty shillings—"Would twenty shillings have ruined his fortune? No—but the payment of half
40 twenty shillings, on the principle on which it was demanded, would have made him a slave." Sir, if, in

acting on these high motives—if, animated by that ardent love of liberty which has always been the most prominent trait in the Southern character, we should
45 be hurried beyond the bounds of a cold and calculating prudence, who is there with one noble and generous sentiment in his bosom, who would not be disposed in the language of Burke[2], to exclaim, "you must pardon something to the spirit of liberty!"

Passage 2

50 If the gentleman had intended no more than to assert the right of revolution, for justifiable cause, he would have said only what all agree to. But I cannot conceive that there can be a middle course, between submission to the laws, when regularly pronounced
55 constitutional, on the one hand, and open resistance, which is revolution, or rebellion, on the other. I say, the right of a State to annul a law of Congress, cannot be maintained, but on the ground of the unalienable right of man to resist oppression; that is to say, upon
60 the ground of revolution. I admit that there is an ultimate violent remedy, above the Constitution, and in defiance of the Constitution, which may be resorted to, when a revolution is to be justified. But I do not admit that, under the Constitution, and in conformity
65 with it, there is any mode in which a State Government, as a member of the Union, can interfere and stop the progress of the General Government, by force of her own laws, under any circumstances whatever.

70 This leads us to inquire into the origin of this Government, and the source of its power. Whose agent is it? Is it the creature of the State Legislatures, or the creature of the People? If the Government of the United States be the agent of the State
75 Governments, then they may control it, provided they can agree in the manner of controlling it; if it be the agent of the People, then the People alone can control it, restrain it, modify, or reform it. It is observable enough, that the doctrine for which the honorable
80 gentleman contends, leads him to the necessity of maintaining, not only that this General Government is the creature of the States, but that it is the creature of each of the States severally; so that each may assert the power, for itself, of determining whether it acts
85 within the limits of its authority. It is the servant of four-and-twenty masters, of different wills and different purposes, and yet bound to obey all. This absurdity (for it seems no less) arises from a misconception as to the origin of this Government and
90 its true character. It is, sir, the People's Constitution,

the People's Government; made for the People; made
by the People; and answerable to the People. The
People of the United States have declared that this
Constitution shall be the Supreme Law. We must
95 either admit the proposition, or dispute their authority.

1 John Hampden (1595–1643), an English politician
who resisted the King and helped bring about the
English Civil War.

2 Edmund Burke (1729–1797), an Irish statesman who
was supportive of the American Revolution as a
member of the English Parliament.

1

As used in line 9, "submit" most nearly means

A) present.

B) offer.

C) refer.

D) agree.

2

Based on Passage 1, Hayne would be most likely to
agree with which claim about the federal government?

A) Its powers are shared equally by Congress and the
Supreme Court.

B) It cannot be constrained unless the states have a
means of overruling unconstitutional laws.

C) It is an essential impediment to the expansion of
oppressive taxation.

D) It is responsible for preserving the Union and
protecting the People from violent revolutions.

3

Which choice provides the best evidence for the
answer to the previous question?

A) Lines 5-7 ("It makes … power")

B) Lines 7-13 ("If the … powers")

C) Lines 22-25 ("The measures … ruin")

D) Lines 36-41 ("These … slave")

4

In the final paragraph of Passage 1, the main purpose
of Hayne's reference to Hampden is to

A) outline the conditions under which the People
have a right to rebel against their government.

B) suggest that compromise is unlikely when matters
of principle are at stake.

C) use a historical example to create an analogy with
the present situation.

D) cite an authority who agrees with Hayne's
argument that the federal government should be
limited.

5

In Passage 2, Webster makes which point about the
relationship between the Constitution and violent
revolution?

A) The Constitution lists the differences between
revolution and rebellion.

B) The Constitution can only be overruled by a
revolution of the People.

C) The Constitution allows for revolution in cases
where the states are oppressing the People.

D) The Constitution prohibits revolution by the
People against the federal government.

6

As used in line 65, "mode" most nearly means

A) trend.

B) style.

C) manner.

D) status.

Which choice best states the relationship between the two passages?

A) Passage 2 attacks a central assumption of the argument made in Passage 1.

B) Passage 2 provides historical context for the scenario described in Passage 1.

C) Passage 2 states explicitly ideas that were merely implied in Passage 1.

D) Passage 2 examines possible solutions to the problems discussed in Passage 1.

8

Hayne would most likely have responded to Webster's claim that there can be no "middle course" (line 53) by asserting that

A) the People have chosen to submit to the power of the federal government rather than revolt.

B) Southern morality values compromise over conflict.

C) state governments intend to challenge the constitutionality of laws in the courts.

D) South Carolina's resistance to the federal government serves to sustain the Union.

Which choice provides the best evidence for the answer to the previous question?

A) Lines 1-5 ("Sir ... States")

B) Lines 16-22 ("In all ... usurpation")

C) Lines 25-26 ("But ... complaints")

D) Lines 46-49 ("who ... liberty")

10

Based on the passages, both Hayne and Webster would agree with which of the following claims?

A) The people have sole authority to determine the constitutionality of a law.

B) There are situations when resistance to government is justified.

C) Businesses should not be subjected to unnecessary government control.

D) Sovereignty is shared equally by the federal government and the states.

Based on Passage 2, Webster would most likely say that basing the federal government on the "sovereignty and independence of the States" (lines 4-5, Passage 1) would have which effect?

A) It would cause different states to give the federal government conflicting instructions.

B) It would enhance the People's ability to establish just laws.

C) It would ensure that the federal government becomes the victim of violent revolution.

D) It would prevent the federal government from unfairly imposing new taxes.

Evidence

The Basics

Evidence is information that supports a claim. Evidence is <u>not</u> simply a restatement of the claim. If you understand this distinction, you'll have an easier time with the Evidence questions. Still, these are genuinely difficult. The Evidence Pairs have a lot of moving parts. It's okay to struggle with them.

The Twists

At a certain point, you just have to accept that the Reading section of the SAT won't ever feel "scientific". Unlike Writing and Math, the rules aren't as set in stone. The passages and the vocabulary are not very predictable. You might get lucky and have five easy-to-understand passages, or you could end up with a double passage written in the 1700s. Success on the Reading section is about confidence. You can't let one hard question or passage distract you. This is especially true with Evidence questions, which take time and can make you feel lost.

Using the Reading rules will help. The **Chronology Rule** also applies to Evidence questions, so if you're stuck between two line references, pick the one that fits in with the chronology of the surrounding questions. Also, **POE** still works on the first evidence question, so eliminate choices with **Strong Words**, even if you're not entirely sure what the line references are saying.

Most importantly, remember that the question, line reference, and choices all need to match. Get rid of line references that restate the claim in the question without providing evidence of why the claim is true. Eliminate line references that are completely irrelevant, but do not worry about finding one correct line reference immediately. It's okay to have two or three that you're considering. Once you use POE to sort through the answer choices, you might better understand line references that made no sense to you before. Success on Evidence questions comes from being flexible and having an open mind.

Packets

- <u>unpaired evidence</u>
- <u>evidence pairs (parts 1 and 2)</u>

approximately 20 questions per test

worth approximately 100 points total

Reading		LR	LR	LR	LR
noLR	noLR	noLR	LR	LR	LR
noLR	noLR	WP	WP	WP	WP
ev1	ev1	ev1	both	both	both
ev1	ev1	ev2	ev2	ev2	evU
ev1	ev1	ev2	ev2	ev2	evU
ev1	ev1	ev2	ev2	ev2	Rfig
Rvoc	Rvoc	Rvoc	Rvoc	Rfig	Rfig
Rvoc	Rvoc	Rvoc	Rvoc	Rfig	Rfig

Important Ideas

What is evidence?

Evidence proves or supports a claim. It's vital that you understand this definition. The SAT will frequently offer you line references that repeat the question but do not provide evidence for the answer. Here's part of an example Evidence Pair:

Question from Part 1:

Fitzgerald believed that the rats had developed resistance to the worms because

[choices omitted]

Question and two Line References from Part 2:

Which choice provides the best evidence for the answer to the previous question?

A) "Fitzgerald's team found that some of the rats became immune to the worm after a few weeks."

B) "When dead worms began to appear in the rats' waste, he speculated that the rats were able to deprive the worms of the nutrients needed to survive inside their hosts."

Line Reference A is <u>not</u> evidence. It merely restates the question. This is sometimes called a **"what"** choice because it only tells you what you already know.

Line Reference B is a great example of evidence. It supports the idea that is stated in the question. This is sometimes called a **"why"** choice because it goes beyond the question and explains why the claim is true.

In other words, the question told you that the rats developed immunity. The question wants to know <u>how</u> Fitzgerald knew this. His evidence was the dead worms in the waste, and your evidence is the line reference that says this.

Typically you only need to read the exact lines given to you in the choices. The +1 Sentence Rule does <u>not</u> apply on Evidence questions. However, **read extra whenever you need to clarify what a pronoun is referring to or which person is being quoted.**

Unpaired Evidence

Underline key ideas in the question. It's important to understand the claim you're asked to support.

Beware **copy/paste** choices that simply repeat phrases from the question. Match ideas, not words.

Unpaired Evidence questions **break the Chronology Rule** more than other question types. When in doubt, stick to the Chronology Rule, but if you feel strongly that an out-of-order line reference is correct, it's okay to break the rule.

Evidence Pairs

Continue to use the QLC Method:

1. **Question** (from Part 1)
   - underline key words in the question so that you are reading the line references with purpose.

2. **Line References** (from Part 2)
   - eliminate line references that are completely unrelated to the question
   - keep line references that are even slightly relevant
   - do not eliminate line references just because you do not understand them
   - it's not necessary to get down to one answer at this point; keep your options open

3. **Choices** (from Part 1)
   - use POE to get rid of choices that do not match any of your remaining line references
   - remember that three things must match — the question, the line reference, and the choice

Pacing

Evidence questions, especially Evidence Pairs, are often the most time-consuming questions on the Reading section. If you're pressed for time, you can quickly guess using SAT strategies:
   - Use the **Chronology Rule** to eliminate out-of-order line references. Guess from what's left.
   - Find and eliminate answer choices with obvious **Strong Words**. Guess from what's left.

Unpaired Evidence

evidence

The Basics

There aren't many Unpaired Evidence questions on the test, but they are very useful for learning the strategies that you'll use on the Evidence Pairs.

First, it's important to know what the SAT means by "evidence". You need to pick the line that proves the question true. Look for matching ideas, but be careful of exact copies of words and phrases. **The SAT likes to copy/paste distinctive phrases from the passage to trick you.** Correct answers tend to use synonyms of key phrases.

Normally, you'll need to go to the listed line references in the passage, but this example lists them in the choices for simplicity.

Example 1

Which choice best supports the idea that the human health effects of microplastics are poorly understood?

A) Lines 1-4 ("A recent study has given scientists a frightening look at the threat posed by microplastics, the tiny plastic particles that find their way into our air, water, and soil.")

B) Lines 13-17 ("A one liter sample of soil contained nearly 17,000 grains that were greater than 10 micrometers in diameter, which is still small enough to be absorbed by the large intestine.")

C) Lines 18-22 ("The study confirmed that there is no shortage of ways for these particles to enter our bodies, yet very little is known about how the chemicals that they are composed of interact with living tissue.")

D) Lines 44-46 ("Ludlow hopes her research alerts the public to the danger that microplastics pose to human health and our fragile ecosystems.")

The Twists

The trickiest choices will seem to capture the idea mentioned in the question, but they won't qualify as true evidence of that idea. **Typically, the problem will be that the line reference states what the author knows instead of explaining why she knows it.** Always read all of the choices so that you don't get tricked.

Example 2

Which choice best explains how microplastics enter the soil in areas that are far from population centers?

A) Lines 6-12 ("Theresa Ludlow, a climatologist at the Hamilton Center for Climate Change Mitigation, devised the study to better understand how microplastics were entering drinking water reservoirs hundreds of miles from the urban centers they supported.")

B) Lines 30-35 ("Ludlow's team surveyed soils in a variety of places: densely populated cities, quiet suburbs, agricultural communities, national parks, and some of the most remote landscapes on Earth. In all of them—every single one—they found microplastics.")

C) Lines 36-39 ("The culprit is trade winds that keep the tiniest particles aloft, carrying everything from flecks of varnish to microscopic threads of nylon hundreds of miles from their source.")

D) Lines 41-42 ("The pollution will only get worse as plastic waste proliferates.")

It's also worth noting that **Unpaired Evidence questions tend to break the Chronology Rule** more than other question types. There isn't really a good reason why, and it doesn't happen every time, but you should be aware of it. The good news is that Unpaired Evidence questions typically have fairly obvious answers, so you will be more confident that you're breaking the Chronology Rule for a valid reason.

Exercise: Unpaired Evidence

1

Which choice best supports the claim that populist movements are linked to periods of government centralization?

A) Lines 61-65 ("Although these movements lacked the political power to bring about the changes they sought, they did see moments of strength when governments nationalized a major industry or instituted new social programs.")

B) Lines 65-68 ("Rural areas, in particular, found themselves undergoing change at a pace that hadn't been seen since the Industrial Revolution.")

C) Lines 76-78 ("Candidates on both the left and the right have made populist appeals by criticizing elites.")

D) Lines 78-82 ("Since the elites are typically perceived to belong to the same political party that controls the government, populism may be more a tactic for minority groups than a coherent political philosophy.")

2

Which choice best supports the claim that the narrator has an unpleasant history with Mrs. Reed?

A) Lines 41-46 ("I soon rose, quietly took off my bonnet and gloves, uninvited, and said I would just step out to Bessie—who was, I dared say, in the kitchen—and ask her to ascertain whether Mrs. Reed was disposed to receive me or not tonight.")

B) Lines 55-57 ("I did not need to be guided to the well-known room, to which I had so often been summoned for chastisement or reprimand in former days.")

C) Lines 57-59 ("I hastened before Bessie; I softly opened the door: a shaded light stood on the table, for it was now getting dark.")

D) Lines 63-64 ("Well did I remember Mrs. Reed's face, and I eagerly sought the familiar image.")

3

Which choice best supports the conclusion that Bobby feels uncomfortable among his new coworkers?

A) Line 14 ("Bobby waited for the right moment.")

B) Line 14-17 ("He had only been there a week, but they already acted like he knew the ins and outs of the daily routine.")

C) Lines 19-22 ("Not knowing the lingo, he was afraid to join in.")

D) Lines 22-24 ("They talked about "the file zone," which was either a real place where real files were stored or some sort of zen-like office worker state of mind.")

4

Which choice best supports the view of the "critics" (line 17)?

A) Lines 48-51 ("While 72% of subjects performed significantly better on the grid-based memory test, another 19% showed the same level of recall on the color-based test.")

B) Lines 51-53 ("The control group did not show a significant improvement on the randomized test.")

C) Lines 58-61 ("However, when the color group was given a second test that also included a spatial component, recall improved even further.")

D) Lines 71-74 ("Waverley points out that whether the test was grid-based or color-based had a significant impact on the subject's ability to remember the answers.")

Note: This question obviously requires one extra step — you need to go to the line reference in the question and figure out what the critics believe. But once you do, it's just another Evidence question. The relevant lines are below:

Lines 14-19

One theory holds that something deep in the structure of the brain relates abstract concepts to physical locations, which makes all memories fundamentally spatial. However, some critics contend that memory mapping is a technique that some—but not all—people develop in their adolescence. In other words, it's just one strategy for forming memories among many.

Evidence Pairs

evidence

The Basics

Evidence Pairs suck. It's not that they're necessarily harder. It's more that they're annoying because there is so much information to keep track of. It's important that you work through these questions with a plan. You should continue to use the **QLC Method** to move through the Evidence Pairs methodically:

1. **Question** (from Part 1)
   - read it and understand it
   - underline key words that you'll keep in mind as you sort through the line references
   - it's important that you read the line reference with purpose, searching for the ideas that are mentioned in the question

2. **Line References** (from Part 2)
   - you can use the Chronology Rule to guide you, but go back to <u>all of the references</u>, regardless of the line numbers
   - read <u>only</u> the indicated lines, and eliminate any choices that do not relate to the question
   - if you're confused by a mysterious pronoun or an unknown speaker, read a little extra to gain context
   - jot down **dumb summaries** to help you remember the main idea of the line reference
   - you do <u>not</u> need to pick an answer at this point

3. **Choices** (from Part 1)
   - read them, compare them to the remaining line references, and use POE to eliminate any choices that do not relate to the question or the evidence.
   - remember that you are looking for a <u>pair</u> of correct answers!
   - if you have to guess, use the **Chronology Rule** and avoid **Strong Words**

The Twists

All three parts need to match.

Example 1

Despite the promise of lepidopterase, there are a number of reasons that the medical community should
45 not celebrate just yet. "Our results are preliminary," says Ulrich. "They still need to be independently verified, and that process will likely take years."

Even if Ulrich's findings are corroborated, there's no guarantee that lepidopterase can be collected and
50 implemented as a treatment on a large scale. Ulrich's team found that in 26 percent of cases, the enzyme became denatured for unknown reasons, rendering large quantities unusable. In some cases, the problem was only discovered after it had been injected into
55 patients, despite rigorous quality control testing.

Ulrich notes that harvesting enough lepidopterase to conduct sufficient trials to satisfy federal regulators will require an exorbitant investment, which would mean taking funds away from other breakthrough
60 treatments at a time when the pharmaceutical industry is already cutting its research and development budget. What's more, there's a concern that pursuing lepidopterase research could put butterfly populations in jeopardy. "Many of these species are already
65 vulnerable from habitat loss and climate change," says Ulrich, and the increased pressure on their populations "could push them over the brink."

1

The passage indicates that a problem involved with future lepidopterase research is that

A) other areas of study could be ignored.

B) the next phase has a long timeframe.

C) there are not enough butterflies left to harvest.

D) executives have blocked further experimentation.

2

Which choice provides the best evidence for the answer to the previous question?

A) Lines 43-45 ("Despite … yet")

B) Lines 50-53 ("Ulrich's … unusable")

C) Lines 56-62 ("Ulrich … budget")

D) Lines 62-64 ("What's … jeopardy")

Exercise: Evidence Pairs

Questions 1-12 are based on the following passage.

This passage is adapted from Sinclair Lewis, *Babbitt*, originally published in 1922.

To George F. Babbitt, as to most prosperous citizens of Zenith, his motor car was poetry and tragedy, love and heroism. The office was his pirate
Line ship but the car his perilous excursion ashore.
5   Among the tremendous crises of each day none was more dramatic than starting the engine. It was slow on cold mornings; there was the long, anxious whirr of the starter; and sometimes he had to drip ether into the cocks of the cylinders, which was so
10 very interesting that at lunch he would chronicle it drop by drop, and orally calculate how much each drop had cost him.

This morning he was darkly prepared to find something wrong, and he felt belittled when the
15 mixture exploded sweet and strong, and the car didn't even brush the door-jamb, gouged and splintery with many bruisings by fenders, as he backed out of the garage. He was confused. He shouted "Morning!" to Sam Doppelbrau with more cordiality than he had
20 intended.

Babbitt's green and white Dutch Colonial house was one of three in that block on Chatham Road. To the left of it was the residence of Mr. Samuel Doppelbrau, secretary of an excellent firm of
25 bathroom-fixture jobbers. His was a comfortable house with no architectural manners whatever; a large wooden box with a squat tower, a broad porch, and glossy paint yellow as a yolk. Babbitt disapproved of Mr. and Mrs. Doppelbrau as "Bohemian." From their
30 house came midnight music and obscene laughter; there were neighborhood rumors of bootlegged whisky and fast motor rides. They furnished Babbitt with many happy evenings of discussion, during which he announced firmly, "I'm not strait-laced, and
35 I don't mind seeing a fellow throw in a drink once in a while, but when it comes to deliberately trying to get away with a lot of hell-raising all the while like the Doppelbraus do, it's too rich for my blood!"

On the other side of Babbitt lived Howard
40 Littlefield, Ph.D., in a strictly modern house whereof the lower part was dark red tapestry brick, with a leaded oriel, the upper part of pale stucco like spattered clay, and the roof red-tiled. Littlefield was the Great Scholar of the neighborhood; the authority

45 on everything in the world except babies, cooking, and motors. He was a Bachelor of Arts of Blodgett College, and a Doctor of Philosophy in economics of Yale. He was the employment-manager and publicity-counsel of the Zenith Street Traction Company. He
50 could, on ten hours' notice, appear before the board of aldermen or the state legislature and prove, absolutely, with figures all in rows and with precedents from Poland and New Zealand, that the street-car company loved the Public and yearned over its employees; that
55 all its stock was owned by Widows and Orphans; and that whatever it desired to do would benefit property-owners by increasing rental values, and help the poor by lowering rents. All his acquaintances turned to Littlefield when they desired to know the date of the
60 battle of Saragossa, the definition of the word "sabotage," the future of the German mark, the translation of "hinc illae lachrimae," or the number of products of coal tar. He awed Babbitt by confessing that he often sat up till midnight reading the figures
65 and footnotes in Government reports, or skimming (with amusement at the author's mistakes) the latest volumes of chemistry, archeology, and ichthyology.

But Littlefield's great value was as a spiritual example. Despite his strange learnings he was as strict
70 a Presbyterian and as firm a Republican as George F. Babbitt. He confirmed the business men in the faith. Where they knew only by passionate instinct that their system of industry and manners was perfect, Dr. Howard Littlefield proved it to them, out of history,
75 economics, and the confessions of reformed radicals.

Babbitt had a good deal of honest pride in being the neighbor of such a savant, and in Ted's intimacy with Eunice Littlefield. At sixteen Eunice was interested in no statistics save those regarding the ages
80 and salaries of motion-picture stars, but—as Babbitt definitively put it—"she was her father's daughter."

The difference between a light man like Sam Doppelbrau and a really fine character like Littlefield was revealed in their appearances. Doppelbrau was
85 disturbingly young for a man of forty-eight. He wore his derby on the back of his head, and his red face was wrinkled with meaningless laughter. But Littlefield was old for a man of forty-two. He was tall, broad, thick; his gold-rimmed spectacles were engulfed in the
90 folds of his long face; his hair was a tossed mass of greasy blackness; he puffed and rumbled as he talked; his Phi Beta Kappa key shone against a spotty black vest; he smelled of old pipes; he was altogether funereal and archidiaconal; and to real-estate
95 brokerage and the jobbing of bathroom-fixtures he added an aroma of sanctity.

1

Throughout the passage, George F. Babbitt is portrayed as someone who is

A) curious about how things work.

B) judgmental about other people's conduct.

C) charitable toward his neighbors.

D) eager to help those in need.

2

Which choice best supports the claim that the ideology of Zenith's business men was partially based on assumptions?

A) Lines 3-4 ("The office … ashore")

B) Lines 28-29 ("Babbitt … Bohemian")

C) Lines 72-75 ("Where … radicals")

D) Lines 93-96 ("he was … sanctity")

3

As used in line 16, "brush" most nearly means

A) graze.

B) clean.

C) paint.

D) wipe.

4

Based on the discussion of Babbitt's car in the beginning of the passage (lines 1-20), it is reasonable to infer that Babbitt would consider a problem with the car's ignition to be

A) an unanticipated and frustrating obstacle.

B) the result of neglecting regular maintenance.

C) a satisfying start to his daily routine.

D) an opportunity to bond with his neighbors.

5

Which choice provides the best evidence for the answer to the previous question?

A) Lines 1-3 ("To George … heroism")

B) Lines 5-6 ("Among … engine")

C) Lines 13-18 ("This … garage")

D) Lines 18-20 ("He shouted … intended")

6

The narrator uses the phrase "no architectural manners" (line 26) to emphasize that the Doppelbrau's house is

A) disrespectful.

B) inviting.

C) spacious.

D) unsightly.

7

It can be most reasonably inferred from the passage that Howard Littlefield's use of statistics is

A) contrived, because he argues that contradictory ideas are simultaneously true.

B) impressive, because he can recite scientific facts more eloquently than the experts.

C) unappreciated, because legislators use other sources of information when making decisions.

D) novel, because few people have the time to research a wide variety of subjects.

8

Which choice provides the best evidence for the answer to the previous question?

A) Lines 49-54 ("He could ... employees")

B) Lines 56-58 ("that whatever ... rents")

C) Lines 58-63 ("All ... tar")

D) Lines 63-67 ("He awed ... ichthyology")

9

Based on the passage, Babbitt is portrayed as being

A) fascinated by numbers.

B) intolerant of his neighbors.

C) passionate about education.

D) steadfast in his convictions.

10

The narrator suggests that one reason Babbitt admires Littlefield is that Littlefield

A) hosts entertaining parties that strengthen Zenith's sense of community.

B) convinces many in the neighborhood of the rightness of their beliefs.

C) is a successful businessman who also makes time for public service.

D) displays complete devotion to his daughter's success.

11

Which choice provides the best evidence for the answer to the previous question?

A) Lines 32-38 ("They furnished ... blood")

B) Lines 43-46 ("Littlefield ... motors")

C) Lines 68-69 ("But ... example")

D) Line 71 ("He ... faith")

12

As used in line 79, "save" most nearly means

A) protect.

B) conserve.

C) except.

D) store.

Quick Questions

The Basics

If you consistently run out of time on the SAT Reading, you need to develop strategies that maximize the number of correct answers. The No Reading strategy works because it saves you about 15 minutes that you would normally spend reading the passages. You'll still need to read the line references for each question, but you would have done that anyway. It's true that you may get a few more questions wrong here and there. However, one or two extra mistakes on the first four passages would be worth it if you get most of the fifth passage right instead of leaving it blank. If you still can't finish the final passage, skip directly to the Quick Questions to add some relatively easy points.

The Twists

Although these questions are quick, they still hide tricks and traps, so you need to be careful. In fact, the SAT is hoping that you move too quickly through these questions to notice that you're getting tricked. But if you know how the SAT is trying to manipulate you, you're more likely to beat them at their own game. As always, knowing the SAT's special rules is half the battle.

Reading Vocab questions ask about common words with multiple definitions. However, the correct answer is usually an uncommon meaning of the common word. The best way to avoid getting tricked is to read the line reference as if the vocab word were a blank and **guess your own word** that captures the same meaning. Compare your guess to the choices.

Reading Figures questions are almost always about the graph or chart, even when they also reference the passage. At the least, you should start with the figure because it's easier to read than the passage. Read everything — titles, axis labels, legends, and footnotes. Use POE to sort through the choices. If the figure doesn't mention a word or idea from the choice, then it's probably not right. Remember that the figure itself needs to be evidence of the answer. You should not have to make inferences or guesses about what the data means.

Packets

- reading vocab
- reading figures

approximately 13 questions per test

worth approximately 70 points total

Reading	LR	LR	LR	LR
noLR	noLR	noLR	LR	LR	LR
noLR	noLR	WP	WP	WP	WP
ev1	ev1	ev1	both	both	both
ev1	ev1	ev2	ev2	ev2	evU
ev1	ev1	ev2	ev2	ev2	evU
ev1	ev1	ev2	ev2	ev2	Rfig
Rvoc	Rvoc	Rvoc	Rvoc	Rfig	Rfig
Rvoc	Rvoc	Rvoc	Rvoc	Rfig	Rfig

Important Ideas

Pacing

These are called Quick Questions because they can be solved quickly. Duh!

If you reach the fifth and final passage with less than 10 minutes remaining, you should skip directly to the Vocab and Figure questions. They require very little reading, and they are typically among the easiest questions in the Reading section.

Overall, if you're pressed for time, you should answer the final passage questions in this order:
1. Reading Vocab
2. Reading Figures
3. Line Reference (read +1 Sentence)
4. Unpaired Evidence
5. No Line Reference (use Chronology Rule)
6. Both Passages (skim, use dumb summaries)
7. Whole Passage (skim, use dumb summaries)
8. Evidence Pairs (use Chronology Rule)

Reading Vocab

Follow the QLC Method:

1. **Question** — read it <u>without</u> looking at the answer choices to avoid getting biased

2. **Line Reference**
   • read the sentence that contains the vocab word
   • treat the vocab word as a blank, and try to **guess a replacement** word that captures the meaning
   • use or steal clue words from the sentence to help you come up with an accurate guess

3. **Choices** — pick the answer that best matches your guess

Reading Vocab questions typically ask about common words with multiple meanings. Coming up with your own guess prevents you from getting tricked. Do <u>not</u> simply pick the definition that you're most familiar with. You need to prove it using the context.

Reading Figures

Focus on the graph or chart. The passage is almost never needed to answer Reading Figures questions. Try to answer it using the graph first, then only go to the passage if necessary.

First, check for **accuracy**. Do the choices reflect the data in the figure? Sometimes only one of the choices will match the data.

Second, check for **relevance**. Which choice fits with the main idea of the passage? Use a dumb summary to compare with the choices.

Make sure you read:
   • graph or chart title
   • rows and columns
   • x- and y-axis labels
   • legend
   • footnotes

Pay very close attention whenever the figures involve **percentages**. The SAT loves to trick people who confuse percentages with absolute numbers. Here's an example:

Graduates by Major

Major	Total Number of Graduates	Percent Graduating with Honors
Philosophy	254	56%
Political Science	1,827	33%

C) More Philosophy majors than Political Science majors graduated with honors.

This choice is <u>not</u> accurate. A greater <u>percentage</u> of Philosophy majors graduated with honors, but the total number of honors graduates is significantly larger for Political Science majors because 56% of 254 is around 125, whereas 33% of 1,827 is around 600. You should not need a calculator to see this.

Reading Vocab

quick questions

The Basics

Your goal is to find the word that is closest in meaning to the word in context. The word in the passage will most likely be a common word that has multiple definitions. Use the **QLC Method** so you don't get tricked:

1. Question

All reading vocab questions are phased the exact same way:

> As used in line X, "WORD" most nearly means

Do NOT read the choices yet!

If you need to, physically cover them with your hand. The SAT is trying to trick you. You don't want the choices to bias you before you have a chance to read the line reference and understand the context for the vocabulary word.

2. Line Reference

Usually, you only need to read the sentence that contains the word.

Guess the answer!

When you read the sentence, treat the vocabulary word as a blank and replace it with your own guess. The sentence will often contain "clues" that give away the definition.

3. Choices

Your guess usually won't be a choice, but it will help you NARROW YOUR FOCUS to the correct meaning. You want the choice that is the closest match to your guess.

Do <u>not</u> eliminate hard words!

If you don't know the meaning of one of the choices, skip it. If one of the easier choices matches your prediction, then the hard word didn't matter. But if you can't find a choice that matches your prediction, then don't be afraid to pick the hard word.

The Twists

Every **Reading Vocab** question has the same twist. Essentially, the word will **rarely have the most familiar meaning**, so you have to use the context to determine the correct answer. Always go back to the line reference. Guess as best you can, and at the least, plug the choices back into the sentence to see which one makes sense.

Example 1

Maria was constantly telling papa that she was a terrific cook. "If only you'd give me a chance!" she'd say. After two years under her roof, I had tasted many of Maria's "specialties" and found them wanting. Yet I held my tongue for fear of her other specialty—rage.

———————————————————————

As used in line 4, "wanting" most nearly means

A) desiring.

B) craving.

C) lacking.

D) wishing.

Example 2

Excerpt from Thomas Paine, *Common Sense*, published in 1776.

For were the impulses of conscience clear, uniform, and irresistibly obeyed, man would need no other lawgiver; but that not being the case, he finds it necessary to surrender up a part of his property to furnish means for the protection of the rest; and this he is induced to do by the same prudence which in every other case advises him out of two evils to choose the least. Wherefore, security being the true design and end of government, it unanswerably follows that whatever form thereof appears most likely to ensure it to us, with the least expense and greatest benefit, is preferable to all others.

———————————————————————

As used in line 9, "end" most nearly means

A) destruction.

B) fragment.

C) deadline.

D) intention.

Exercise: Reading Vocab 1

Questions 1-25 are based on the following passage.

This passage is the full text of *The Gettysburg Address*, a speech delivered by President Abraham Lincoln in 1863 during the American Civil War. The speech was given four and a half months after Union forces defeated the Confederacy at Gettysburg, Pennsylvania. Lincoln was at the battlefield to dedicate a new cemetery for the fallen soldiers. Earlier that year, Lincoln had signed the Emancipation Proclamation, which freed the majority of slaves in the United States.

    Four score and seven years ago our fathers brought forth on this continent, a new nation, conceived in Liberty, and dedicated to the proposition that all men
Line are created equal.
5   Now we are engaged in a great civil war, testing whether that nation, or any nation so conceived and so dedicated, can long endure. We are met on a great battle-field of that war. We have come to dedicate a portion of that field, as a final resting place for those
10 who here gave their lives that that nation might live. It is altogether fitting and proper that we should do this.
    But, in a larger sense, we can not dedicate—we can not consecrate—we can not hallow—this ground. The brave men, living and dead, who struggled here, have
15 consecrated it, far above our poor power to add or detract. The world will little note, nor long remember what we say here, but it can never forget what they did here. It is for us the living, rather, to be dedicated here to the unfinished work which they who fought
20 here have thus far so nobly advanced. It is rather for us to be here dedicated to the great task remaining before us—that from these honored dead we take increased devotion to that cause for which they gave the last full measure of devotion—that we here highly
25 resolve that these dead shall not have died in vain— that this nation, under God, shall have a new birth of freedom—and that government of the people, by the people, for the people, shall not perish from the earth.

1

As used in line 1, "score" most nearly means

A) markings.

B) reckonings.

C) groups of twenty.

D) points earned.

2

As used in line 2, "conceived" most nearly means

A) impregnated.

B) founded.

C) believed.

D) held.

3

As used in line 3, "proposition" most nearly means

A) question.

B) idea.

C) solicitation.

D) scheme.

4

As used in line 5, "engaged" most nearly means

A) involved.

B) matched.

C) pledged.

D) betrothed.

5

As used in line 5, "civil" most nearly means

A) courteous.

B) formal.

C) communal.

D) domestic.

Exercise: Reading Vocab 2

6

As used in line 7, "long" most nearly means

A) desire to.

B) for an extended period.

C) verbosely.

D) as outstretched.

7

As used in line 7, "met" most nearly means

A) introduced.

B) acquainted.

C) fused.

D) gathered.

8

As used in line 8, "dedicate" most nearly means

A) sanctify.

B) restrict.

C) open.

D) sign.

9

As used in line 9, "portion" most nearly means

A) serving.

B) part.

C) quantity.

D) destiny.

10

As used in line 10, "gave" most nearly means

A) gifted.

B) collapsed.

C) allowed.

D) sacrificed.

11

As used in line 11, "fitting" most nearly means

A) snug.

B) appropriate.

C) desirable.

D) comfortable.

12

As used in line 12, "sense" most nearly means

A) touch.

B) feeling.

C) understanding.

D) tact.

13

As used in line 13, "ground" most nearly means

A) field.

B) foundation.

C) reason.

D) conductor.

14

As used in line 14, "dead" most nearly means

A) indifferent.

B) exhausted.

C) absolute.

D) deceased.

15

As used in line 15, "poor" most nearly means

A) impoverished.

B) inadequate.

C) unhappy.

D) barren.

16

As used in line 16, "note" most nearly means

A) write down.

B) acknowledge.

C) annotate.

D) compose.

17

As used in line 18, "living" most nearly means

A) alive.

B) metabolizing.

C) income.

D) celebrating.

18

As used in line 18, "dedicated" most nearly means

A) consecrated.

B) honored.

C) committed.

D) founded.

19

As used in line 19, "work" most nearly means

A) project.

B) chore.

C) occupation.

D) function.

20

As used in line 20, "advanced" most nearly means

A) furthered.

B) state-of-the-art.

C) raised.

D) loaned.

21

As used in line 22, "take" most nearly means

A) steal.

B) grasp.

C) receive.

D) stick.

22

As used in line 23, "cause" most nearly means

A) explanation.

B) action.

C) origin.

D) objective.

23

As used in line 24, "measure" most nearly means

A) calculation.

B) rhythm.

C) size.

D) amount.

24

As used in line 25, "resolve" most nearly means

A) decide.

B) separate.

C) reduce.

D) transform.

25

As used in line 25, "in vain" most nearly means

A) selfishly.

B) needlessly.

C) proudly.

D) foolishly.

Reading Figures

quick questions

The Basics

Read the figure. All of it. The title, the legend, the axis labels, the units... Most of the time, the answer is staring you in the face, even without the context of the passage.

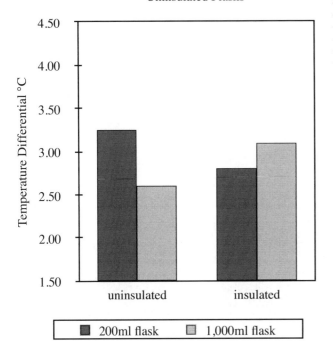

Temperature Differential for Insulated and Uninsulated Flasks

Example 1

The graph following the passage demonstrates that the temperature differential for insulated flasks is most strongly correlated with

A) the temperature differential of the uninsulated flasks.

B) the volume of the flask.

C) the boiling point of the liquid.

D) the density of the insulation.

The Twists

If a Reading Figures question asks you to refer back to the passage, you should read what it tells you to. But usually, the reference is nothing more than an annoying hurdle. The important information will be fairly explicit. For the question below, you'd actually have to go to the lines in the passage to read the text — the annoying hurdle — but the references have been included in the choices to show you that the full passage isn't needed.

Example 2

Which statement from the passage is most directly reflected by the data presented in the graph?

A) Lines 22-26 ("The scientists presented their results at the Fairfax Emporium, a biannual conference focusing on changes in the field of thermodynamics.")

B) Lines 33-36 ("Francis concluded, 'The problem is that insulation can be beneficial, but it depends on the experiment being performed.'")

C) Lines 38-45 ("Interestingly, coating the flask reduced the difference in heat loss between the two sizes.")

D) Lines 56-58 ("'Now we have information that could affect how researchers across the globe design future experiments.'")

This next question seems like you'd need to have read the full passage, but remember that the focus is actually on the graph!

Example 3

The data in the graph provide support for which idea from the passage?

A) Using insulated flasks introduces error into experiments.

B) The effectiveness of insulation is variable.

C) Scientists favor larger flasks for temperature-dependent experiments.

D) Uninsulated flasks are safer to use.

Exercise: Reading Figures

Note: Some of these questions can be answered using only the chart. If you're stuck, then you probably need to find the relevant information in the passage. The box on the bottom right includes excerpts that should help. Notice how clearly the information is presented. On the actual SAT, the hardest part will be finding the lines, but once you do, the answers to the Reading Figures questions should be fairly obvious.

Mass of Chemical Compounds in Fruit in Micrograms

Fruits	prictose	biofin	nuclide
pear	13.1	9.6	19.2
strawberry	15.6	8.4	15.9
pineapple	5.7	14.3	28.7
orange	9.8	10.4	20.1
grape	13.4	8.1	16.7
peach	14.4	10.1	19.9
plum	9.5	11.8	23.0
banana	6.7	12.4	24.5
apple	14.9	11.2	22.8

1

Data in the table indicate that the amount of prictose is greater than the amount of biofin for which fruit?

A) pineapple

B) orange

C) strawberry

D) plum

2

Based on the table and the passage, which choice gives the correct amounts of hexagonal compounds in grapes and plums?

A) 8.1 and 10.1

B) 8.1 and 11.8

C) 9.5 and 13.4

D) 13.4 and 14.4

3

Do the data in the table support the author's conclusion about the relationship between the compounds in fruit?

A) Yes, because for each fruit, the amount of nuclide is approximately double the amount of biofin.

B) Yes, because for each fruit, the amount of nuclide is approximately double the amount of prictose.

C) No, because for each fruit, the amount of nuclide is approximately double the amount of biofin.

D) No, because for each fruit, the amount of nuclide is approximately double the amount of prictose.

4

According to the table, which of the following compound masses in pineapple provides evidence in support of the previous question?

A) 5.7 and 14.3

B) 5.7 and 28.7

C) 11.2 and 22.8

D) 14.3 and 28.7

5

The data in the table best serve as evidence of

A) "the acidity and relative sweetness of the fruit" (line 29)

B) "variability of the chemical content from species to species" (line 38)

C) "catalysts for organic reactions" (lines 56-57)

D) "the insufficiency of previous theories" (line 79)

---

from the passage

"The compounds are identified by their molecular structures—biofin and nuclide have a tetrahedral structure, while prictose is hexagonal."

"Because the nitrosynthesis process is linear, the fruit will always contain twice as much nuclide as biofin."

Writing Packets

I recommend that you start with a plan. Take a full practice test and pick the packets for the questions you got wrong. If you are just diving in, remember that there are detailed lessons and explanations in the back of the book.

Ideas

The Basics

Ideas questions have more in common with Reading questions than they do with the other Writing questions. Grammar does not matter. Style does not matter. Focus on the ideas that the question is asking for. These questions are surprisingly scientific, in that you can almost always point to specific words in the sentence or paragraph that prove the correct answer. For this reason, you should try not to pick an answer simply because it "feels" right. Support your choice with evidence.

The Twists

Sometimes the question will explicitly ask for specific ideas. Always accomplish the stated goal. When the goals are more vague, you'll need to use the surrounding sentences to figure out what the SAT is really asking for. Use **dumb summaries** to boil down sentences and paragraphs into simpler ideas. Use positive and negative connotations to understand Transitions. Find anchor words so you can more easily place a sentence near related sentences.

One of the most common obstacles on Ideas questions is your own laziness. A question tells you to find the choice that best supports the main idea of the paragraph, but you're too lazy to read the entire paragraph. Another question asks whether you should add or delete a sentence, but you go with your hunch without ever scrutinizing the "becauses" in the choices. Or, craziest of all, you're asked for the most accurate interpretation of the graph, but you don't even look at the graph! Students are especially lazy when the sentence or paragraph continues onto the next page. The SAT is doing this intentionally! They know that some students are too lazy to flip the page. **They've purposely designed the question to punish you for being lazy.**

Let this also be a reminder to always read all of the answer choices. The SAT loves to make Choice B pretty good, hoping that you'll just pick it because you're too lazy to read the rest. Maybe Choice D was obviously better, but you never gave it a chance.

Packets

- accomplish the goal
- add or delete
- transitions
- combine sentences
- sentence placement
- writing figures

approximately 19 questions per test

worth approximately 100 points total

Writing				goal	goal
goal	goal	goal	goal	goal	goal
AD	AD	trans	trans	trans	comb
comma	Wfig	Wfig	place	place	comb
apstv	punc+	pron	pron	conc	conc
list	punc+	verb	verb	Wvoc	Wvoc
apost	punc+	sym	sym	Wvoc	FCW
FRO	FRO	sym	mod	dict	dict

Important Ideas

Ideas Questions

The vast majority of Ideas questions will ask a specific question, instead of simply giving you four answer choices for the underlined portion. Always read the question! Follow the instructions.

You will not need to worry about grammar or style. Focus on the ideas contained in the sentences and the goals provided in the questions.

Accomplish the Goal

Some goals will be very clear. The SAT does not care what <u>you</u> would write or what <u>you</u> think sounds best. You <u>must</u> give them the sentence <u>they</u> ask for.

Other goals will be more general. If the question tells you to read something, read it. Here are some examples:

- "provides the most relevant information" means read the surrounding sentences

- "establishes the main idea" means find a broad topic sentence that summarizes the paragraph

- "supports the main idea" means find a narrow example that matches the repeated ideas in the paragraph

- "provides the most effective transition" means read the current paragraph and previous/next paragraph

- "add another example" means pick the choice that repeats the surrounding ideas without repeating the exact same examples

Add or Delete

Read the sentence, and decide whether you would add or delete it. Check the "becauses" to make sure that you're adding or deleting it for a good reason. If the "becauses" don't make sense, you may need to rethink whether to add or delete.

Transitions

Transitions questions look like Grammar questions, but they're not.

Always read the sentence that contains the underlined transition and the sentence before it. Use dumb summaries and connotations to predict the relationship between the sentences.

Use the transition category boxes to quickly sort through the answer choices. If two choices belong to the same category, you can usually eliminate them both: if they mean the same thing, they can't both be right. (But if you're sure of the relationship between the sentences, it's okay to break this rule.)

Combine Sentences

These questions are almost <u>never</u> about grammar. Your goal is to **combine the ideas**.

Semicolons and "and" do not sufficiently combine the ideas. Essentially, you still have two separate sentences. Colons and stronger transitions are better.

Make sure the ideas flow. Avoid comma clauses that interrupt the flow. Keep related ideas together.

Sentence Placement

First, read the sentence that they want you to move. Underline any **anchor words** that will force the sentence into a particular position.

Next, read the paragraph without the sentence you're moving. Listen for gaps that need to be filled or for phrases that match your anchor words.

Finally, make sure placing the sentence does not accidentally break up other sentences that need to be together.

Writing Figures

See the Reading Figures description in the Quick Questions chapter.

Accomplish the Goal

The Basics

Your instincts might tell you to read the choices and see which one sounds best in context. **Try this first example by only reading the choices below.** Which one would you choose for the underlined portion?

Saving the Sarangi

Most Westerners are familiar with violins, violas, and cellos, but few had heard of the *sarangi*—another bowed instrument—until Ram Narayan brought it out of India to the wider world in the 1960s. **1** The instrument is also popular in neighboring Nepal, where it is an essential part of the country's folk music tradition. Sarangi music was considered a dying art-form in India when Narayan first learned to play as a child. **2** He grew up at a time when information was spread quickly through the new technology of radio. If not for Narayan, this fascinating instrument, which has been a major part of Hindustani classical music since the 12th century, might not have survived the 20th century.

Example 1 — Answer Choices

A) NO CHANGE

B) This medium-sized instrument emits an unforgettable sound when the bow is drawn across the strings.

C) About two feet long and six inches wide, the sarangi is thought to sound more like a human voice than any other instrument.

D) In fact, the sarangi is almost twice as old as the violin, which first appeared in Italy in the 16th century.

The Twists

Does Example 1 become any easier after you read the question that should have gone with it?

Example 1 — Question

The writer wants to provide the most specific information about the sarangi's physical and musical characteristics. Which choice best accomplishes this goal?

The most important thing to remember about Accomplish the Goal questions is that **the question tells you what to do**. Pay attention to the goal!

But not every Goal question will be as explicit. Remember that Ideas questions are the exception where you may actually need to read significant portions of the passage. Follow the instructions.

Example 2

Which choice most logically follows from the previous sentence?

A) NO CHANGE

B) The sitar, another Indian string instrument, is not played with a bow because its strings are plucked.

C) The sarangi has been featured in songs by the Western rock bands Aerosmith and Def Leppard.

D) It has since seen a resurgence, largely because of the new international interest.

A few other Goal questions: Which choice...

- provides the best introduction to the paragraph?
- best establishes the main idea of the paragraph?
- best supports the main point of the paragraph?
- adds the most relevant supporting information to the paragraph/sentence?
- most effectively sets up the examples in the following sentences?
- provides the best transition between paragraphs?
- is most consistent in style and content with the rest of the passage/paragraph/sentence?

Exercise: Accomplish the Goal

Worldwide, the most famous Hindustani classical instrument is probably the sitar, **1** and Narayan often played alongside sitarists both before and after he became internationally famous. When he was six years old, Narayan found a sarangi and asked his musically gifted father to teach him how to play. His father was reluctant because the sarangi is notoriously difficult to learn, and its connection to courtesan music gave the instrument a low social status. **2** Eventually, he relented and found his son a tutor, putting Narayan on a path that would one day lead to mastery of this unique instrument.

3 At about ten years of age, Narayan studied under Uday Lal of Udaipur, who was well-versed in *dhrupad*, the oldest type of classical Hindustani music. He ultimately studied under several different teachers, but repeatedly left those apprenticeships to pursue other opportunities. At one point, he gave up on the sarangi altogether and traveled to

1

The writer wants to establish a link between Narayan and the sarangi that also contrasts with the beginning of the sentence. Which choice best accomplishes this goal?

A) NO CHANGE

B) which is played not with a bow like the sarangi, but by plucking the strings.

C) so it's likely that Narayan grew up listening to sitar music.

D) but the sarangi is well-known in the north of India where Narayan was born.

2

Which choice provides the most logical introduction to the sentence?

A) NO CHANGE

B) One day, he searched high and low and

C) Since he also lived in northern India, he

D) Using the family's financial resources, he

3

Which choice best establishes the main idea of the paragraph?

A) NO CHANGE

B) Despite his tenacity and talent, Narayan initially struggled to make a career out of playing the sarangi.

C) The *ganda bandhan* is a traditional Indian ceremony of acceptance between a teacher and his pupil.

D) Narayan's brother was also musically gifted, but he played the *tabla*, a drum-like instrument.

Lahore to audition for a local radio station as a singer. He didn't get the job, but the station manager noticed distinctive grooves on Narayan's <u>fingernails.</u> **4** The manager hired him on the spot as a sarangi player instead, and it wasn't long before Narayan began to outshine the radio singers that he was supposed to be backing up.

5 <u>Even though he was busy raising his four children,</u> Narayan finally broke through when he embarked on an international tour to Europe and America in 1964. For the first time, the sarangi was brought to the attention of a worldwide audience.

4

Which choice adds the most relevant supporting information to the paragraph?

A) fingernails; the manager rigorously studied applicants before hiring them.

B) fingernails, a result of the unusual way the sarangi is played.

C) fingernails, which had been there for some time.

D) fingernails; the manager would later become one of the biggest supporters of Narayan's career.

5

The writer wants to add a supporting detail to indicate that Narayan had previously tried to achieve independent success. Which choice best accomplishes this goal?

A) NO CHANGE

B) After several failed attempts at a solo career in the 1950s,

C) Despite never having been outside of Asia,

D) While other Indian musicians were competing for airtime,

Narayan continued to perform internationally over the next few decades, exposing thousands of listeners to a new instrument. **6** Through his efforts, Narayan increased the status of the sarangi to that of a modern concert solo instrument and made it known outside of India. Surprisingly, Narayan does not see himself as the instrument's savior. He acknowledges that wider Indian appreciation of the sarangi only began after Western audiences became interested. What's more, Narayan doubts that his chosen instrument will continue to survive.

7 Chinese musician Wang Guotong has brought another traditional bowed instrument, the *erhu*, to the attention of an international audience.

6

At this point, the writer wants to add another example of how Narayan promoted sarangi music. Which choice best accomplishes this goal?

A) He also took on teaching roles at several Indian universities and created a scholarship for young sarangi players.

B) He often played at large venues with other world famous musicians.

C) He visited many cities better known for Western classical music, including Berlin and Vienna.

D) Whenever he traveled, Narayan brought several sarangis, just in case one malfunctioned during a concert.

7

Which choice most clearly ends the passage with a hopeful conclusion that recalls an earlier claim?

A) NO CHANGE

B) There are many other Hindustani classical instruments, and perhaps one of them will eclipse the sarangi in importance.

C) Despite Narayan's effort, Western orchestras continue to be dominated by violins, violas, and cellos.

D) Yet with all the work that he has done to promote the sarangi, it seems likely that another talented and dedicated performer will pick up the torch and carry sarangi music into the 21st century.

Add or Delete

ideas

The Basics

Add or Delete questions are essentially Accomplish the Goal questions where the goal is in the answer choices. The "becauses" provide reasons for adding or deleting the sentence. First decide whether you would add or delete it yourself, then make sure that the "because" makes sense. You can use **Process of Elimination** to help.

Saving the Sarangi

Most Westerners are familiar with violins, violas, and cellos, but few had heard of the *sarangi* [1] —another bowed instrument—until Ram Narayan brought it out of India to the wider world in the 1960s. About two feet long and six inches wide, the sarangi is thought to sound more like a human voice than any other instrument. Sarangi music was considered a dying art-form in India when Narayan first learned to play as a child. It has since seen a resurgence, largely because of the new international interest. If not for Narayan, this fascinating instrument, which has been a major part of Hindustani classical music since the 12th century, might not have survived the 20th century.

Worldwide, the most famous Hindustani classical instrument is probably the sitar, but the sarangi is well-known in the north of India where Narayan was born. [2] When he was six years old, Narayan found a sarangi and asked his musically gifted father to teach him how to play. His father was reluctant because the sarangi is notoriously difficult to learn, and its connection to courtesan music gave the instrument a low social status. Eventually, he relented and found his son a tutor, putting Narayan on a path that would one day lead to mastery of this unique instrument.

The Twists

Most of the time, you'll know whether to add or delete a sentence simply by reading it. But occasionally, it won't be obvious. Always make sure that you add the sentence because it accomplishes the right goal, or that you delete it for the right reason. That may mean fighting your instincts if the "becauses" don't match with the situation. In other words, if you want to add the sentence, but the "becauses" do not provide good reasons for adding it, then you need to consider deleting it. Don't be stubborn.

Exercise: Add or Delete

1

The writer is considering deleting the underlined portion (adjusting the punctuation accordingly). Should the underlined portion be kept or deleted?

A) Kept, because the underlined portion defines a term that is important to the passage.

B) Kept, because the underlined portion gives an example of a dying art-form.

C) Deleted, because the underlined portion detracts from the paragraph's focus on Narayan.

D) Deleted, because the information in the underlined portion is provided later in the paragraph.

2

At this point, the writer is considering adding the following sentence.

> The *tambura* is also popular, especially in the *dhrupad* style.

Should the writer make this addition here?

A) Yes, because it provides a detail that supports the main topic of the paragraph.

B) Yes, because it serves as a logical transition to the next sentence.

C) No, because it does not take into account that there are other instruments in *dhrupad* music.

D) No, because it provides background information that is irrelevant to the paragraph.

Despite his tenacity and talent, Narayan initially struggled to make a career out of playing the sarangi. He ultimately studied under several different teachers, but repeatedly left those apprenticeships to pursue other opportunities. At one point, he gave up on the sarangi altogether and traveled to Lahore to audition for a local radio station as a singer. **3** He didn't get the job, but the station manager noticed distinctive grooves on Narayan's fingernails, a result of the unusual way the sarangi is played. The manager hired him on the spot as a sarangi player instead, and it wasn't long before Narayan began to outshine the radio singers that he was supposed to be backing up. After several failed attempts at a solo career in the 1950s, Narayan finally broke through when he embarked on an international tour to Europe and America in 1964. For the first time, the sarangi was brought to the attention of a worldwide audience.

Narayan continued to perform internationally over the next few decades, exposing thousands of listeners to a new instrument. He also took on teaching roles at several Indian universities and created a scholarship for young sarangi players. Through his efforts, Narayan increased the status of the sarangi to that of a modern concert solo instrument and made it known outside of India. **4** Surprisingly, Narayan does not see himself as the instrument's savior. He acknowledges that wider Indian appreciation of the sarangi only began after Western audiences became interested. What's more, Narayan doubts that his chosen instrument will continue to survive. Yet with all the work that he has done to promote the sarangi, it seems likely that another talented and dedicated performer will pick up the torch and carry sarangi music into the 21st century.

3

At this point, the writer is considering adding the following sentence.

> Back then, Lahore was part of India because the predominantly Muslim region it belonged to had not yet formed the separate country of Pakistan.

Should the writer make this addition here?

A) Yes, because it provides historical context for the events described in the passage.

B) Yes, because it explains that the station manager was Muslim.

C) No, because it blurs the focus of the paragraph by introducing loosely related information.

D) No, because it undermines the main claim of the paragraph.

4

At this point, the writer is considering adding the following sentence.

> In 2005, the Indian President awarded Narayan the country's second highest civilian honor in recognition of his lifetime of dedication to the sarangi.

Should the writer make this addition here?

A) Yes, because it describes an event that logically follows the preceding sentences.

B) Yes, because it introduces a counterargument for balance.

C) No, because it blurs the focus of the paragraph by introducing a new idea that is not clearly explained.

D) No, because it distracts from the paragraph's emphasis on Narayan's teaching roles.

Transitions

ideas

The Basics

Transitions are the only Ideas questions that do not have a literal question. They look like Grammar and Style questions, but they're not. Instead, you're looking to accomplish one very specific goal: connect two related sentences with the appropriate connector word. You should always **read the sentence before the underlined transition and the sentence that contains the underlined transition**. Use dumb summaries to capture the connotation and key ideas.

Example 1

Activists are trying to remove coral-bleaching chemicals from sunblocks. Subsequently, many scientists say that it may be too late to save the reefs.

A) NO CHANGE
B) Furthermore,
C) Therefore,
D) However,

The Twists

The relationship between the two sentences won't always be obvious. Plus, some of the transition words might not be familiar to you. Use the categories to the right to help you sort through the choices.

Example 2

Kahlo has achieved far greater fame in death than she ever did in life. Therefore, Kahlo's home is now one of the most popular museums in Mexico City, with thousands of admirers visiting every month.

A) NO CHANGE
B) Thus,
C) Indeed,
D) Despite this,

Categories

Generally, you can **eliminate choices that have the same meaning**. But some words (to the right of the dashed line) are different enough from the main group that this doesn't always work.

but		
however	regardless	alternatively
conversely	nevertheless	instead
in contrast	nonetheless	still
although	despite this	on the other hand

and		
in addition	moreover	similarly
furthermore	also	likewise

so		
therefore	consequently	subsequently
thus	accordingly	next
hence	as a result	then

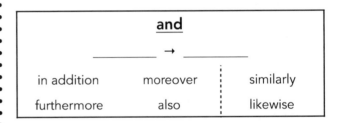

for example		
for instance	specifically	in short

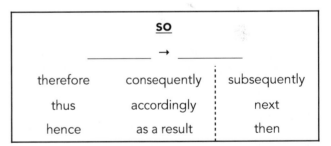

emphasis		
indeed	in fact	surely
truly	in reality	certainly

Exercise: Transitions

1

Art conservation once fell to the artists themselves, who simply painted over faded areas. <u>As a result,</u> restoration is more science than art, as modern chemistry plays a vital role in understanding how works of art degrade over time.

A) NO CHANGE

B) Regardless,

C) Specifically,

D) Today,

2

Greco-Roman wrestling, claiming to be a link to the Olympics' ancient past, has been part of the modern games since their inception in 1896. <u>Consequently,</u> true Ancient Greek wrestling was quite different from today's version.

A) NO CHANGE

B) Likewise,

C) However,

D) By the same token,

3

Luce's brand of feminism was leading by example as she routinely advanced in fields dominated by men— author, legislator, and diplomat. <u>Moreover,</u> as a philanthropist, she donated a large portion of her fortune to create a program that would promote the entry of women into the sciences and mathematics.

A) NO CHANGE

B) Nonetheless,

C) Nevertheless,

D) In short,

4

Conservationists recommend preserving and increasing pollinator habitats so that butterflies have more places to breed and lay their eggs. <u>Subsequently,</u> a few organizations encourage people to plant "butterfly gardens" that include favored food sources, such as milkweed.

A) NO CHANGE

B) However,

C) To this end,

D) Conversely,

5

E-readers were thought to be a sign of the apocalypse for the publishing industry. Book sales, <u>therefore,</u> continue to be robust, even if many of those sales come from digital devices.

A) NO CHANGE

B) for example,

C) in fact,

D) however,

6

Artifacts from Tut's tomb have been famously exhibited in Egypt and around the world. <u>Besides that,</u> the international tours attract millions of visitors and boost museum admissions.

A) NO CHANGE

B) Nonetheless,

C) Basically,

D) DELETE the underlined portion and begin the sentence with a capital letter.

7

Mr. Rogers believed that children's programming was an essential part of emotional and social education. <u>Accordingly,</u> he testified in Congress on behalf of increased funding for public broadcasting.

A) NO CHANGE

B) Likewise,

C) Despite this,

D) However,

8

The race to invent the telephone came down to the wire. On the exact same day in 1876, Gray filed a caveat (essentially, an announcement that he intended to file a patent at a later date), <u>whereas</u> Bell filed a full patent application for the telephone. History would remember the man with the stronger paperwork.

A) NO CHANGE

B) alternatively

C) or

D) for

Combine Sentences

ideas

The Basics

These questions are intimidating because it's hard to figure out what they're testing. Grammar? Vocabulary? Well, it's a little of both, but mostly neither. Combine Sentences questions test a little of everything, but they still follow fairly predictable rules like the rest of the SAT. Here's what you should think about when you're sorting through the choices:

Grammar? Mostly no. Almost all of the answer choices will be grammatically correct. You won't need to consider the complex rules, like Pronouns or Verb Agreement, but Modifier placement matters a little. Punctuation almost never matters, but it will seem like it does. (More on Punctuation in The Twists.)

Style? A little. Diction can matter, but you'll usually hear those errors. **The most important rule is Concision.** When only a small part of the two sentences is underlined, the shortest answer is almost always the right answer.

Example 1

Allison Dolby and Pauline Indio, authors of a series of self-help books for the social media addicted, maintain that technology companies design their products with built-in feedback loops, which most people don't even <u>notice. The technology companies create those products to get</u> users to log in more frequently.

Which choice best combines the sentences at the underlined portion?

A) notice, which is what technology companies create those products to do when they get

B) notice, by which the technology companies get

C) notice and create products to get

D) notice, to get

The Twists

Sometimes they underline two full sentences! The choices will be too long to know which one is truly the shortest. So if Grammar and Style don't matter, what does?

Ideas? Yes! That's why Combine Sentences questions are in the Ideas chapter. More than anything, you need to make sure you're combining the ideas contained in the two sentences. There are a lot of ways to use punctuation to combine two sentences, but some punctuation marks connect sentences without actually connecting the ideas.

Example 2

<u>Besides being costly and ineffective, these fuel additives release harmful chemicals. These harmful chemicals cause respiratory and other health problems in humans.</u>

Which choice most effectively combines the underlined sentences?

A) Besides being costly and ineffective, these fuel additives release harmful chemicals; they cause respiratory and other health problems in humans.

B) Besides being costly and ineffective, these fuel additives release harmful chemicals, and the harmful chemicals cause respiratory and other health problems in humans.

C) Besides being costly and ineffective, these fuel additives release harmful chemicals: the effect being that they cause respiratory and other health problems in humans.

D) Besides being costly and ineffective, these fuel additives release harmful chemicals, which cause respiratory and other health problems in humans.

Exercise: Combine Sentences

1

Opponents of plastic bag bans, however, claim the opposite is <u>true. They claim</u> that because of their higher plastic content, reusable shopping bags are actually worse for the environment.

Which choice best combines the sentences at the underlined portion?

A) true—

B) true, such

C) true, it being

D) true; they believe

2

<u>Nature documentaries are frequently given narrative structure to make the information more digestible to lay audiences. Popular psychology books are often written to help readers understand complex theories.</u>

Which choice most effectively combines the underlined sentences?

A) To make the information more digestible to lay audiences, nature documentaries, which are frequently given narrative structure, are similar to popular psychology books, which are often written to help readers understand complex theories.

B) Just as nature documentaries are frequently given narrative structure to make the information more digestible to lay audiences, popular psychology books are often written to help readers understand complex theories.

C) Popular psychology books are often written to help readers understand complex theories, while nature documentaries are frequently given narrative structure to make the information more digestible to lay audiences.

D) Popular psychology books are much like nature documentaries in being frequently given narrative structure to make the information more digestible to lay audiences and often written to help readers understand complex theories.

3

Roosevelt thought that there was a need for new progressive government action to alleviate New York's many <u>problems. He</u> had an idea about who could lead the charge.

Which choice best combines the sentences at the underlined portion?

A) problems—in effect, he

B) problems; and Roosevelt

C) problems, and he

D) problems, and likewise he

4

<u>Unsurprisingly, the policy is very controversial. Law enforcement would have unrestricted access to citizens' personal home security devices.</u>

Which choice most effectively combines the underlined sentences?

A) With the policy being unsurprisingly very controversial, law enforcement would have unrestricted access to citizens' personal home security devices.

B) Law enforcement would have unrestricted access to citizens' personal home security devices, and the policy is unsurprisingly very controversial.

C) Unsurprisingly, the policy is very controversial: law enforcement would have unrestricted access to citizens' personal home security devices.

D) Law enforcement would have unrestricted access, an unsurprisingly very controversial policy, to citizens' personal home security devices.

Sentence Placement

ideas

The Basics

These can be really tough because it feels like there's a lot to think about. Follow these steps:

1. **Read the sentence.** Look for "anchors" that you can use to lock the sentence in one place.

   But Einstein approached the task with enthusiasm, completing a draft paper in only a year.

   These concerns made it difficult to pass the law, but support for environmentalism increased throughout the 1970s.

   Jansen inspected each hive for signs of disease, recording the number of bees and making note of any unusual behavior.

   The exhibit features the world's largest collection of scrimshaw: engraved whale bone from the 1800s, the height of the whaling industry.

2. **Read the paragraph.** Skip the placement sentence when you read, but think about the "anchors" and how they might fit in with the rest of the paragraph. Listen for gaps in logic or information.

3. **Check for linked sentences.** Make sure that placing your sentence doesn't accidentally break up other ideas that need to go together.

The Twists

It's easier said than done.

Example 1

[1] When it opened in 1984, the Monterey Bay Aquarium was already ahead of its time. [2] It was the first truly regional aquarium, focusing specifically on the nearby bay ecosystem, which had once supported a thriving fishing industry. [3] The pelagic, or open ocean, exhibit is the Aquarium's largest, featuring sea turtles, sting rays, and a swarm of sardines. [4] But the real open ocean is just outside, as the Aquarium is perched on the edge of Monterey Bay. [5] Today, Monterey Bay's diverse wildlife is protected, and every year, the Aquarium gives millions of people the opportunity to see that wildlife up close. [6] Visitors can spot local marine mammals such as otters, sea lions, and humpback whales, all of which somehow depend on the bay's most important inhabitant—the kelp. **1**

To make this paragraph most logical, sentence 5 should be placed

A) where it is now.

B) before sentence 1.

C) after sentence 1.

D) after sentence 2.

Exercise: Sentence Placement

1

[1] Growing at the astonishing rate of ten inches per day, kelp carpets Monterey Bay, the tall fronds clearly visible on the surface of the water. [2] These dense underwater forests shelter hundreds of species of fish and invertebrates, creating one of the most diverse ecosystems on Earth. [3] When the Monterey Bay Aquarium was first proposed, biologists knew they wanted to showcase this unique environment. [4] The problem was that no aquarium had ever attempted to grow and maintain a live kelp forest. [5] They envisioned a huge tank that would house a miniature kelp forest and its accompanying wildlife. [6] Designing the tank would prove to be a new scientific and engineering challenge. 1

To make this paragraph most logical, sentence 4 should be placed

A) where it is now.

B) before sentence 1.

C) after sentence 2.

D) after sentence 5.

2

[1] First, engineers needed to find a way to simulate the kelp's natural environment. [2] Monterey Bay features strong oceanic currents, which constantly replenish nutrients that are essential for the kelp to survive. [3] All that pumping stirs up microscopic particles, making the water cloudy, so sand filters are used during the day to increase visibility. [4] Engineers found a way to mimic these currents, creating a surge machine that pushes water through the exhibit. [5] At night, unfiltered sea water is pumped into the tank, which encourages the growth of small invertebrates and allows the kelp's reproductive spores to settle on the bottom. 2

To make this paragraph most logical, sentence 3 should be

A) placed after sentence 1.

B) placed after sentence 4.

C) placed after sentence 5.

D) DELETED from the paragraph.

3

[1] Aesthetics also factored into the design. [2] Previously, ecosystem-sized tanks had been constructed only for research purposes. [3] Scientists could study their specimens by diving into the tank, viewing it from the top, or using small windows on the sides. [4] However, the Monterey Bay Aquarium wanted to immerse visitors in the kelp forest. [5] The windows were made from cast acrylic instead of glass, which allowed designers to maximize panel size, minimize weight, and achieve the clearest views through the 18-centimeter thickness required. [6] Overcoming these structural challenges was worth it to give visitors a view of the bay that they otherwise would never see. [7] Experiencing the kelp forest in this way leaves people awed by the tremendous diversity of life that exists only a few miles from shore and instills in them the desire to preserve this wondrous ecosystem. 3

Where is the most logical place in the is paragraph to add the following sentence?

The Aquarium's tank was designed with massive windows so that the 28-foot tall exhibit could be viewed from two levels.

A) After sentence 1

B) After sentence 2

C) After sentence 3

D) After sentence 4

Writing Figures

ideas

The Basics

Just like on the Reading section, Writing Figures questions are more about the chart or graph than the content of the passage. Always start by checking the **accuracy** of the choices:

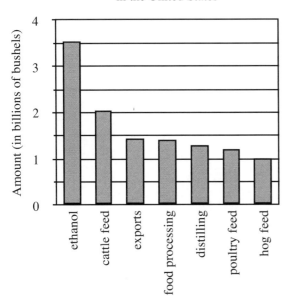

Yearly Estimates of Corn Use
in the United States

Amount (in billions of bushels)

Uses for corn

Example 1

Even though many people probably imagine that those vast fields of corn eventually end up on their dinner tables, cattle feed uses twice as much corn as human food production.

Which choice provides an accurate interpretation of the graph?

A) NO CHANGE

B) more corn is used in distilling than in food processing.

C) ethanol production actually constitutes the largest portion of annual corn use.

D) the majority of corn produced in the United States is exported to other countries.

The Twists

Sometimes you'll also need to consider whether the choices are **relevant** to the point being made in the passage. You should still start by eliminating inaccurate statements, but then NARROW YOUR FOCUS to the main idea of the paragraph to pick the one correct answer:

Example 2

Ethanol policies, however, are complex. Governments must weigh a variety of environmental concerns. Some studies have shown that ethanol production requires more energy than it provides when burned for fuel. Additionally, land used to grow crops for ethanol could be used to produce food for human consumption, a tradeoff that some see as irresponsible when millions of people around the world are at risk of starvation. One estimate found that **2** food production uses nearly 1.5 million bushels of corn annually. Since ethanol additives make up only a small percentage of biofuels, the claims that it's a renewable alternative to petroleum might be more about marketing than good policy.

At this point, the writer wants to add specific information that supports the main topic of the paragraph. Which choice adds the most relevant and accurate information based on the graph?

A) NO CHANGE

B) far more corn is used to feed cattle, hogs, and poultry than human beings.

C) turning corn into ethanol costs more than every other form of corn production.

D) over 3.5 billion bushels of corn per year are pumped into gas tanks instead of feeding hungry families.

Exercise: Writing Figures

The speed with which digital streaming services have been adopted has shocked the entertainment industry. In 2009, digital entertainment **1** (raking in less than $3 billion in revenue) was dwarfed by the much larger DVD and Blu-ray market. However, digital sales **2** did not exist before 2009 and had eclipsed physical sales by 2014. Since then, digital entertainment has dominated, and similar declines in the sale of DVD and Blu-ray players suggest that consumers no longer feel the need to own "hard" copies of their entertainment. One reason for this change might be that consumers have many more places to watch their favorite movies—laptops, phones, and tablets—compared to the stationary television set that had been the bastion of home entertainment for 50 years. **3**

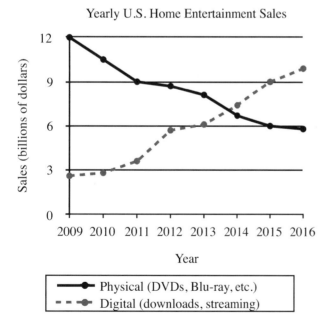

Yearly U.S. Home Entertainment Sales

Legend:
— Physical (DVDs, Blu-ray, etc.)
- - Digital (downloads, streaming)

1

Which choice provides an accurate interpretation of the graph?

A) NO CHANGE

B) (with not even 3 billion downloads)

C) (comprising $12 billion of yearly sales)

D) (representing 3 out of every 12 sales)

2

Which choice provides the most relevant and accurate information from the graph?

A) NO CHANGE

B) had leveled off by 2012

C) had increased slightly by 2010

D) took off in 2011

3

At this point, the writer is considering adding the following sentence.

Interestingly, while digital sales increased and physical sales declined, the total number of movies and shows purchased by consumers remained relatively constant at around 15 billion.

Should the writer make this addition here?

A) Yes, because it raises and responds to a potential criticism of the main argument made by the writer.

B) Yes, because it provides context helpful in understanding the trends discussed in the paragraph.

C) No, because it is not an accurate interpretation of the data in the graph.

D) No, because it introduces irrelevant information that blurs the focus of the paragraph.

Punctuation

The Basics

Most Punctuation questions are easy to recognize because all four answer choices will contain the exact same words. The only difference will be the placement and types of punctuation marks. In general, punctuation indicates a pause, so you can sometimes "hear" whether you need a comma, period, or dash.

The Twists

But not always. Sometimes you'll hear a pause, but you won't know which type of punctuation to use. That's why it's essential to know the purpose and function of each punctuation mark.

The **semicolon** and **colon** have very clear rules. If you memorize the rules, you'll be able to quickly "test" whether semicolons and colons are acceptable for the situation. In both cases, the rules revolve around the idea of a complete sentence. In fact, most Punctuation questions are about the structure of the sentences — what's essential and what's extra?

Run-on sentences are particularly difficult because they will often be impossible to hear. A Run-on is just two complete sentences that are joined together with only a comma. When you say a run-on out loud, it will sound fine because it will sound like two separate sentences. But writing is different than speaking. Whenever the choices mess with commas, periods, and semicolons, you need to check for run-ons. Sometimes the choices won't include punctuation, but the question will still be about the structure of the sentence. If the underlined portion is even near a comma, you should check for run-ons, especially when the choices include pronouns and/or "which".

The SAT also knows that you know certain rules, and they'll design the questions to push the limits of those rules. For example, they know that you know that colons are associated with lists, so they'll give you the option to use a colon in a sentence that contains a list. But there are times when you cannot use a colon with a list. It depends on the structure!

Packets

- general comma rules
- appositives
- lists & examples
- apostrophes
- advanced punctuation
- fragments & run-ons

approximately 9 questions per test

worth approximately 50 points total

Writing				goal	goal
goal	goal	goal	goal	goal	goal
AD	AD	trans	trans	trans	comb
comma	Wfig	Wfig	place	place	comb
apstv	punc+	pron	pron	conc	conc
list	punc+	verb	verb	Wvoc	Wvoc
apost	punc+	sym	sym	Wvoc	FCW
FRO	FRO	sym	mod	dict	dict

Important Ideas

Commas

Commas separate extra ideas from the main core of the sentence.

Unfortunately, there are very few words that always need commas. In fact, the SAT likes to ask about situations that seem to break many of the rules that you think you know.

Whether you use a comma is actually much more about the structure of the sentence. Would using a comma create a run-on? Is a clause necessary? Does a clause interrupt the main sentence?

Here are a few of the most commonly tested situations. There may be exceptions to these rules!

Do not use commas with prepositions.

✗ I like to sing, in the shower.

Do not use commas with "that".

✗ The boat, that sank last night, was full of holes.

Use commas with "which"…

✔ The boat, which sank last night, was full of holes.

…except when "which" is not extra.

✔ Do you know which boat sank last night?

Use commas for introductory clauses.

✔ After the party, we couldn't find our car.

Use commas for direct quotations.

✔ Vincent asked, "are you sure we drove here?"

Do not use commas for summary quotes.

✗ Connie said, she was pretty sure that we did.

Use commas for lists of 3 or more.

✔ Teddy has a dog, cat, and guinea pig.

Do not use commas for lists of 2.

✗ Jay only has a dog, and a cat.

Appositives

Use commas when an explanation or definition is extra and interrupts the sentence.

✔ Bill, my friend from school, bought a new car.

Do not use commas when the appositive cannot be cut out of the sentence.

✗ My friend, Bill's, new car has a sun roof.

Lists & Examples

Colons can be used to start lists, but they also provide an answer or explanation to a question implied in the sentence.

✔ I have only one fear: clowns.

Apostrophes

For most nouns, apostrophes show possession. But pronouns only get apostrophes for contractions.

✔ The dog's bark is worse than its bite.

Advanced Punctuation

Semicolons are essentially periods. They separate two complete sentences.

The part before a **colon** must be a full sentence.

✗ I like a few vegetables, such as: carrots and peas.

Dashes can be used as every other punctuation mark, but they're most often used to separate out an extra clause that interrupts the sentence.

Fragments & Run-ons

A comma is not sufficient to join two sentences.

✗ Fran sings beautifully, she hits all the notes.

Use a conjunction, another connector word, or turn the second sentence into a dependent clause.

✔ Fran sings beautifully, and she hits all the notes.

✔ Fran sings beautifully when she hits all the notes.

✔ Fran sings beautifully, hitting all the notes.

General Comma Rules

The Basics

Don't let the answer choices bully you into using a comma. If there isn't a pause, you probably don't need a comma.

Example 1

Increased funding could lead to the development of more eco-friendly materials and better <u>strategies for combatting climate change, on remote islands or in populated</u> coastal cities.

A) NO CHANGE

B) strategies, for combatting climate change on remote islands or in populated

C) strategies for combatting climate change on remote islands or in populated

D) strategies for combatting climate change on remote islands, or in populated,

Example 2

The grades on the project were so <u>bad, that the teacher said,</u> "I think I may have made the students dumber."

A) NO CHANGE

B) bad, that the teacher, said

C) bad that the teacher, said

D) bad that the teacher said,

The Twists

Sometimes you need to look beyond the underlined portion. Pay attention to unnecessary and introductory clauses.

Example 3

While singing in the shower may seem <u>strange and embarrassing, this habit</u> has been shown to relieve stress and increase happiness.

A) NO CHANGE

B) strange and embarrassing this habit,

C) strange and, embarrassing, this habit

D) strange, and embarrassing this habit

Example 4

If nothing changes in the next ten years, experts <u>say then</u> the supply of oil will eventually fail to meet the demand.

A) NO CHANGE

B) say. Then

C) say; then

D) say, then

Exercise: General Comma Rules

1

Two years ago, Dr. Jenkins <u>waited</u> for the results of the experiment in his laboratory, but now he has lab assistants who do the work for him.

A) NO CHANGE

B) waited,

C) waited;

D) waited —

2

Pierre Charles L'Enfant, who designed the original layout for the United States capital <u>city in the 1790s</u> worked on plans for other American cities throughout the early 1800s.

A) NO CHANGE

B) city in the 1790s,

C) city, in the 1790s,

D) city in the 1790s —

3

<u>Television commercials that are simple, and catchy are the most effective</u> while too much information can confuse consumers.

A) NO CHANGE

B) Television commercials, that are simple and catchy, are the most effective

C) Television commercials, that are simple and catchy are the most effective,

D) Television commercials that are simple and catchy are the most effective,

4

During the <u>speech several protestors interrupted, with chants and</u> slogans that drowned out the candidate and brought the campaign event to a halt.

A) NO CHANGE

B) speech, several protestors interrupted with chants and

C) speech, several protestors interrupted, with chants and

D) speech, several protestors interrupted with chants, and

5

Every year, millions of people visit Yellowstone National <u>Park; a</u> nature preserve larger than the states of Delaware and Rhode Island combined.

A) NO CHANGE

B) Park; that is a

C) Park, a

D) Park. A

6

Many <u>people regardless of where they're from believe,</u> that Southern California is heaven on Earth.

A) NO CHANGE

B) people: regardless of where they're from, believe

C) people, regardless of where they're from, believe

D) people regardless, of where they're from, believe

7

In the early <u>2000s, music videos made a brief comeback</u> with the establishment of the *MTV Hits* channel, which only played Top 40 songs.

A) NO CHANGE

B) 2000s, music videos made a brief, comeback

C) 2000s music videos, made a brief comeback

D) 2000s — music videos made a brief comeback

8

Early exit polls showed that Congressman Jackson, who had campaigned on a promise to reform <u>entitlements in the first year, of his presidency had</u> pulled into second place.

A) NO CHANGE

B) entitlements in the first year of his presidency, had

C) entitlements, in the first year of his presidency had

D) entitlements, in the first year of his presidency, had

Appositives

punctuation

The Basics

An appositive is a relatively short noun phrase that identifies another noun in a different way. Often, appositives tell you more about who a person is:

Right

Barry Goldwater, the junior senator from Arizona, received the Republican nomination in 1964.

Example 1

After crossing the river, the hikers could see the most difficult part of their journey, the mountain <u>peak;</u> directly ahead of them.

A) NO CHANGE

B) peak—

C) peak,

D) peak

Example 2

Famed <u>novelist Charles Dickens,</u> was paid to write by the word, which explains why many of his novels are filled with long chapters that seem to be irrelevant to the plot.

A) NO CHANGE

B) novelist, Charles Dickens,

C) novelist, Charles Dickens

D) novelist Charles Dickens

The Twists

The main issue with appositives is that they don't always need commas. Sometimes, the information is "essential" to the sentence. **Try to cross out the appositive to figure out if it's extra and needs commas.** The SAT knows that you know this rule, so they'll try to trick you with it. Notice how similar these examples are to the Basics:

Right

Arizona senator Barry Goldwater received the Republican nomination in 1964.

Arizona senator Barry Goldwater's platform was the most conservative in history.

Wrong

Arizona senator, Barry Goldwater, received the Republican nomination in 1964.

Arizona senator, Barry Goldwater's, platform was the most conservative in history.

Appositives are also useful when you need to fix run-on sentences:

Example 3

The governor introduced Erica Willoughby, <u>she is</u> an artist whose sculptures can be found in public parks across Europe.

A) NO CHANGE

B) Willoughby is

C) her being

D) DELETE the underlined portion.

Exercise: Appositives

1

Bill <u>Marshall, the head of the university's engineering department</u> decided to resign his position so he could have more time to bring his invention to life.

A) NO CHANGE

B) Marshall, the head, of the university's engineering department

C) Marshall, the head of the university's engineering department,

D) Marshall the head of the university's engineering department

2

I couldn't wait to see <u>magician The Amazing Hubert's</u> latest illusion.

A) NO CHANGE

B) magician, The Amazing Hubert's

C) magician The Amazing Hubert's,

D) magician, The Amazing Hubert's,

3

The darkness of the temple made it difficult to see, but the priest performed the ablution, <u>or ritual washing— as</u> if he'd done it thousands of times before.

A) NO CHANGE

B) or, ritual washing, as

C) or ritual washing as,

D) or ritual washing, as

4

Known for his knowledge of Italian <u>cuisine, celebrity chef Jamie Oliver, owns</u> several restaurants in the United States and around the world.

A) NO CHANGE

B) cuisine celebrity chef, Jamie Oliver, owns

C) cuisine, celebrity chef Jamie Oliver owns

D) cuisine celebrity chef Jamie Oliver owns

5

The woman who wrote <u>it, diarist, Mary Chesnut</u> is still credited for her well-balanced account of the South's experience during the war.

A) NO CHANGE

B) it, diarist, Mary Chesnut,

C) it diarist Mary Chesnut,

D) it, diarist Mary Chesnut,

6

The artist's first commissioned work, a <u>sculpture,</u> received mixed reviews.

A) NO CHANGE

B) sculpture;

C) sculpture:

D) sculpture

7

In extreme circumstances, <u>"impeachment" the process of removal from office outlined in the Constitution,</u> can be the only way to stop the abuse of power.

A) NO CHANGE

B) "impeachment," the process of removal from office outlined in the Constitution,

C) "impeachment," the process of removal from office outlined in the Constitution

D) "impeachment" the process of removal from office outlined in the Constitution

8

Even though print journalism is in decline, many Americans are comfortable receiving their news from digital media, like a <u>blog or a podcast.</u>

A) NO CHANGE

B) blog, or a podcast.

C) blog or, a podcast.

D) blog; or a podcast.

Lists & Examples

punctuation

The Basics

There are a lot of comma rules, but the simplest has to do with lists. You've known this rule for a long time, so don't let the fact that it's now on the SAT make you doubt yourself. Items in a list are separated by commas:

Example 1

The Spartan C5 featured a number of engineering improvements, including strut braces, a fully-enclosed <u>cabin and,</u> spatted main-wheels.

A) NO CHANGE

B) cabin, and

C) cabin; and

D) cabin and;

But don't get confused between items in the list and adjectives describing those items:

Example 2

As soon as guests entered the hall, they were overwhelmed by the beauty of the <u>brilliant gold accents</u> and large watercolor portraits.

A) NO CHANGE

B) brilliant, gold accents,

C) brilliant, gold, accents,

D) brilliant gold accents—

The Twists

You know that a colon is somehow involved in making lists, but you can't use it in every situation. Generally, use a colon when there's a clear separation between the main sentence and the list of examples:

Example 3

The advent of steamships and refrigeration gave Europeans their first widespread access to several tropical <u>fruits;</u> bananas, kiwis, and guavas.

A) NO CHANGE

B) fruits:

C) fruits,

D) fruits

But be careful. Many list-beginning phrases connect the list to the rest of the sentence, so we don't need the hard stop of a colon.

Example 4

Many families use their attics to store items they no longer need but don't want to part <u>with, such as:</u> old clothes, childhood toys, and family heirlooms.

A) NO CHANGE

B) with such as:

C) with such as,

D) with, such as

Exercise: Lists & Examples

1

Members of both parties sought to implement long-overdue tax reforms, which included adjusting rates, consolidating tax <u>brackets: and</u> closing deduction loopholes.

A) NO CHANGE

B) brackets and,

C) brackets, and

D) brackets; and

2

The Library of Congress has one of the largest collections in the world, and it includes not only <u>books: but also</u> maps, films, sound recordings, and newspapers.

A) NO CHANGE

B) books, but also:

C) books but also

D) books; but also

3

Athletes are fighting a constant struggle against their own bodies, which, partly due to hereditary <u>traits such as genes that influence height and muscle elasticity</u> can limit or enhance various aspects of athleticism.

A) NO CHANGE

B) traits, such as genes that influence height and muscle elasticity,

C) traits such as: genes that influence height and muscle elasticity,

D) traits such as, genes that influence height and muscle elasticity,

4

On a cold winter's night, there are two things I'm always thankful <u>for, a roaring fire, and</u> a good book.

A) NO CHANGE

B) for, a roaring fire and

C) for; a roaring fire and

D) for: a roaring fire and

5

Accountants need to meticulously record every aspect of a company's <u>finances: income, expenses, and the details of each purchase—</u>so that management can make informed decisions.

A) NO CHANGE

B) finances—income, expenses, and the details of each purchase—

C) finances: income, expenses, and the details of each purchase,

D) finances; income, expenses, and the details of each purchase;

6

Many people have switched from disposable water bottles to refillable ones for a variety of <u>reasons such as,</u> a hope to reduce the amount of plastic in landfills and a personal desire to save money.

A) NO CHANGE

B) reasons, such as,

C) reasons, such as

D) reasons, such as:

7

Stradivarius violins are prized for their color, <u>shape, and tone,</u> all of which make them as treasured today as they were in the 17th century.

A) NO CHANGE

B) shape and, tone,

C) shape, and, tone

D) shape, and tone;

8

Even though Franklin Roosevelt was the only President who served more than two terms, a few <u>others:</u> Teddy Roosevelt, Ulysses Grant, and Woodrow Wilson—ran for a third term but were defeated.

A) NO CHANGE

B) others;

C) others,

D) others—

Apostrophes

punctuation

The Basics

Apostrophes indicate possession:

regular plural

The dogs are large.

singular possessive

The dog's owner is large.

plural possessive

The dogs' owner is large.

The dogs' owners are large.

multiple possessives

The dog's owner's house is large.

The dogs' owner's house is large.

The dog's owners' house is large.

The dogs' owners' house is large.

The dogs' owners' houses are large.

But don't get bullied by the choices into using an apostrophe. Ask what owns or possesses anything.

Example 1

As climate change increases ocean temperatures, unusually powerful storms will permanently <u>erode beaches</u>, threatening communities along the coast.

A) NO CHANGE

B) erode beach's,

C) be eroding beaches,

D) erode beaches',

The Twists

Possessive pronouns do <u>not</u> get apostrophes.

possession	contraction	not a thing
its	it's	its'
his	he's	his'
her hers		her's hers'
your yours	you're	your's yours'
their theirs	they're	their's theirs'
our ours		our's ours'
whose	who's	whos'

Example 2

The battalion hadn't received <u>it's</u> instructions from central command, so there was nothing to do but wait.

A) NO CHANGE

B) its

C) its'

D) their

Also, be careful how you use apostrophes with irregular plurals:

Example 3

Because the shelves were overstocked, the department store decided to put all <u>womens'</u> shoes on sale.

A) NO CHANGE

B) womens

C) women's

D) womans

Exercise: Apostrophes

1

Research is being conducted by the <u>nations premier scientists,</u> who consider their work to be of the utmost importance.

A) NO CHANGE

B) nations' premier scientists',

C) nation's premier scientists,

D) nation's premier scientist's,

2

Today, <u>tourist's entering</u> foreign countries are subjected to numerous security and immigration checks.

A) NO CHANGE

B) tourists entering

C) tourists enter

D) tourists' entering

3

The city council intends to vote on a redevelopment plan that includes the expansion of public transit routes to connect the city's center with areas on the outer <u>edges of it's</u> furthest suburbs.

A) NO CHANGE

B) edge's of its'

C) edge's of it's

D) edges of its

4

Often a subject of intense study and disagreement, the United <u>States' market's</u> economy is still considered by many to be a fundamental aspect of American democracy.

A) NO CHANGE

B) States' market

C) States market's

D) State's market

5

Although Steve had wanted to see the movie, he changed his mind after he heard a <u>coworker comment,</u> "That was supposed to be a comedy, but I didn't laugh once."

A) NO CHANGE

B) coworker's comment,

C) coworkers' comment,

D) coworker commented,

6

It's not surprising that children everywhere admire <u>astronaut's:</u> the job is dangerous, and very few people get the opportunity to do it.

A) NO CHANGE

B) astronauts,

C) astronaut's;

D) astronauts—

7

The entire neighborhood was outside helping to look for <u>Rose's son's</u> dog, which had managed to escape through a hole in the fence.

A) NO CHANGE

B) Rose's sons

C) Roses son's

D) Roses sons'

8

The other team's pitcher was starting to show signs of fatigue, but <u>our's was</u> determined to stay in the game for a few more innings.

A) NO CHANGE

B) ours was

C) ours' was

D) ours' were

Advanced Punctuation

punctuation

The Basics

Most "Advanced" questions are just regular punctuation questions with lots of complicated choices. Know what the punctuation marks do.

Commas and dashes separate unnecessary clauses:

Example 1

With her infamous cheerfulness and <u>determination:</u> Leslie Knope led a scrappy team at the Parks Department.

A) NO CHANGE

B) determination,

C) determination, and

D) determination:

Example 2

Even though it's difficult to see the connection between investigative journalism and public policy, the story about the chemical company—published in a major news <u>magazine)</u> could lead to dramatic new regulations that prevent the problem from recurring.

A) NO CHANGE

B) magazine,

C) magazine—

D) magazine

The Twists

Lots of people have trouble with colons. Remember that colons introduce lists or examples, but only when there's a clear break in the sentence:

Example 3

Orcas Island is home to a few small towns, museums, and historical sites, but its most popular attraction is also <u>its least developed</u> the 5,000 acre Moran State Park.

A) NO CHANGE

B) it's least developed—

C) its least developed;

D) its least developed:

Colons can also separate two complete sentences, kind of like a semicolon. Generally, **the part after a colon answers or explains something from the part before the colon.** The first part <u>must</u> be a complete sentence, but the second part can be a sentence or just a fragment:

Example 4

Only a few years after the Oregon Treaty supposedly resolved the boundary between the United States and British Columbia, a new conflict arose from the most unlikely <u>source: an American farmer shot an Irishman's pig on San Juan Island,</u> setting off a chain of events that would eventually settle the boundary once and for all.

A) NO CHANGE

B) source. An American farmer shot an Irishman's pig on San Juan Island:

C) source. An American farmer shot—an Irishman's pig on San Juan Island

D) source, an American farmer shot an Irishman's pig on San Juan Island,

Exercise: Advanced Punctuation

1

Many experts argue that classical music, especially 19th century classical <u>music—</u>is not as conservative and traditional as it seems.

A) NO CHANGE

B) music:

C) music;

D) music,

2

Not all wine grapes are grown on sun-bathed Mediterranean slopes. The pinot gris variety grows in cool <u>climates, for example:</u> and other grapes are well-suited to inland soils.

A) NO CHANGE

B) climates: for example,

C) climates, for example,

D) climates; for example,

3

By diverting the spring water to a number of <u>troughs; the</u> miners were able to set aside a water supply that would sustain them through the dry season.

A) NO CHANGE

B) troughs. The

C) troughs, the

D) troughs—the

4

The "tough-kid" genre featured stories that frequently found the gang in the same <u>situation—escaping,</u> dirty, oppressive reform schools that the kids had been unfairly forced to attend.

A) NO CHANGE

B) situation, escaping,

C) situation; escaping

D) situation—escaping

5

With the deadline looming, Jenkins miraculously came up with an idea that would save the <u>project: larger</u> windows.

A) NO CHANGE

B) project, larger

C) project. Larger

D) project; larger

6

As the amount of plastic in the oceans has grown, the use of <u>microfibers:</u> synthetic threads with diameters less than 10 micrometers—has come under increased scrutiny as a source of plastic pollution.

A) NO CHANGE

B) microfibers,

C) microfibers—

D) microfibers;

7

Records allow biologists to <u>know;</u> which specimens were made by Nelson himself and which were purchased by the museum after his death.

A) NO CHANGE

B) know

C) know,

D) know:

8

Ecologists must constantly ask themselves if killing one endangered organism <u>will help protect the species in the long run?</u>

A) NO CHANGE

B) will help protect the species in the long run.

C) will it help protect the species in the long run.

D) will it help protect the species in the long run?

Fragments & Run-ons

punctuation

The Basics

Learn to distinguish FRO questions from other Punctuation questions. Punctuation choices will often have identical wording but change the punctuation type and placement. FRO questions will have shorter choices that vary the wording, if only slightly. In general, you can avoid run-on sentences by **removing unnecessary pronouns**:

Example 1

Some people dislike English literature because it can be long-winded, but there's a large fanbase for *Pride and Prejudice, this is a* favorite of students and teachers alike.

A) NO CHANGE

B) *Prejudice*. A

C) *Prejudice*, a

D) *Prejudice*, this being a

In addition to removing pronouns, run-o sentences can be fixed by **adding a "which"**:

Example 2

Sommers invented a uniquely shaped cone, this keeps ice cream from melting onto your hands.

A) NO CHANGE

B) that

C) which

D) it

The Twists

Sometimes, avoiding a run-on means using an unusual phrase:

Example 3

The bill is supported by two candidates, both of whom are polling in the single digits.

A) NO CHANGE

B) of which both

C) both of them

D) both

Not Only ... But Also

For some reason, the SAT loves this sentence construction:

Example 4

Harbor improvements are required to accommodate large cruise ships, but there are benefits not only for tourists but it also benefits local residents.

A) NO CHANGE

B) and also for

C) and also benefitting

D) but also for

Just As ... So Too

Not as common, but more confusing:

Example 5

Just as television revolutionized elections in the 1960s, and Twitter changed politics in 2016.

A) NO CHANGE

B) so too

C) also

D) but

Exercise: Fragments & Run-ons

1

The panic on Wall Street impacted many different stocks, some <u>of them</u> lost 25 percent of their value in a matter of minutes.

A) NO CHANGE

B) stocks

C) of which

D) DELETE the underlined portion.

2

Not only was the fireworks display meant to celebrate the spirit of the occasion, <u>also allowing</u> the company to show off its latest innovations in pyrotechnics.

A) NO CHANGE

B) but also allowing

C) but it also allowed

D) but also allowed

3

The host introduced Cynthia Rogers, <u>she is</u> a business owner and inventor with several patents to her name.

A) NO CHANGE

B) Rogers is

C) her being

D) DELETE the underlined portion.

4

<u>After the</u> concert was over, the entire crowd headed toward the parking lot at the same time, creating a bottleneck.

A) NO CHANGE

B) The

C) Afterward, the

D) Following the

5

The flies and mosquitos, in the midst of their breeding season, are swarming near stagnant <u>water, they</u> are biting whatever they can.

A) NO CHANGE

B) water, the flies and mosquitos

C) water and

D) water,

6

In honor of veterans, <u>donating</u> a portion of their profits to the local VFW post.

A) NO CHANGE

B) having donated

C) to donate

D) these businesses donate

7

The Grand Canyon was carved by natural forces over eons, and it has become a modern day natural <u>wonder, it awes</u> the millions of tourists who visit each year.

A) NO CHANGE

B) wonder, awing

C) wonder; awing

D) wonder, its awing

8

Elephants use their trunks to grasp <u>food, and</u> their tusks can be used to dig for water and roots.

A) NO CHANGE

B) food, so

C) food,

D) food

Consistency

The Basics

The most complicated grammar rules on the SAT are about consistency. On the one hand, these rules are very formulaic — the answer will be indisputably correct if you just apply the rule. Unlike Punctuation rules, which can sometimes feel more like a personal choice, Consistency rules have very few exceptions. But on the other hand, **Consistency questions will frequently defy your instincts**. You will often be unable to trust the sound of a sentence. In fact, the correct answer will sometimes sound much worse than the wrong answers. The SAT is doing this on purpose.

The Twists

You use the Consistency rules every single day. Every sentence you say or write involves Verb Agreement. And you actually get these rules right the vast majority of the time! But the SAT is not testing the simple situations that you encounter every day. They are deliberately asking about the weird circumstances when things don't turn out as we would expect. If you can master the Consistency rules, however, you're significantly more likely to get a 35 or better on the Writing section.

The key to mastery is being able to recognize when they're testing Consistency. Look first to the answer choices. If they're pronouns or verbs, you need to think about singular versus plural. If there's a list or a comparison, you need to think about symmetry. If the underlined portion is near a descriptive clause, you need to think about modifiers. Once you know they're testing a Consistency rule, you can usually fight your instincts and follow the formula, no matter how right or wrong the sentence sounds.

The most important thing to note is that "their" is <u>not</u> a singular pronoun. "Their" is plural because it refers to multiple things or people. We often use "their" to refer to one person whose gender we do not know, but this is incorrect. We <u>should</u> say "his or her", but we don't, and the SAT knows it!

Packets

- <u>pronouns</u>
- <u>verb agreement</u>
- <u>symmetry</u>
- <u>modifiers</u>

approximately 8 questions per test

worth approximately 40 points total

Writing				goal	goal
goal	goal	goal	goal	goal	goal
AD	AD	trans	trans	trans	comb
comma	Wfig	Wfig	place	place	comb
apstv	punc+	pron	pron	conc	conc
list	punc+	verb	verb	Wvoc	Wvoc
apost	punc+	sym	sym	Wvoc	FCW
FRO	FRO	sym	mod	dict	dict

Important Ideas

Pronouns

Whenever the answer choices include pronouns, check to see if they refer to singular or plural nouns.

its	→	singular
their	→	plural
his or her	→	singular
this	→	singular
that	→	singular
these	→	plural
those	→	plural

Do not rely on the sound of the sentence when pronouns are involved. You frequently get this rule wrong when you speak, so the right answer will not always sound correct.

- ✘ A teacher should help their students
- ✔ A teacher should help his or her students.

Ambiguous pronouns: If it's unclear what a pronoun is referring to, you probably should not use a pronoun at all. On the SAT, if you're given the option to specify a pronoun, you probably should.

Symmetry

All parts of a **list** must be symmetrical.

- ✘ I like running, jumping, and to skip.
- ✔ I like running, jumping, and skipping.
- ✔ I like to run, jump, and skip.
- ✘ I like to run, jump, and to skip.

Verb **tenses** must be symmetrical. Find another verb to match with the underlined verb. However, many questions that seem like they're about tense are actually about Verb Agreement, so check singular and plural first.

Comparisons must be symmetrical.

- ✘ Bob's cake tastes better than Erica.
- ✔ Bob's cake tastes better than Erica's.
- ✔ Bob's cake tastes better than Erica's cake.
- ✔ Bob's cake tastes better than that of Erica.

Verb Agreement

Just like nouns and pronouns, verbs can be singular or plural. All singular verbs end with S.

sings	→	singular
sing	→	plural
thinks	→	singular
think	→	plural
is	→	singular
are	→	plural
was	→	singular
were	→	plural
has	→	singular
have	→	plural

Singular subjects need singular verbs, and plural subjects need plural verbs.

- ✔ The dog barks loudly.
- ✔ The dogs bark loudly.
- ✘ The dogs barks loudly.

Only verbs in the present tense can be singular or plural. The only exceptions are was/were and has/have. Verbs in the past or future tense will be the same, regardless of whether they're singular or plural.

- ✔ The dog barked loudly.
- ✔ The dogs barked loudly.
- ✔ The dog will bark loudly.
- ✔ The dogs will bark loudly.

Cross out unnecessary clauses, especially prepositional phrases, to help you find the subject.

- ✘ The meaning of his tweets are unknown.
- ✔ The meaning of his tweets is unknown.

Modifiers

Make sure descriptive clauses are near the things they describe. Be careful of apostrophes.

- ✘ Searching desperately, Tom's glasses were lost.
- ✔ Searching desperately, Tom lost his glasses.

Pronouns
consistency

The Basics

Make sure that singular pronouns replace singular nouns and that plural pronouns replace plural nouns:

Example 1

The restaurant's menu was determined by the availability of the ingredients as well as <u>its</u> freshness and cost.

A) NO CHANGE

B) it's

C) their

D) they're

The hardest part about this rule is that it will often sound wrong to say the right thing. When the choices are pronouns, you need to doubt your instincts and follow the rule no matter what:

Example 2

Today, a teacher has the ability to share information and engage with a topic in ways unknown to <u>its</u> predecessors.

A) NO CHANGE

B) his or her

C) one's

D) their

The Twists

Occasionally you need to make the singular/plural choice for words that aren't technically pronouns:

Example 3

When war was finally declared, any civilian who could claim to be the owner of a boat instantly became <u>members of the navy.</u>

A) NO CHANGE

B) a member of the navy.

C) navy members.

D) as members to the navy.

Also, be careful of pronouns that don't seem to refer to anything specific. **Ambiguous pronouns** are almost always wrong because you don't want to sacrifice clarity for the sake of concision. When given the option to use a specific noun instead of a pronoun, you probably should choose the longer, more precise answer.

Example 4

Trees use their roots to absorb nutrients and keep the soil in place. Scientists were aware of, but did not fully appreciate, just <u>how important they are</u> in preventing soil erosion.

A) NO CHANGE

B) how important it is

C) how important tree roots are

D) that they are important

Exercise: Pronouns

1

The university does not base <u>their</u> admission decisions on a student's financial need.

A) NO CHANGE

B) there

C) its

D) it's

2

With the collapse of the Roman Empire, a previously crucial trading partner, Ethiopian scholars of the medieval period increasingly found <u>oneself</u> isolated from foreign ideas and influences.

A) NO CHANGE

B) himself or herself

C) themselves

D) their selves

3

Because of <u>their</u> wide variety of uses, corn continues to be a major crop in the United States and around the world.

A) NO CHANGE

B) they're

C) it's

D) its

4

The ancient symbol had been first found on a cave wall in Spain, likely carved into the rock 2,000 years ago. However, <u>they believe that it originated</u> before then and was brought to Spain by mariners from the Levant.

A) NO CHANGE

B) it originated, they believe,

C) many anthropologists believe that it originated

D) many anthropologists believe its origin is

5

The advertising campaign was so successful that the bookstore was able to double <u>it's</u> sales in just four months.

A) NO CHANGE

B) its

C) their

D) they're

6

The BBC inaugurated a trend toward independent public broadcasting in the Commonwealth countries, which continued to support public stations after the war. Other countries around the world continued <u>this</u> by either chartering new public stations or supporting those already in existence.

A) NO CHANGE

B) it

C) them

D) this trend

7

Before the auction, the jeweler polished the gold and silver, hoping to increase <u>its</u> luster and, thus, his profits.

A) NO CHANGE

B) it's

C) there

D) their

8

Due to a wave of anti-establishment feeling, a candidate can succeed even without experience as <u>politicians or government employees.</u>

A) NO CHANGE

B) a politician or government employee.

C) both politicians or government employees.

D) either politicians or government employees.

Verb Agreement
consistency

The Basics

Verbs are actions. The **subject** is the noun that performs the action. We all know that nouns can be singular or plural, but we often forget that verbs can be singular or plural, too. Singular verbs <u>always</u> end with S.

Singular

<u>The penguin</u> <u>waddles</u> across the ice.
    subject   *verb*

Plural

<u>The penguins</u> <u>waddle</u> across the ice.
    subject   *verb*

When a singular subject is paired with a singular verb, we say that the verb **agrees** with the subject. Verb Agreement is one of the most difficult grammar rules on the SAT. One problem is that you might not recognize that they're testing singular versus plural. Many people look at the question below and think that it's about tenses. Sometimes the SAT does test tenses (see the Symmetry packet), but **you should always check Verb Agreement first.**

Example 1

State budgets have seen significant, if not drastic, cuts in recent years, but <u>there is</u> many ways for legislators to increase tax revenue.

A) NO CHANGE

B) there are

C) there has been

D) there was

The Twists

Verb Agreement questions are almost never straightforward. They try to hide the subject from you. Don't let **unnecessary comma clauses** distract you from the subject. And remember, the subject is the noun that performs the action:

Example 2

These portraits, which constitute some of the artist's most realistic depictions of his wife, <u>has not been</u> publicly displayed since 1953.

A) NO CHANGE

B) not being

C) was not

D) have not been

Prepositional Phrases

This is hard. A **prepositional phrase** is a short, descriptive clause. They blend in because they aren't separated out with commas, but they usually start with small, seemingly insignificant words. Subjects can't be within prepositional phrases:

Example 3

Despite all the theories, accusations, and denials, the meaning of his tweets <u>is</u> unknown.

A) NO CHANGE

B) are

C) being

D) would have been

Exercise: Verb Agreement

1

An understanding of the various nuances in Weber's poetry <u>lead</u> to a greater appreciation of his originality.

A) NO CHANGE

B) are leading

C) have led

D) leads

2

Scientists are studying how animals that feed at night <u>is relying</u> on their other senses to "see" in the dark.

A) NO CHANGE

B) was relying

C) rely

D) relies

3

The last few minutes of the speech to the delegates <u>features</u> anecdotes, jokes, and one-liners that are meant to make the candidate more relatable.

A) NO CHANGE

B) feature

C) featuring

D) was featuring

4

All of the trophies <u>represents</u> the dreams of childhood that would never be realized.

A) NO CHANGE

B) has represented

C) represented

D) representing

5

The crisis became unmanageable when the portion of the population showing symptoms <u>was recovering</u> in city hospitals.

A) NO CHANGE

B) were recovering

C) recovering

D) recovers

6

Students at the State University of New Jersey <u>protested</u> the smoking ban that was implemented last week.

A) NO CHANGE

B) is protesting

C) has protested

D) was protesting

7

Hurricanes cause changes in sea level that simultaneously <u>erodes natural barriers and threaten</u> beachfront property.

A) NO CHANGE

B) erodes natural barriers and threatens

C) erode natural barriers and threatens

D) erode natural barriers and threaten

8

Commitment to multiple activities, including sports, <u>create</u> a stronger resume that can be submitted to colleges.

A) NO CHANGE

B) creates

C) created

D) was creating

Symmetry

consistency

The Basics

Writers often want their sentences to follow a pattern or maintain a rhythm. This is most obvious when a sentence contains a **list** of items or actions:

Example 1

Sensing that the public is demanding reforms, the party has released a platform with a number of progressive ideas: it calls for an end to tax breaks for corporations, demands equal pay for equal work, and <u>it prioritizes</u> tax cuts for the middle class.

A) NO CHANGE

B) prioritizing

C) prioritized

D) prioritizes

Even when verbs aren't in a list, you need to maintain consistency. Usually there will be another verb in the sentence that indicates the correct **tense**:

Example 2

Revolutionary forces overtook the federal police garrison stationed in the old courthouse near the town square and then <u>beginning</u> the long process of negotiating with local officials.

A) NO CHANGE

B) will begin

C) had begun

D) began

The Twists

The other type of Symmetry question is a little different, but the idea is the same — match the underlined portion to another part of the sentence. When making **comparisons**, it's important to compare two things that can actually be compared:

Rebecca's hair is longer than Mike.

Comparison questions are tricky because you can easily tell what the writer is trying to say, so you might not notice that anything is wrong. However, the choices will almost always give it away and remind you to make sure the comparison is symmetrical:

Example 3

Since almost all industrially produced bananas are of the same variety, diseases and parasites affecting the banana crop are potentially more harmful than <u>other fruits.</u>

A) NO CHANGE

B) that affecting other fruits.

C) those affecting other fruits.

D) those other fruits.

Exercise: Symmetry

1

The intricate design of the jewelry reflected the care that went into making it, but the many chips and scratches <u>had revealed</u> the inferiority of the metal it was made from.

A) NO CHANGE

B) has revealed

C) revealed

D) will reveal

2

The airport's size and layout resembled <u>that of</u> large international terminals in major cities, but the low number of yearly passengers has kept it from becoming more than a local facility.

A) NO CHANGE

B) these of

C) those of

D) DELETE the underlined portion.

3

Many people fear that modern cellphones could be hacked to steal passwords and personal information, access bank accounts, and <u>secretly recording</u> conversations.

A) NO CHANGE

B) to secretly record

C) secretly record

D) recording secretly

4

The church's unique design featured a steep roof to prevent snow from accumulating and <u>dispensed</u> with the symmetrical layout that was common at the time.

A) NO CHANGE

B) dispensing

C) dispenses

D) had dispensed

5

Petroglyphs can be found throughout the American West in a wide variety of locations, including on cave walls, in Native American ruins, and <u>drawn on</u> isolated rock formations.

A) NO CHANGE

B) on

C) they were drawn on

D) DELETE the underlined portion.

6

The town's mayor contends that the cultural society not only promotes folklore that would otherwise die out but also <u>it entertains</u> local residents with plays and dances.

A) NO CHANGE

B) entertaining

C) to entertain

D) entertains

7

The railroad brought change to every settlement along its route, but perhaps no transformation was more obvious than <u>these</u> from a small town to a major city.

A) NO CHANGE

B) those

C) that

D) DELETE the underlined portion.

8

The band's desire to mix their own songs with tracks from other artists has met resistance from the band manager, who fears that sampling other people's music might anger the group's fans, as well as <u>violated</u> copyright laws.

A) NO CHANGE

B) violating

C) has violated

D) violate

Consistency

Modifiers

The Basics

Introductory clauses, or modifiers, should be followed by what they introduce, or modify.

Wrong

His tail wagging playfully, <u>the mailman was greeted by the happy dog.</u>

Right

His tail wagging playfully, <u>the happy dog greeted the mailman.</u>

Example 1

Having left his job to travel the world, <u>little income was now available to do so.</u>

A) NO CHANGE

B) income was now important to do so.

C) doing so now required available income.

D) he now lacked the income to do so.

Be careful of possessive phrases.

Example 2

Speaking about his decades of experience, the <u>professor's lecture</u> was both engaging and informative.

A) NO CHANGE

B) professor delivered a lecture that

C) lecture by the professor

D) professor's delivery of the lecture

The Twists

Modifiers don't always have to be at the beginning of a sentence. Basically, anytime you add a descriptive clause, you need to make sure it's near the thing you're describing.

Example 3

<u>The historian, hidden among the old books, was surprised to discover an antique map of the United States from just after the Revolution.</u>

A) NO CHANGE

B) The historian hidden among the old books was surprised to discover an antique map of the United States from just after the Revolution.

C) The historian was surprised to discover, hidden among the old books, an antique map of the United States from just after the Revolution.

D) Hidden among the old books, the historian was surprised to discover an antique map of the United States from just after the Revolution.

Example 4

Although <u>semaphore is used by few people today,</u> which uses two flags in various positions to represent letters and numbers, it was once necessary for sending messages long distances.

A) NO CHANGE

B) few people today know how to communicate using semaphore,

C) communicating with semaphore is used by few people today,

D) few people today know how to use semaphore for communication,

Exercise: Modifiers

Covered with symmetrical bumps, the biologist was intrigued by an unusual salamander and its skin.

A) NO CHANGE

B) The biologist, covered with symmetrical bumps, was intrigued by an unusual salamander and its skin.

C) The biologist covered with symmetrical bumps was intrigued by an unusual salamander and its skin.

D) The biologist was intrigued by an unusual salamander and its skin, covered with symmetrical bumps.

Good for both the environment and the economy, organic food production can be a smart way for farmers to improve their yield.

A) NO CHANGE

B) the start of organic food production

C) you should start organic food production because it

D) starting to produce organic food

For thousands of years, many cultures participated in the ambergris trade (a waxy substance produced in the digestive system of sperm whales) because its fragrant odor made it ideal for perfumes and traditional medicines.

A) NO CHANGE

B) many cultures traded other luxury goods for ambergris

C) many cultures acquired ambergris by trading their own luxury goods

D) the ambergris trade involved many cultures that exchanged their own luxury goods

For his first catering job, the cake from the bakery used all natural ingredients.

A) NO CHANGE

B) bakery's cake

C) baker's cake

D) baker made a cake that

With its emphasis on rules and logical reasoning, geometry can be a frustrating yet important way to improve critical thinking.

A) NO CHANGE

B) studying geometry can be

C) you should study geometry as

D) the study of geometry can be

The paintings of Claude Monet featured water lilies as their chief subject—the founder of Impressionism—after he built himself an elaborate garden with ponds and bridges.

A) NO CHANGE

B) Water lilies became the chief subject of paintings by Claude Monet—

C) The chief subject of Claude Monet's paintings became water lilies—

D) Water lilies became the chief subject of Claude Monet's paintings—

With her student debt piling up, it was in Cindy's best interest to get a second job.

A) NO CHANGE

B) a second job was in Cindy's best interest.

C) Cindy realized it was in her best interest to get a second job.

D) Cindy's best interest was to get a second job.

Consistency

Style

The Basics

There is almost always more than one way to write a sentence. For some Style questions, the wrong answer choices will not be grammatically incorrect. Rather, they'll be too wordy or too confusing. If you don't know the SAT's rules, then these questions can be difficult, but once you know what the SAT prefers, Style questions become much easier. **In general, be concise and be clear.**

The Twists

Even though the SAT prefers shorter choices, there will be exceptions because of the Punctuation and Consistency rules in the previous chapters. Also, Ideas questions are never about Style or Concision. But when you've checked the question for all of the grammar rules and you can't find a problem, you're probably fine to just pick the shortest choice.

Writing Vocab questions are a little different from Reading Vocab questions because most of the choices will have the same basic definition. Your task is to pick the word that is most appropriate for the context, usually based on the word's level of difficulty. Some people think that complicated words are better because they make you sound smart, but the SAT prefers words that are clear and easily understood by the average reader.

Diction questions can be difficult because there might not be a good reason why certain words are used in certain situations. Sometimes we just say things one way and not others. **With Style questions, you can usually trust your instincts.** If something sounds good, it probably is. If it sounds weird, then it's probably wrong. The more you read, the better your instincts.

But there are still a few cases where words cannot be used interchangeably. The end of this chapter includes several exercises with **Frequently Confused Words**. The odds of any particular rule coming up on your SAT are pretty low. But even seeing a rule once might be enough to guarantee you those 10 points on the test if it does happen to show up!

Packets

- concision
- writing vocab
- diction
- frequently confused words

approximately 8 questions per test

worth approximately 40 points total

Writing				goal	goal
goal	goal	goal	goal	goal	goal
AD	AD	trans	trans	trans	comb
comma	Wfig	Wfig	place	place	comb
apstv	punc+	pron	pron	conc	conc
list	punc+	verb	verb	Wvoc	Wvoc
apost	punc+	sym	sym	Wvoc	FCW
FRO	FRO	sym	mod	dict	dict

Important Ideas

Concision

Shorter is better!

- ✘ The SAT has a preference for choices that are shorter.
- ✔ The SAT prefers shorter choices.

Avoid redundancy.

- ✘ If you can, omit needless words when you're able.
- ✔ If you can, omit needless words.

But remember that there are times when the shortest choice will not be correct. Some other grammar rules override the Concision rule:

- ambiguous pronouns
- symmetry with lists
- symmetry with comparisons
- fixing run-on sentences

Also, remember that the Concision rule does <u>not</u> apply to Ideas Questions.

Writing Vocab

Usually, all four words will have the same basic definition. You are deciding which word fits best based on the context.

Consider the **usage**, or the subtle differences in meaning. For example, "build" and "construct" are typically synonyms:

- ✔ They're building a new library.
- ✔ They're constructing a new library.

But they can't always be used interchangeably:

- ✔ The author builds suspense.
- ✘ The author constructs suspense.

Consider the **difficulty**. Words can be placed on a spectrum, and you want to pick words close to the middle. Don't be too informal or too fancy:

slangy ↔ academic ↔ pedantic

When in doubt, trust your instincts.

Diction

Sometimes you have to say things a certain way because that's just how people say things.

- ✔ Get in the car.
- ✔ Get on the plane.
- ✘ Get on the car.
- ✘ Get in the plane.

If you read a lot, then your brain will instinctively know which choice is correct. Don't over-think it.

Frequently Confused Words

Memorize a few key rules and definitions so that you don't lose points on these questions.

its	→	possessive
it's	→	it is
their	→	possessive
they're	→	they are
whose	→	possessive
who's	→	who is
who	→	people
which	→	things
than	→	comparisons
then	→	time
affect	→	verb
effect	→	noun
passed	→	verb
past	→	not a verb
too	→	"also", "extra"
to	→	everything else
fewer	→	countables
less	→	uncountables

Concision

style

The Basics

Don't repeat yourself by saying the same thing twice.

Example 1

Scientists were amazed when they discovered not one but two colonies of the <u>rare and uncommon</u> chameleon living on the island.

A) NO CHANGE

B) rare, uncommon

C) rare and not particularly common

D) rare

Sometimes, difficult words or long sentences will make you question whether something is redundant. Trust your knowledge of the SAT. It's probably best to go with the shortest answer.

Example 2

Knowing he had no choice but to answer, James prevaricated, <u>when he deliberately misstated the facts,</u> forcing the detectives to seek evidence elsewhere.

A) NO CHANGE

B) by misstating deliberately,

C) in that he made deliberate misstatements,

D) DELETE the underlined portion.

The Twists

Some Concision questions aren't noticeably redundant. They don't repeat words as obviously, but the general rule is the same — pick shorter choices.

Example 3

<u>Unfortunately,</u> the *USS Columbus* was scuttled by retreating Union forces in 1861 as the Confederate army advanced toward Norfolk.

A) NO CHANGE

B) The circumstances being unfortunate,

C) In circumstances that would be unfortunate,

D) Unfortunate as the circumstances were,

Example 4

Professional birdwatchers can identify the species <u>and identify the</u> sex of most birds because of differences in size, shape, and color.

A) NO CHANGE

B) plus also the

C) and the

D) with the

Exercise: Concision

1

Modern air travel makes it easier to find flights to more remote locations, where the high cost of the plane ticket can be offset by <u>hotels and restaurants that do not charge a premium for their services.</u>

A) NO CHANGE

B) relatively inexpensive food and lodging.

C) the lower prices that various tourism-related services charge their customers in these locations.

D) hotels as well as restaurants that are inexpensive compared to those in other places.

2

Closely guarded secrets <u>hidden from most citizens</u> allow governments to better protect the public, but they can also breed distrust if overused.

A) NO CHANGE

B) undisclosed to almost all people

C) withheld from nearly everyone

D) DELETE the underlined portion.

3

The service allows customers to post reviews, rate account managers, and make suggestions, all without leaving a company's homepage. While most of this data is logged digitally so that support staff can analyze it later, there is also a feature that allows customers to immediately <u>speak with a live representative.</u>

A) NO CHANGE

B) speak with a representative in a manner that is live.

C) speak with a live representative, who can help them post reviews, rate account managers, and make suggestions.

D) and not at a later date speak with a live representative.

4

Long after the temple had fallen into disuse, a committee was established to decide what to do with the structure; several artifacts were chosen <u>to be restored by them.</u>

A) NO CHANGE

B) for their restoring.

C) for them to restore.

D) for restoration.

5

Instead of focusing on treating patients, preventative medicine attempts to help people avoid disease in the first place by informing them about potential causes, including <u>inherited conditions,</u> family medical history, environmental factors, and lifestyle choices.

A) NO CHANGE

B) where they live,

C) personal habits,

D) DELETE the underlined portion.

6

The company must undergo an annual audit, which is conducted by an outside accounting firm <u>each year.</u>

A) NO CHANGE

B) every year.

C) yearly.

D) DELETE the underlined portion and end the sentence with a period.

7

Due to its rarity, platinum has been used in several cultures <u>as a substitute that replaces</u> gold in coinage and jewelry.

A) NO CHANGE

B) as a substitute and replacement for

C) as a replacement for

D) to replace as a substitute for

Writing Vocab

style

The Basics

Reading Vocab questions have clear instructions:

As used in line 16, "operate" most nearly means…

You are looking for the word that *means* the right thing in that sentence. Writing Vocab questions rarely have an explicit question. With fewer instructions, there are more things to think about:

Meaning

BUTTERFLY ⇔ MOTH

Difficulty

SLANGY ⇔ ACADEMIC ⇔ PEDANTIC

Sound

TRUST YOUR INSTINCTS

Example 1

Before the early 1910s, there was no system in place to audit icebergs to protect ships from collisions, most likely because they weren't considered a serious threat back then.

A) NO CHANGE

B) supervise

C) monitor

D) keep an eye on

The Twists

For Reading Vocab questions, you can usually substitute the choices into the sentence, and only one will make sense. That can still help on Writing, but sometimes words will have nearly identical meanings except that they can't be used in the same context:

Example 2

Eager to get back on the road, Kevin went into the store to buy snacks while Peter injected the gas and cleaned the windshield.

A) NO CHANGE

B) poured

C) pumped

D) inserted

Example 3

Marjorie brought out five cups of hot water and let her guests choose their favorite from a variety of teabags. She encouraged everyone to help themselves to pastries while they waited for their tea to steep.

A) NO CHANGE

B) pickle.

C) marinate.

D) bathe.

Memorizing flashcards won't help you here. Trust your instincts, even if you can't quite explain your reasoning. The more you read and have diverse experiences, the better you'll be at these.

Exercise: Writing Vocab

Because of the Civil War in the 1860s, many people assume that most of the political **1** ruckuses in the antebellum United States were about slavery. As it turns out, this isn't perfectly accurate. Most of the early debates were over the role of the federal government and the side that the United States should take in the wars between Britain and France. In fact, the first great slavery crisis **2** occurred in 1820, when Missouri sought to enter the Union as a slave state. Many worried that the issue would lead to civil war, but Speaker of the House Henry Clay led both sides to a compromise that would **3** outlast for over 30 years.

Clay himself was a slaveholder from Kentucky, but he also believed in a strong national Union. He understood the conflict well—both slave and free states wanted to **4** maintain balance in the federal government so that neither side would have the advantage. While **5** rough population growth had led to Northern dominance of the House of Representatives, the Senate had the same number of free and slave states. Missouri statehood **6** menaced to change that.

1
A) NO CHANGE
B) tugs-of-war
C) conflicts
D) competitions

2
A) NO CHANGE
B) exposed
C) befell
D) turned up

3
A) NO CHANGE
B) endure
C) linger
D) sustain

4
A) NO CHANGE
B) persevere
C) nurture
D) keep up

5
A) NO CHANGE
B) uneven
C) capricious
D) spotty

6
A) NO CHANGE
B) pressured
C) warned
D) threatened

Diction

The Basics

Diction is all about choosing the right words — just like Writing Vocab questions — but there isn't always a good reason why the right answer is right. Most of the time, the correct answer to a Diction question is right because… well… it sounds best.

Example 1

The princes became increasingly independent and <u>included in the expansion of their territory</u> most of the outlying agricultural lands.

A) NO CHANGE

B) expanded their territory to include

C) expanding their territory included

D) the territory's expansion included

Other times, even the right answer won't sound great.

Example 2

The legislature didn't go <u>as far to</u> completely ban the chemical, but the new regulation limited the amount that could be released into the atmosphere.

A) NO CHANGE

B) so far as to

C) too far to

D) far and

The Twists

Diction questions can be frustrating because there might be just one small word that makes all the difference.

Example 3

In preparation <u>with</u> the national holiday, streets were lined with ceremonial bunting and festive lights.

A) NO CHANGE

B) of

C) to

D) for

If you're not a native English speaker, these questions can feel impossible. Dictionaries won't really help you understand the answers any better. These are the kinds of rules that you learn over the course of a lifetime reading, speaking, and hearing English. If you want to practice Diction, you're better off watching *Friends* or *The Office* than reading Shakespeare or Dickens.

Another way to make these easier is to **cross out** extra phrases to get down to the core of the sentence. Sometimes the correct word is easier to "hear" when there are fewer distractions:

Example 4

Historians attribute the decline of the Roman Empire <u>with</u> the overextension of the army and costly foreign wars.

A) NO CHANGE

B) after

C) to

D) from

Exercise: Diction

1

The new technology has <u>already played a role in</u> a wave of medical breakthroughs that could save millions of lives.

A) NO CHANGE

B) already role-played in

C) role-played already for

D) already played a role for

2

Road safety advocates point out that sleep-deprived drivers caused a disturbingly high number of accidents last <u>year when they fall</u> asleep at the wheel.

A) NO CHANGE

B) year by falling

C) year, and they fall

D) year since falling

3

In 1756, Austria and France formed a new alliance <u>in what was known as</u> the Diplomatic Revolution.

A) NO CHANGE

B) knowing it was

C) in that it was known as

D) as it was known as

4

After a number of high-profile scandals, universities have shown a willingness <u>for reversing</u> admissions decisions when a student engages in unethical behavior.

A) NO CHANGE

B) in reversing

C) for reversals of

D) to reverse

5

Scientists have long believed that some identifiable part of the human brain is solely responsible for our species' dominance. However, after comparing human brains to those of other animals, neuroscientists now conclude that no particular feature stands <u>for.</u> Anatomically, we are not unique.

A) NO CHANGE

B) out.

C) in.

D) up.

6

The failure of international efforts to limit carbon emissions has given environmentalists little <u>reason to</u> optimism.

A) NO CHANGE

B) reasoning to

C) reason for

D) reasoning for

7

There is a certain stigma around the idea of a president seeing a therapist, so those who hold the office often <u>talk as</u> their advisors or family members instead.

A) NO CHANGE

B) confide on

C) confide in

D) talk on

8

Long periods of oxygen deprivation can leave many patients who suffer traumatic brain injuries <u>to</u> permanent damage that forever alters how they perceive the world around them.

A) NO CHANGE

B) with

C) for

D) by

Style

Frequently Confused Words

The Basics

You can find lists of Frequently Confused Words online. They usually have similar meanings or spellings, but they can't be used interchangeably. They're often a secondary part of Pronoun questions:

Example 1

Regardless of intent, the decision was wrong, and now people are demanding that the committee reverse <u>their</u> decision.

A) NO CHANGE

B) they're

C) it's

D) its

But most Frequently Confused Words get to the kinds of mistakes that you probably make when you type essays or send text messages:

Example 2

In the 21st century, college students are living further from home <u>then their</u> 20th century counterparts.

A) NO CHANGE

B) then there

C) than there

D) than their

The Twists

Unfortunately, almost every Frequently Confused Words question is twisted in some way. There are just a lot of rules!

Test out your instincts by answering the examples without help. But when you check your answers, **write down any rules that you want to study later.**

Example 3

Everyone in the neighborhood loved calling on Mrs. Johansson, <u>whose</u> homemade cherry pies were said to be the most delicious in the county.

A) NO CHANGE

B) who's

C) that's

D) her

You'll also notice that after you decide which of the Frequently Confused Words is correct, you sometimes need to solve a mini Diction question.

Example 4

The experimental treatment did not have a significant <u>effect on</u> the disease.

A) NO CHANGE

B) affect on

C) affect for

D) effect for

Exercise: Frequently Confused Words

1

Just as a machine needs regular maintenance, <u>so to</u> the human body needs regular checkups to detect health problems before they become severe.

A) NO CHANGE

B) also to

C) also too

D) so too

2

Just a few miles <u>past these</u> tranquil and verdant pastures, a cluster of industrial smokestacks billows a thick, black cloud.

A) NO CHANGE

B) passed these

C) passed this

D) past this

3

Roger had a tendency <u>to loose</u> his keys, so he installed a hook near the door where he would always leave them.

A) NO CHANGE

B) for loosing

C) for losing

D) to lose

4

The study suggested that the drought will have the greatest effect on the people <u>whom live</u> within 10 miles of the affected area.

A) NO CHANGE

B) whom lives

C) who lives

D) who live

5

The fields had been so over-farmed that nothing <u>could of</u> made them fertile again in time for the next planting season.

A) NO CHANGE

B) could have

C) might have

D) might of

6

This is a major problem for archaeologists, <u>they</u> often find themselves excavating in inhospitable areas with poor access to emergency medical care.

A) NO CHANGE

B) that

C) who

D) which

Exercise: Frequently Confused Words 2

7

The boxer's boasting could intimidate his opponent, but it's also <u>rising</u> expectations beyond a point where they can be met.

A) NO CHANGE

B) arising

C) raising

D) arisen

8

While the arrangement was not what either party had wanted, the need for compromise forced them <u>by accepting</u> the proposal.

A) NO CHANGE

B) to accept

C) to except

D) for excepting

9

The memorial is frequently surrounded by flowers and other tokens of remembrance that visitors <u>lie</u> down at its base.

A) NO CHANGE

B) lies

C) lay

D) lays

10

The general decided to stand <u>to principal</u>, so he deliberately refused to carry out the order.

A) NO CHANGE

B) on principal

C) on principle

D) to principle

11

Many teachers agree that students shouldn't <u>waist their</u> time on "busy work," but administrative rules often require daily homework assignments.

A) NO CHANGE

B) waist his or her

C) waste his or her

D) waste their

12

While scholars enjoy debating the effect that Nixon's decisions had on the <u>course of</u> history, they also recognize that some events were truly beyond his control.

A) NO CHANGE

B) coarse of

C) coarse in

D) course in

13

The ingenious design of the cup allows people to <u>pore its</u> contents back into the jar for easy transport.

A) NO CHANGE

B) pore it's

C) pour its

D) poor its

14

All of the courses contained locally-sourced ingredients, including the <u>dessert, which</u> featured ice cream made from dairy cows on a nearby farm.

A) NO CHANGE

B) dessert, that

C) desert, which

D) desert, which was

15

Mandatory sentencing guidelines can keep violent drug offenders in prison, but <u>in this instance,</u> the regulation is needlessly imposing a long prison term.

A) NO CHANGE

B) in this instants,

C) instantly,

D) for these instances,

16

With nothing but a compass, the scoutmaster <u>lead</u> his troop out of the wilderness to a highway, where they waved down a car for help.

A) NO CHANGE

B) had lead

C) could lead

D) led

17

Construction on the bypass road created miles of congestion and limited <u>access for</u> the beach during the height of tourist season.

A) NO CHANGE

B) access to

C) excess to

D) excess for

18

Sometimes it can be helpful to <u>reed allowed</u> so you can hear errors more easily.

A) NO CHANGE

B) read allowed

C) read aloud

D) reed aloud

Exercise: Frequently Confused Words 4

19

Many people find rats disgusting, and I know that they often carry disease. <u>Furthermore,</u> I think they are adorable.

A) NO CHANGE

B) As a rule,

C) Irregardless,

D) Regardless,

20

The park was as pristine as ever. There was nothing to indicate that it had been the <u>cite of</u> a crowded music festival only a few days earlier.

A) NO CHANGE

B) cite for

C) sight of

D) site of

21

The two boxers faced off seven times during their long careers. The fights were always close, but ultimately Osmond would end up with the <u>best</u> record.

A) NO CHANGE

B) better

C) larger

D) largest

22

Not usually a sentimental person, Jeremy found it difficult to express to Regina that her gift meant <u>alot</u> to him.

A) NO CHANGE

B) allot

C) a lot

D) allott

23

Even though she hadn't studied, Judy did surprisingly <u>good</u> on the exam and was able to pass the class.

A) NO CHANGE

B) goodly

C) well

D) we'll

24

No matter what the comedian tried, he could not <u>elicit so</u> much as a giggle from the audience.

A) NO CHANGE

B) elicit too

C) illicit too

D) illicit so

Exercise: Frequently Confused Words 5

25

Historians continue to debate whether the development of Norse mythology <u>proceeded</u> the settlement of the northernmost areas of Scandinavia.

A) NO CHANGE

B) proceeding

C) preceding

D) preceded

26

Even though he was the only one who ruled against the plaintiff, the judge's blistering <u>descent</u> gained more attention than the decision of the majority.

A) NO CHANGE

B) decent

C) dissent

D) descend

27

Most planets are incredibly luminous in the night's sky, but it's usually too bright for Uranus to be <u>visual to</u> the human eye.

A) NO CHANGE

B) visual for

C) visible for

D) visible to

28

<u>Formally of</u> the Arizona Diamondbacks, Joey Torino found his stride once he became clean-up hitter for the Cleveland Indians.

A) NO CHANGE

B) Formerly of

C) Formerly to

D) Formally to

29

As the two men stared each other down, Goodrich tried to <u>defuse</u> the situation with humor.

A) NO CHANGE

B) defusing

C) diffusing

D) diffuse

30

Bertha hadn't been home in years, but as soon as she walked into the reunion, she knew she was <u>toward</u> friends.

A) NO CHANGE

B) towards

C) among

D) between

Exercise: Frequently Confused Words 6

31

The Democratic Unionist Party lost substantial support when veterans and farmers walked out of the convention. The <u>former</u> ultimately started their own Agricultural Workers Party.

A) NO CHANGE

B) latter

C) foremost

D) later

32

Designers are constantly rethinking the qualities that are essential for a car that is both practical and <u>desirous.</u>

A) NO CHANGE

B) desired.

C) desirable.

D) desiring.

33

A mid-winter heat wave created warmer temperatures that caused a noticeable <u>recline</u> in snow cover.

A) NO CHANGE

B) reclining

C) declining

D) decline

34

Increased interest in organic foods has proven to be a <u>boon to</u> small farmers who specialize in pesticide-free farming

A) NO CHANGE

B) boon at

C) bane at

D) bane for

35

Both of the boys got in trouble, even though Victor had eaten <u>far fewer</u> cookies.

A) NO CHANGE

B) much fewer

C) much less

D) far less

36

After the accident, Professor Billings decided that he needed to move <u>foreword with</u> his plans to return to work.

A) NO CHANGE

B) foreword to

C) forward to

D) forward with

37

Kevin kept noticing that the the other students seemed to be <u>alluding to</u> some inside joke that he wasn't privy to.

A) NO CHANGE

B) alluded to

C) eluding to

D) eluding from

38

She thought she saw another reflection in the mirror, but it was just an <u>allusion caused by</u> the light.

A) NO CHANGE

B) illusion caused by

C) illusion caused with

D) allusion caused with

39

Since he was first, George Washington set more <u>precedents than any president.</u>

A) NO CHANGE

B) presidents than any other precedent.

C) presidents than any precedent.

D) precedents than any other president.

40

The mushroom sauce <u>complemented</u> the herbs in the roast chicken perfectly.

A) NO CHANGE

B) complementing

C) complimenting

D) complimented

41

With his <u>dominate</u> hand in a cast, Tony had no choice but to scribble his name with his left.

A) NO CHANGE

B) dominated

C) dominant

D) dominating

42

The refugees were able to claim asylum because they had been <u>prosecuted and</u> oppressed by their previous government.

A) NO CHANGE

B) prosecuted, and

C) persecuted, and

D) persecuted and

43

Town councils across the state are struggling <u>to ensure</u> worried citizens that their tax dollars are being well spent.

A) NO CHANGE

B) to assure

C) to insure

D) at insuring

44

The doctor's <u>patients</u> had worn thin as the day went on and the majority of his staff still had not shown up for their shifts.

A) NO CHANGE

B) patients'

C) patient's

D) patience

45

Shelby was <u>on the peak</u> of her career when she decided to give it all up and move to the Caribbean.

A) NO CHANGE

B) on the peek

C) at the peek

D) at the peak

46

Contrary to popular belief, the story that NASA spent millions of dollars to invent a pen that could write in space while the Russians simply used a pencil is neither true, as the pen cost far less to develop and produce, <u>or</u> complete, since a pencil would actually be dangerous to use in a space capsule because the graphite is flammable and conducts electricity.

A) NO CHANGE

B) but

C) yet

D) nor

47

Environmentalists argue that the true cost of beef is hidden from consumers because tax benefits allow beef producers <u>to deduct</u> a large portion of their expenses, which creates artificially low prices.

A) NO CHANGE

B) to deduce

C) reducing

D) a reduction

48

Those who learn a second language will <u>fair much better</u> in the modern economy, which, more than ever before, crosses international boundaries.

A) NO CHANGE

B) fare much better

C) fare much greater

D) fair much greater

Exercise: Frequently Confused Words 9

49

Toxins that leach out of plastics enter the food chain and <u>affecting</u> the development of animals that absorb too much of certain chemicals.

A) NO CHANGE

B) effecting

C) can effect

D) can affect

50

The Apollo program successfully landed men on the Moon six times, the last occurring in 1972, but no manned missions have taken place <u>from then.</u>

A) NO CHANGE

B) since then.

C) since than.

D) from than.

51

Many people <u>whom receive</u> greeting cards report throwing them away within a mere twenty-four hours, suggesting that the practice is both unappreciated and wasteful.

A) NO CHANGE

B) which receive

C) who receive

D) receive

52

It is long <u>past</u> time that governments around the world address the crisis caused by over-fishing in international waters.

A) NO CHANGE

B) passed

C) passing

D) pasted

53

The once-thriving penguin colony has been reduced to <u>less then</u> 500 individuals, probably because it has become more difficult for penguins to hunt the fish that they feed to their chicks.

A) NO CHANGE

B) less than

C) fewer than

D) fewer then

54

Despite Jackson and DeAngelo's long preparation ahead of the experiment, <u>there was no way they're</u> team could plan for every possible outcome.

A) NO CHANGE

B) there was no way their

C) there was no way there

D) their was no way their

Style

Lessons and Answers

Remember to try the Examples on your own first. It's okay if you feel lost and confused. You need to learn how to get past that feeling!

SAT Reading lesson

The Basics

As we go through this practice passage, we'll see these same questions again. You'll notice that most of them give you a line reference...

The Twists

... and that's why you can get away with not reading the passage to start. I know it's scary. And if you hate it, that's okay — you can always go back to spending the first 4 minutes of each passage reading the full text. **But you need to try the No Reading Strategy for this lesson and on at least one full SAT Reading section from a practice test.** If you end up getting a similar score, then you'll know that the No Reading Strategy isn't as risky as it might seem. In fact the first time they try it, most of my students tell me that they <u>think</u> the No Reading Strategy made them do worse, and then when I grade their practice section, they <u>actually</u> end up doing the same or better. Regardless, you need to incorporate new strategies, processes, and ideas into your Reading section plan. If you keep using your old strategy, you'll keep getting your old score. Change your strategy, change your score!

Whole Passage

Always save Whole Passage questions for last, even if you decide to read the passage first. Just don't forget to go back to them after you're done with all of the other questions. You don't want to accidentally leave them blank.

Line Reference

`2`

Most people find this question fairly easy. **The answer is Choice A,** and it just feels right. There are still probably difficult vocabulary words in the passage that make this hard to perfectly understand, but you get the main idea. The narrator is clearly

talking about John Reed. We learn that he doesn't look good, even if we don't understand every single word. That's okay! **Dumb summaries** help you work around difficult phrasing.

But this question was meant to be easy. Others will be much harder, so we should use this easy example to put a new process in place.

POE

Process of Elimination is essential if you want to change your Reading score. In my experience, students who don't improve their scores almost universally struggle with POE. No matter how much I beg them, they continue to treat the Reading section like the questions are asking for their opinion. They're not! Nobody cares what you think! The correct answers will always be provable and — more importantly — the wrong answers will always be provably wrong.

For #2, each wrong answer choice has a few problem words:

- Choice B is wrong because we don't really get any <u>historical context</u>. That would be information about the time period, like who was king of England at the time or what current events were taking place. This paragraph is about one boy, John Reed.

- Choice C is close to being right. They definitely discuss <u>education</u>, since they mention that John is a schoolboy and the Master, or principal, of the school has some opinions. But they never discuss the <u>merits</u> of education, which would be saying why education as a whole is a good thing. This paragraph is about only one boy's education, not the whole educational system.

- Choice D is also close to being right because they definitely talk about the <u>past</u>. But an <u>event</u> is a specific moment in the past. They aren't talking about that quite yet. This is more of a general overview of John. They never talk about specific dates or moments. However, they will later in this passage. And that's a good reason why the No Reading Strategy can be very helpful — we don't get tempted to pick choices that are about other parts of the passage.

Show Your Work

Again, there's a clear split among my students based on whether they adopt this strategy. Students who show their work on Reading (and Writing) consistently score higher than students who "do the work in their heads". Showing your work is how you train your brain to use POE. It's not enough to only cross off bad answers; you also need to underline the problem words and phrases. Train your brain to NARROW YOUR FOCUS to small parts of each choice.

3

This question is much harder than the previous one. One way to use POE is to turn the parts of the choices into simple yes-or-no questions:

- Choice A
  - Do they talk about eating <u>large quantities</u> of food? Yes. He <u>gorges</u> himself.
  - Are these foods <u>unhealthy</u>? Probably. John is kind of fat.
  - Is it about <u>children</u>? Not really. It's about one child — John Reed.
  - Choice A is what I sometimes call a "bumper sticker" choice. It's a short piece of wisdom that's not controversial and makes you feel good. Of course children shouldn't eat a lot of unhealthy foods! But that's not the point of this paragraph. It's about one specific person.

- Choice B
  - Do they talk about John Reed's <u>physical attributes</u>? Yes. He's fat and ugly.
  - Seems pretty good. Most people keep this choice in the mix.

- Choice C
  - Is there a <u>behavior</u>? Yes. John gorges himself.

  - Does the narrator <u>witness</u> it? Seems so. She's describing it pretty well.
  - Does she witness it <u>repeatedly</u>? Hmm… Hard to say. Seems pretty good otherwise, though.

- Choice D
  - Is there an <u>illness</u>? Seems like it. The +1 Sentence says he has <u>delicate health</u>.
  - Does it <u>affect his appearance</u>? Seems like it. He's fat and ugly, and it seems like that's because he eats a lot.
  - Most people pick Choice D.

But most people are wrong. **The answer to #3 is actually Choice C.** And the reason is entirely because of…

Strong Words

The lesson focuses on Choice B, but C and D also have Strong Words. In Choice B, <u>only</u> is all it takes to make the answer wrong. The narrator is concerned with more than <u>only</u> John's physical attributes.

Choice D says John has a <u>chronic</u> illness, but that's way too strong compared to <u>delicate health</u>. A <u>chronic</u> illness is something like cancer, or maybe he's in an iron lung. Regardless, we'd expect to find evidence that his health condition is chronic, but there aren't any lines that provide the evidence.

Choice C also has the strong word <u>repeatedly</u>. That word carries a lot of meaning, and we would want evidence from the passage that supports it. Does the narrator <u>repeatedly</u> witness John's behavior? Yes, because he <u>habitually</u> gorges himself. It's not the exact same word, but they both suggest that something is done multiple times. That's all the evidence we need to prove Choice C correct.

In general, it would be great if we could spend time proving every word of the correct answer and disproving at least one word in every incorrect answer. But time is valuable, so you sometimes need to use POE to do the best you can and then guess from whatever choices are left. The more you use POE, the more likely you'll guess right.

Try to notice Strong Words. They are often words that we would normally ignore, but they can make all the difference on hard questions.

Which is stronger?

1. most — this specifically means "more than half", whereas "some" can refer to just a few people

2. all — this means "everybody, without any exception", which is stronger than "many", even though "many" is also kind of strong

3. only if — "only" is a strong word that you'll likely see on your test

4. confirms — proof is hard to come by in science and on the SAT; "confirms" means that the hypothesis is 100% true, but science is mostly about supporting ideas because very few things are actually 100% true

5. argues that — some authors will take a clear position on their topics, but others won't; always pay attention to the author's opinion, especially when he mentions another person, because the other person's opinion might not be shared by the author

+1 Sentence Rule

A point worth emphasizing is that this rule only applies to questions that mention a line reference in the question itself. Evidence questions have line references, but they're usually contained in the answer choices. As we'll see on the next question, we typically stick to the exact lines given in the evidence choices and don't read extra. There are occasionally exceptions to this because the evidence might include a mysterious pronoun or speaker. In those cases, it's okay to read extra, but you generally want to stick to the lines when the line reference is in the choices like in #5.

Evidence Pairs

These are typically the hardest questions on the SAT Reading because they involve a lot of decisions. The first step should be to underline key parts of the question so that you know what you're reading for. This is called **reading with purpose**.

Imagine you're in school, reading Shakespeare or something complicated. Your teacher calls on you. Which question would you want to be asked?

- What was the last scene about?
- Was the last scene about love?

Most people would prefer the second question because it's less open-ended. You might not know what a scene is about because of all the difficult language, but you would probably be able to tell if it was about love, right? We want to do the same thing on the SAT Reading. When you read line references, don't try to summarize them like you would in school. Create **dumb summaries** that capture the ideas in the lines in just a word or two. And if you underline key ideas in the question, you can NARROW YOUR FOCUS to just those ideas when you read the line references. When you read with purpose, you're asking, "are these lines about love?" instead of "what are these lines about?"

4

The key ideas in this question are "John Reed is not currently at school because…"

5

Eliminate any line references that have nothing to do with not being at school.

- Line Reference A is irrelevant. Who cares how old he is? That doesn't explain why he's not at school.

- Line Reference B is good. They even say that his mom took him home from school. This seems to match with the question perfectly.

- Line Reference C is okay. It's a little hard to figure out what they're saying, but it talks about the master and being taken home. That's good enough for now. In fact, don't bother re-reading this to understand it better. When you read with purpose, you're putting off the summarizing until later. It might not matter what Line Reference C means if Line Reference B matches with an answer choice.

- Line Reference D is irrelevant. This says nothing about school.

Getting rid of two line references is pretty good. Our goal at this point is <u>not</u> to find the one correct answer. We're simply narrowing down our options so that we can more easily find a match when we look at the choices for #4.

4

Again, use POE to NARROW YOU FOCUS to the individual words in the choices.

- Choice A is wrong because his age doesn't matter. (But notice that Line Reference A also had to do with John's age. This is why we eliminate bad line references first. We don't want to be tempted by them when we get to the choices.)

- Choice B is close, but we have to be very careful. Just like in #3, we have a strong word in <u>constant</u> medical attention. <u>Delicate health</u> is one thing, but <u>constant</u> medical attention is way stronger than the passage suggests. Students who do not use POE will pick this choice because they are paying more attention to the words that match (<u>medical</u> and <u>health</u>) than to the words that do not match (<u>constant</u> and <u>delicate</u>).

- Choice C has two things we can check: is John <u>spoiled</u>? And is his <u>mother</u> responsible? Line Reference C suggests that his mom is sending him <u>cakes and sweetmeats</u>. That sounds like she's spoiling him.

- Choice D is wrong because we have no evidence that he's <u>bullying</u> other students. But once again, this choice matches with a Line Reference that we correctly eliminated earlier. Even though Choice D matches Line Reference D, they don't match the original question because they don't explain why <u>John isn't at school</u>.

The answer to #4 is Choice C, and the supporting Line Reference from #5 is C. This isn't what we expected when we looked at the line references first, but that's why Evidence Pairs are about being flexible. Sometimes you'll understand the line reference better after you've read the answer choices. It's okay to have a favorite line reference, but abandon it if you find something better.

No Line Reference

Whenever a question doesn't have a line reference, you <u>must</u> look ahead to the next question or two. Sometimes it'll be like #5 and give you line references. But if not, you can still use the **Chronology Rule** to NARROW YOUR FOCUS to a smaller portion of the passage.

In this case, the line references from #5 and #7 suggest that the answer to #6 can be found between lines 16 and 41. Once we adjust for the paragraphs, we're looking at lines 17-42. That's still a lot of text, but it's better than reading the whole passage. Plus, we're not simply reading the lines — we're reading with purpose. Where do they talk about <u>preventing John from bullying</u>?

6

Some people see the answer in the lines, but you can still use POE if not:

- Choice A is wrong because <u>too preoccupied with reading</u> is very strong. We have no evidence that she's too busy to learn self defense.

- Choice B matches with some key lines from the passage. The middle of that first paragraph talks about the narrator having <u>no appeal whatever.</u> The servants don't want to <u>offend</u> John, and the mother seems to ignore the problem.

- Choice C is one of those "bumper sticker" choices. Of course violence is <u>immoral</u>, but this isn't about that. At no point does the narrator say this. The story is more complicated than that.

- Choice D is wrong because these lines don't mention her <u>injuries</u>. And she doesn't seem <u>too weak.</u>

Choice B is correct because POE gets rid of the other choices, and the ideas in B match with the line reference. The Chronology Rule helped us focus on the right part of the passage.

The Chronology Rule won't work every time. Occasionally the SAT breaks the rule. But don't let that deter you from using it. I often have students who get a question wrong because they followed the Chronology Rule but it didn't work. That's not a good reason to abandon the rule! How many times did following the rule <u>add</u> points on other questions? Ideally, it would work every time and you'd be able to get 100% of the points. But it still works 90% of the time. I'd rather have a process that gets me 90% of the points than no process at all. The 10% of times that the rule fails are worth it. And as you practice, you'll get more confident about breaking the rule when you need to.

Reading Vocab

It's <u>very</u> important that you read the line reference and come up with your own guess <u>before</u> you read the answer choices. Tempting you with common definitions is the SAT's favorite trick, but you can easily prevent it by using the QLC Method.

7

In this case, we can steal words from the sentence to help us understand <u>retired</u>. Here are three perfectly valid guesses:

- I tottered, and on regaining my equilibrium <u>fell</u> back a step or two from his chair.
- I tottered, and on regaining my equilibrium <u>tottered</u> back a step or two from his chair.
- I tottered, and on regaining my equilibrium <u>stepped</u> back a step or two from his chair.

The answer probably isn't going to be <u>fell</u>, <u>tottered</u>, or <u>stepped</u>, but that's not why we were coming up with a guess. We just wanted a placeholder so that we can compare our guess to the actual answers. Ideally, our guess will mean the same thing as the correct answer. **In this case, Choice C is a great synonym for <u>falling</u> or <u>stepping</u> back.**

Finish Up

These questions use the same strategies as before, even though they're a little harder.

8

Focus on the question, and underline key words. We need to know why <u>John thinks it's okay to bully</u> the narrator.

9

- Line Reference A is hard to understand, and it kind of sounds like he's <u>bullying</u> her. Keep it.

- Line Reference B also sounds like <u>bullying</u>. Keep it.

- Line Reference C seems random. Cross it off.

- Line Reference D sounds like someone is getting <u>bullied</u>. Keep it.

Eliminating only one Line Reference may not seem like much, but you've learned a lot. Now you need to find matches in the choices.

- Choice A seems to match with Line Reference D. They both sound like someone is being <u>punished</u>.

- Choice B doesn't seem to have a match. Where is the narrator <u>insulting</u> John? Some people think that Line Reference A is an example of an insult, but it's actually John talking. If we had the full passage, this would be a good reason to read a little extra beyond the line reference to better understand the context. If you're ever unsure who's talking, then it's okay to read more.

- Choice C seems to match with Line Reference B, which talks about the house <u>belonging</u> to John.

- Choice D is too strong. Maybe we would try to match this with Line Reference B, but <u>stole</u> is not the same as <u>rummaged</u>. We also don't have evidence that the items are <u>valuable</u>. They're just books. We can cross this choice off because of POE and Strong Words.

Some people have trouble choosing between the two matches (Choice A with Line Reference D or Choice C with Line Reference B). With the full passage, we could read some extra lines to see if we learn anything new. But you can also answer this correctly using the **Chronology Rule**.

Question #7 told us to look at line 41, and #10 tells us to look at line 72. According to the Chronology Rule, the answer to #9 should be between those two line references. Line Reference D would break the Chronology Rule, so if we had to guess, we should guess Line Reference B and then Choice C to match.

The answer to #8 is Choice C, and the answer to #9 is indeed Line Reference B. If we were to read a little extra around Line Reference D, we would learn that Mrs. Reed is actually ordering her <u>servants</u> to punish the narrator, so Line Reference D does not

match Choice A. Again, if you're a little confused about a person or pronoun that the line reference is talking about, you can read a little extra. But most of the time you can just stick to the exact line reference for Evidence Pairs.

Remember to guess your own word before you look at the choices. Physically cover them with your hand if you need to. In this case, we can't steal a word from the sentence. The sentence is trying to convey a contrast: <u>the terror had passed, but other feelings had</u>… arrived? started? come? All of those are fine guesses.

If you don't know what <u>ensued</u> means, then just move on to Choice B. Do <u>not</u> eliminate Choice A, or any other choice, just because you don't know the meaning of the word. It might be right! Instead, focus on the words you do know. Does <u>conquered</u> mean <u>started</u>? Not really. And neither does <u>abandoned</u> or <u>accomplished</u>. **So by Process of Elimination, Choice A is correct.**

But don't forget that we have one more question!

We skipped the Whole Passage question because we hadn't read any of the passage to start. But now we've answered 9 other questions and read the relevant line references. As you can see, we read about 50% of the passage. Don't read the other 50%! Just try to answer the Whole Passage question based on what you know.

- Choice A is half true. It seems like we read a <u>depiction of the narrator's past</u>. But I don't remember anything about <u>another character's future</u>. Everything seems to be about one moment in the narrator's life.

- Choice B is definitely wrong. This passage was not about <u>education</u>. It was about John's education for a small part, but it quickly moved on to other things.

- Choice C is half true. It seems like we get the narrator's <u>inner thoughts</u>. She's not shy about sharing what she really thinks of John. But we don't really get <u>observations by other characters</u>. The narrator quotes what they say, but that's not the same thing as hearing their observations. We stay in Jane Eyre's head for the whole passage.

- Choice D is all that's left, but we should still double check. <u>Never</u> pick D just because you've eliminated everything else. Take the time to test it. In this case, we definitely started with a <u>description of a character</u>. Recall that question #2 was basically asking that same thing. Was there an <u>altercation</u> between John and the narrator? If you don't know what <u>altercation</u> means, you might not know for sure. An <u>altercation</u> is a fight. And that matches with our dumb summary — Jane does not like John, and so they fight.

Choice D is correct mostly because of POE. But more than that, we truly understood a lot of this passage, even if it didn't feel like it. We didn't need to read all of it to understand most of it. That's because main ideas are repeated throughout a passage. One of the biggest worries students have with the No Reading Strategy is that they'll miss an important piece of information by skipping around. Trust me, that's not likely. Only very rarely does the SAT hide an obscure piece of information somewhere in the passage. If something is important, it'll stand out and it'll be repeated.

Using the No Reading Strategy takes a bit of confidence. Hopefully seeing it in action makes you more willing to try it on your own. Don't worry if it feels scary at first. It gets easier with practice. But if you decide that you prefer to read the passages first, that's okay too. Just remember all of the other rules that we used for these questions: POE, Strong Words, +1 Sentence, Chronology, and the QLC Method. All of these ideas have to be a part of how you change your strategy — and your score — on the Reading section.

SAT Reading — Summary

Use the No Reading Strategy to save time and NARROW YOUR FOCUS to smaller parts of the line references.

Follow the QLC Method on all Reading questions:
1. Question
2. Line Reference(s)
3. Choices

Show your work as you use POE to sort through the choices. Remember to divide the choices into smaller parts that need to be tested against the passage.

Start to notice Strong Words in the choices.

Use the +1 Sentence Rule when the line reference is given in the question. When the line references are in the choices, you can usually read only the line reference.

Use the Chronology Rule to NARROW YOUR FOCUS for No Line Reference questions. It can also help when you need to guess on Evidence Pairs.

Save Whole Passage questions for last, and use the 50% Rule to build your confidence that you can answer them without reading the entire passage.

Answers: Reading Passage

#11 — Answer = C

Whole Passage. Remember to answer this question at the end. Choice A is wrong because this passage is not a <u>list of shortcomings</u>. It's not a list of anything, really. Choice B is wrong because they never discuss the <u>practical applications</u> of the experiment. Choice D is wrong because there is not a new <u>method</u>. Plus, they're not <u>testing the limits</u> of anything. They're conducting an experiment to better understand the experiment described in the first paragraph. That dumb summary matches well with Choice C. <u>Unexpected</u> is a Strong Word, but it matches with <u>surprised</u> in line 8.

#12 — Answer = A

Evidence Pair Part 1. Focus on the question, then skip to #13 to sort through the line references. After that, sort through these choices. Choice B is wrong because they never talk about visual landmarks. That's too specific. We never learn how the mice navigate the maze. Choice C is wrong because the puzzles come later in the passage. Choice D is wrong because the passage never compares how the two groups age. Be careful of words that suggest comparisons. They aren't always wrong, but they're still Strong Words that we need to check. Choice A matches with Line Reference C in #13 because challenges is a synonym for difficult circumstances.

#13 — Answer = C

Evidence Pair Part 2. Remember to do this part before you answer #12. Line Reference A uses the copy/paste trick to lure you into a trap, but they never explain why the wild mice have healthier brains. Line Reference A merely says what we already know. Line Reference B is irrelevant. Line Reference C explains that the change in the mice's brains is the result of the challenges that they face in the wild. That seems relevant. Line Reference D is wrong because it doesn't make a distinction between the wild mice and the lab mice.

#14 — Answer = B

Reading Vocab. There aren't many clue words in the sentence, but you should guess that reflect means something like show. That matches with Choice B.

#15 — Answer = D

Evidence Pair Part 1. This question has no line reference, so we should look ahead to the next question to see if it helps us with one. Sure enough, this is an Evidence Pair. The SAT really likes to split Evidence Pairs over two pages because they know that some people are too lazy or clueless to look ahead. Always look ahead! After sorting through the references in #16, you can use POE to sort through these choices. Be careful with Choice A. The experiment is actually supposed to do the opposite — determine whether the lab mice can show the same structures as wild mice. Choice B is wrong because genetic mutations are never mentioned.

Choice C is tricky because it uses a lot of key words from the passage. But the problem word is how. The experiment is not trying to figure out how the dentate gyrus works. Instead, it's trying to figure out if the dentate gyrus is different between the two groups. That matches better with Choice D, which is asking more of a yes-or-no question. Most of the time, vague and general answer choices are better, and this is a good example of why. Also, long term and short term match with lifetime and training in Line Reference D.

#16 — Answer = D

Evidence Pair Part 2. Line Reference A is about the wrong study! Pay attention to the question. It wants the study that includes Strong and Hoskins, but the study in the first paragraph was only conducted by Burnberry. Line Reference B is also about the first study, but it's also irrelevant to the question. Line References C and D both could be right, so you would not be able to get down to one answer without looking at the choices for #15. Line Reference D is the better match to Choice D in #15. Line Reference C does not talk about short term versus long term, but Line Reference D does.

#17 — Answer = A

Reading Vocab. The sentence helps us out here. We're probably looking for a word similar to simple. Plus, the next sentence tells us more about what a regular feeding schedule would look like. It's okay to read extra if we're confused. Choice A is the best match because we're looking for a simple schedule, which would follow a cyclical pattern.

#18 — Answer = B

No Line Reference. According to the Chronology Rule, we'd expect the answer to #18 to be in between the line references for #17 and #19, so read from 40 to 69. And remember to read with purpose. You want something that compares the two groups of mice. They start to talk about the results of the experiment in line 51. Understand the results as best you can, then use POE. Choice A is wrong because neural connections is way too specific. They never get that detailed. Choice C is wrong because the passage says the opposite — line 52 says there was no difference in the sizes of the brain structures.

Choice D is wrong because the experiment was designed so that the mice started out the same. Plus, the simulated mice were meant to be <u>more</u> like the wild mice, not less. Choice B is correct because it's fairly vague. Line 58 also talks about <u>increased activity</u> in one part of the brain.

#19 — Answer = C

Line Reference. Read +1 Sentence and the answer is basically given away. They say Burnberry was <u>surprised</u>. That matches perfectly with Choice C. Also, Choice A is wrong because the questions never mention <u>reasons</u>. Choice B is wrong because they are not questioning the <u>accuracy</u>. And Choice D is wrong because the questions never <u>explain</u> anything.

#20 — Answer = C

Unpaired Evidence. These questions are like Evidence Pairs where the first part has already been answered for us. Focus on the question. They tell you exactly what they want. Line Reference C is correct because it talks about the <u>pay off</u> from practicing in the cages. They're using their skills in the <u>maze</u>, which is outside the cage. Line Reference B is close because it says the experimental group is now <u>faster</u> at the maze, but they don't speculate that this is because of the practice in the cage. When you are deciding between two answers, pick the choice with more matching ideas.

#21 — Answer = C

Reading Figures. You want to get all of the Figure questions correct. They are easy if you don't make careless mistakes. The question is telling you to look at the far right, light grey column. The top of the bar is around 17 or 18, which is good enough for Choice C. If you looked at the wrong bar, you'd get the wrong answer.

#22 — Answer = A

Reading Figures. This one is a bit harder. If you read all of the graph, you should get it. The note underneath the legend explains that the lines and triangles in the centers of the columns are the <u>maximum</u> and <u>minimum</u> times. Choice A is correct because the top triangle for the second column is higher than the top triangle for the first column. This means that the <u>maximum</u> time for the <u>control</u> was

higher than the <u>maximum</u> time for the <u>experimental</u>. Choice B is wrong for the opposite reason: the bottom triangle in the first column is higher than the bottom triangle in the second column, which means that the shortest time for the experimental group was <u>not</u> less than every time for the control. Choice C is not true because the triangle lines for the <u>control</u> (light grey) are both longer than the triangle lines for the <u>experimental</u> (dark grey). Choice D is wrong because the graph doesn't say anything about the number of <u>wrong turns</u>.

SAT Writing lesson

The Basics

Don't get too caught up in the passages. Read what you need to and no less. You can always read more if you want.

The Twists

But it's extremely important that you read everything that you're told to. The SAT <u>will</u> try to trick you by including wrong answers that would seem right if you didn't read the full paragraph when you're supposed to.

Example 1

This is a vague question, but you should be able to recognize that they're instructing you to read the full paragraph. But don't get too caught up in the details. Make a **dumb summary** that captures the repeated ideas: <u>War</u>, <u>defend</u>, <u>Navy</u>, <u>victories</u>, <u>Lake</u>, <u>lake</u>, <u>defense</u>, <u>port</u>. They're talking about the <u>Navy</u>. Which choice is also about the <u>Navy</u>? **Choice D is correct because it's the only relevant answer.**

The wrong answers sound like introduction sentences, but we need more than that. We need to specifically introduce the ideas in this paragraph. Dumb summaries can help you NARROW YOUR FOCUS to the big, repeated ideas.

Example 2

Sometimes the goals are very specific. In fact, this question is not really about the rest of the passage at all. You can answer with just the underlined sentence. Choice B is a trick choice because it continues the previous sentence's focus on Baltimore, but it does not mention the American Navy suffering defeats. Choice D is also a trick choice because it uses the word defeated just like the question, but it completely reverses the meaning. It says that the Americans did the defeating. Choice C, on the other hand, uses different words to convey the same idea as the question. **Choice C is correct because it talks about the Americans getting blockaded and attacked by the British.**

Your instincts might draw you to Choices B or D because they copy words from the passage and question and paste them into the choices. But you need to be skeptical of your instincts on Ideas questions. They're not asking for the ideas that you think are interesting. They give you a specific goal, and you need to follow the rules to give them exactly what they want.

Example 3

You'll probably eliminate Choices B and C pretty easily. We don't need to pause after difficult or States. But deciding between Choices A and D is trickier. Do you remember what a semicolon does?

This is a clear example of where your instincts can only take you so far. You might be able to "hear" the pauses, but you can't really hear the difference between a semicolon and a comma. You just need to know the rule.

On the SAT, a semicolon separates two complete sentences. Essentially, it's the same as a period. If you're given the option to use a semicolon, you must figure out whether the part before and the part after the semicolon are both complete sentences that could stand on their own. If not, you cannot use a semicolon.

In this case, the first part is a complete sentence. We could end the sentence with France and a period if we wanted to. But the part after the semicolon is just a description. It cannot stand alone as a sentence. It's giving more information about France, so we should attach it to the sentence with a comma. **Choice D is correct.**

Example 4

It's very difficult to "hear" the correct answer to this question. All of the choices probably sound okay. Some people pick Choice C, but they aren't very good at explaining why it's correct. That's because they're using the sound of the sentence. If we know the grammar rules, it becomes much easier to know the answer for certain.

Choice C is correct because all of the other answer choices are Run-on Sentences. A run-on occurs when you connect two sentences with only a comma. You can join sentences with semicolons, conjunctions, or other connector words. But you cannot join them with only a comma. Choice A, B, and D sound fine because run-ons won't sound wrong — they'll sound like two complete sentences. But when we write, we need to follow punctuation rules. In this case, all of the wrong answers include pronouns, which start the sentences over with new subjects. Which has a special power to turn a complete sentence into a dependent clause that can be attached to another sentence. In fact, one of the most common ways to fix run-on sentences on the SAT is to replace a pronoun with which.

Example 5

Most people will confidently eliminate Choices A and D because those are contractions (it's = it is; they're = they are). This will 100% come up on your SAT, so you at least need to know the difference between the possessive pronouns and the contractions.

The next part is harder. But when you've eliminated two choices, you can more easily compare the two that remain. What's the difference between its and their?

They're not about people versus things. The only difference is that its is singular and their is plural. In other words, we use its when we want to refer to one thing, and we use their when we want to refer to multiple things.

In this case, the sailors belong to, or are possessed by, Britain, so Britain is what the pronoun stands for. (The technical term for the word a pronoun replaces is an *antecedent*.) Britain has many people in it, but the word is technically singular — there is only one Britain. **So we need to use the singular pronoun, making Choice C correct.**

Pronoun rules can be very difficult because they do not always match our instincts. Many people would say this example with their and never think twice about it. In fact, we very often say the wrong pronoun. What does your gut tell you about this sentence?

A teacher should always help their students.

Does it sound right to you? Probably. It sounds right to me, and I'd probably say it exactly like that if I were talking to a friend. But I'd be wrong. In this case, we're using the plural pronoun their to replace the singular noun a teacher. That's very bad grammar. Technically, we need a singular pronoun, and since we don't know the gender of this mystery teacher, we should say:

A teacher should always help his or her students.

But that probably sounds bad to you. I would never say that sentence! Yet it's the correct way to say it. And this is the hardest part of the grammar section — sometimes you're so used to the wrong way that the right way actually sounds wrong. Success on Writing comes down to knowing when you can trust your instincts and when you have to doubt them.

Example 6

Here's another difficult question. Most people eliminate Choices C and D because they are the wrong tense. But once again, the remaining two choices are very similar. What's the difference?

Just like nouns and pronouns, verbs can be singular or plural. We often forget this rule, but we use it every time we speak. Notice how when we change the number of dogs, the verb bark also changes:

The dog barks loudly.
The dogs bark loudly.

We would never say:

The dogs barks loudly.
The dog bark loudly.

In Example 6, the verbs follow the same rule: was is singular and were is plural. In fact, every singular verb ends with S. That's the opposite of what you'd expect because we usually associate S with plurals. You can always use simple sentences like the ones above to help you remember because our brains understand the verb rules when sentences are straightforward.

We should try to do something similar with Example 6 by removing the extra words and focusing on the verb. Since tributaries was getting sounds wrong and tributaries were getting sounds right, most people pick Choice B. But that's exactly what the SAT was hoping you'd pick.

The actual answer is Choice A because the actual subject of the verb is issue, which is singular. But why is issue the subject? It's very far away from the verb, but the SAT is using one of its favorite tricks to mess with your expectations. You'll learn more about this rule in the Verb Agreement packet, but the issue is the subject because everything in between it and the verb is extra information that can be crossed out of the sentence. The subject of a sentence cannot be in a prepositional phrase, which is an extra clause that starts with a preposition. A preposition is a tiny word that helps describe something in some way. In this case, of is the preposition that lets us cross out a lot of the sentence. We can also cross out the part before the comma because it's an extra clause:

~~While impressment was the primary problem in the eyes of Atlantic merchants,~~ the issue ~~of American sovereignty over the Mississippi River and its tributaries~~ <u>was getting</u> increased attention in the West.

Once we eliminate the extra parts of the sentence, it becomes very easy to hear that Choice A is correct. This rule takes a lot of practice, so don't worry if you're still confused right now. The good news is that Verb Agreement is, in my opinion, the most complicated grammar rule on the SAT, so it doesn't really get any harder than this.

Example 7

Don't over-think this one. What sounds best? **The correct answer is D because it's the shortest.** That's it. That's the whole explanation.

Style questions still involve rules, but they're different than the grammar rules we used on the previous page. Style rules are about finding the best wording, and the SAT follows a rule that shorter choices are better. To be clear, there will absolutely be times when the shortest choice is <u>not</u> correct because some other grammar rule is more important. But in general, when in doubt, you should pick the shortest choice.

In this case, it's not just that Choice D is the shortest. All of the other answers are redundant (they repeat information):

- Choice A is wrong because <u>settlements</u> are <u>places where people live</u>, so there's no need to repeat it.

- Choice B is wrong because <u>settlements</u>, <u>communities</u>, and <u>towns</u> are all the same thing, so there's no need to repeat it.

- Choice C is wrong because we already know that the <u>small settlements</u> were <u>not very large</u>, so there's no need to repeat it.

Example 8

These choices aren't as similar to each other as those in Example 7, but the logic is the same — pick

the most concise answer. **This time, the correct answer is Choice B.**

The main reason students get these questions wrong is that they incorrectly believe that good writing is wordy. I see this all the time when people write SAT essays. They use big words and long sentences because they think it makes them sound smart. Believe me, it doesn't. It makes you sound like you don't know what you're talking about. Good writing is clear and concise. All of the choices in this question convey the same basic idea. Nothing is lost by using fewer words.

Example 9

You probably know that this question is testing vocabulary. But unlike in the Reading section, the Writing Vocab questions aren't really asking for the meaning of the word. In fact, all four of these choices basically mean the same thing. Trust your instincts. Which word would <u>you</u> use if you were writing this sentence for an essay in school?

Most people would choose <u>decline</u>, and Choice C is indeed the correct answer. This question wants you to pick the word that best fits the tone of the passage. In general, words fall on a spectrum:

slangy — academic — pedantic

Choice D is too slangy, or informal. You might use it in a text message, but it doesn't sound great in formal writing. Choice B, on the other hand, is too pedantic, or fancy. It's the kind of word students use when they are trying to sound smart, but that's a bad strategy. Good writing is supposed to be clear and easily understood. Using a pedantic word makes it harder for your audience to understand what you're trying to say. Don't pick complicated words when a more well-known word would effectively convey the same idea. Choice C is academic — it's formal enough for a school paper, but it's also common enough that the average reader would understand it.

Choice A is also pedantic, but there's another problem that comes up on Writing Vocab questions. The answer choices will be synonyms, but that doesn't mean they can be used interchangeably. Enfeeblement might remind you of the word feeble, which is typically used to describe an old or sick person. It wouldn't be used to describe a political party. In this case, you probably wouldn't notice that the usage is wrong, but in other cases you will. Reading for school or even watching TV can teach you about the English language in ways that a textbook or dictionary cannot.

Example 10

Same with this question. **The answer is Choice A because... well... that's just what we say.** Unlike Example 9, this question is about choosing words that don't really have a concise definition. This is a Diction question, and it's almost entirely about which choice sounds best. If you got this wrong, I'm not sure what to say. You were unlucky? Thankfully, there aren't many Diction questions on the SAT. When you encounter one, trust your instincts, pick the best sounding choice, and move on!

Predict the Question

Compare the past three pages. Do you see any differences between the questions? For the Ideas questions, we had to pay attention to the instructions in the literal questions. We ignored our own personal opinions about the choices and the passage. For the Grammar questions, we had to use a lot of complicated rules. In fact, going with our gut got us in trouble on a lot of the questions. But for the Style questions, our gut was basically all we needed.

The overall strategy for the Writing section is to pay attention to the question type — Ideas, Grammar, or Style. If you can recognize the type, you can follow the correct procedure. Mostly, you need to know whether you'll be able to trust your instincts (Style) or have to follow the rules (Grammar).

SAT Writing — Summary

The questions fall into one of three categories — Ideas, Grammar, and Style. If you can identify the category and predict what the question is asking, you'll be less likely to fall into the SAT's traps.

Ideas questions almost always have a literal question (instead of only the answer choices). Always follow the instructions in the question. The correct answer will accomplish a goal that is stated or implied by the question. Grammar does not matter. Your personal preferences do not matter. Match ideas in the text to ideas in the choices.

Grammar questions either test punctuation or consistency within a sentence. You must follow strict grammar rules. Your instincts might lead you into a trap, so you need to learn and memorize the rules. Use the answer choices to predict the relevant rule for each question.

Style questions also follow rules, but they're not as strict as traditional grammar questions. Typically, you can follow your instincts and pick the choice that sounds best. Answers should be clear and concise. But beware: the shortest answer won't always be correct if a grammar rule takes precedence.

Answers: Writing Questions

#1 — Answer = D
Style — Concision. All of the wrong answers repeat information. There is no good reason to say moments or past, since both are already included in the definition of history. Be concise.

#2 — Answer = C
Grammar — Advanced Punctuation. Divide this question into two smaller questions. First, do you need an apostrophe? The Fathers don't own or possess anything, so there's no need for an apostrophe. That eliminates Choices A and D. Next, do you need a comma or a dash? The dash is better in this case because there's a second dash at the end of the list. Like commas, dashes can be used to

separate extra information from the main sentence. Since this extra information is a list with commas, it's less confusing to use dashes so readers know where the list begins and ends.

#3 — Answer = C

Ideas — Add or Delete. Don't get tricked. Just because they mention <u>Lincoln</u> doesn't mean we need more facts about him. Choices C and D essentially tell you to read the full paragraph to better understand the main idea. If you do, you'll see that the paragraph is moving toward introducing <u>Henry Clay</u>. The title of the passage suggests that Clay is the topic, so there's no need for more information about Lincoln. Choice C is better than D because it's weaker. <u>Undermine</u> is a Strong Word, just like in the Reading section. This Lincoln fact gets in the way, but it doesn't attack the central claim.

#4 — Answer = C

Grammar — Appositives. Extra information should be separated from the main sentence with commas. In this case, <u>a largely forgotten statesman</u> is an extra description of <u>Clay</u>, so it should be surrounded by commas.

#5 — Answer = C

Style — Writing Vocab. Trust your instincts. Choices A and B are too slangy. The phrase <u>rose to priority</u> should sound strange. It's just not something that can be said. However, you might have heard <u>rose to prominence</u> at some point. <u>Prominence</u> means notoriety or fame.

#6 — Answer = B

Style — Writing Vocab. This one is harder. Choices A and C are too slangy. People who picked Choice D typically failed to read the entire sentence, which is a requirement for all SAT Writing questions. You <u>must</u> read the full sentence! In this case, the rest of the sentence makes it clear that America is already independent at this time, <u>30 years after the Revolution</u>. So Clay isn't <u>arguing</u> for something that's already true. Instead, Clay hopes the war will help America <u>assert</u>, or stand up for, its independence.

#7 — Answer = A

Grammar — Lists & Examples. The most well-known use of the colon is to start lists. That's exactly how it's being used here. But you'll see in the lesson later on that colons have a much more nuanced purpose. They are used when the second part (after the colon) answers or explains something from the first part (before the colon). In this case, the list is explaining the <u>reasons</u> the war was a <u>failure</u>.

#8 — Answer = B

Ideas — Transitions. These are the only type of Ideas questions that do not have an actual question. Your goal is to connect the ideas contained in the sentence before the transition with those in the sentence that includes the transition. Use dumb summaries to capture the ideas. The first sentence is clearly negative (<u>failure</u>), and the second sentence is clearly positive (<u>victory</u>). That's a contrast, and <u>however</u> is a contrast word.

#9 — Answer = C

Grammar — Pronouns. The choices make it obvious that you need to worry about singular and plural pronouns. Find the word that the pronoun refers to. <u>The nation</u> is the correct noun, and it's singular because it's just one nation. Choice C is the singular pronoun.

#10 — Answer = C

Ideas — Sentence Placement. Focus on the sentence that they're asking you to move. Look for "anchor words" that will help you place it. Sentence 3 mentions <u>this growing region</u> as if it's been introduced before. The same is true of <u>he</u>, which is clearly referencing <u>Clay</u>. Sentence 1 introduces <u>Clay</u> and <u>the West</u>, so Sentence 3 should follow it. We want the pronouns to reference things that are nearby.

#11 — Answer = D

Grammar — General Comma Rules. Commas are basically quick pauses in a sentence. Read the sentence, and you won't really pause anywhere in the underlined portion. That's a good sign that commas aren't necessary. More technically, we don't typically use commas to mark off prepositional phrases like <u>to enter the Union</u>.

#12 — Answer = B

Style — Frequently Confused Words. First, think about <u>who</u> versus <u>that</u>. You can probably hear that <u>that</u> is better, but the real reason is that <u>who</u> is only used for people, not things like <u>states</u>. Next, you need to know that <u>than</u> is used for comparisons, and <u>then</u> is used for time. They're not making a comparison, so <u>then</u> is correct. If you thought that this was a Grammar question, that's okay. There are definitely concrete rules at play here, but I consider it Style because many students start by using their instincts on questions like these

#13 — Answer = A

Grammar — Fragments & Run-Ons. Most punctuation questions have the exact same words in each choice, but the punctuation marks will be different. That's not the case here, but notice that the underlined portion is right next to a comma. That's a clue that you have to worry about run-on sentences. Choices B and C don't sound bad, but they're incorrect because they join two complete sentences together with only a comma. <u>Which</u> has that special power to connect the sentences without creating a run-on, so it's the best answer.

#14 — Answer = B

Ideas — Add or Delete. You might not have a good instinct for whether to add or delete this sentence. That's okay! Focus on the "becauses". Choice A is wrong because it definitely doesn't <u>define a term</u>. Choice D is wrong because it does not <u>repeat information</u>. Now focus on the surrounding sentences. The sentence after suggests that Clay is <u>limiting the expansion of slavery</u>, but that's not talked about in the sentence before. In other words, we need to add this sentence because it connects the two ideas that are already there. It directly discusses <u>prohibiting slavery</u>.

#15 — Answer = A

Style — Frequently Confused Words. Using your instincts, you can probably eliminate Choices C and D because they sound bad. For the rest, you need to know that <u>affect</u> is a verb and <u>effect</u> is a noun. They're talking about <u>the</u> effect, so it's a noun.

#16 — Answer = B

Grammar — Appositive. Once again, we have extra information that needs to be separated out with commas. But make sure you're putting the commas around the extra and not something that's essential to the sentence. You can test your guess by crossing out the part between the commas and reading the sentence without it. If the sentence still sounds okay, then the commas are probably in the right place. <u>Veto</u> is the definition of <u>nullify</u>, so it's the extra clause.

#17 — Answer = A

Ideas — Combine Sentences. Grammar does not really matter for these questions. You want to make sure the ideas flow together. Choice B is wrong because the comma clause interrupts the sentence in a way that makes the sentence hard to follow. Choice C is wrong because it sounds like they're talking about the <u>rate of violence</u>, but the original sentence is talking about the <u>rate of the tariff</u>. Choice D is wrong because <u>their</u> does not really refer to anything. Choice A is clear and concise.

#18 — Answer = C

Style — Writing Vocab. This one is hard. You just need to know the right word from experience. All of these words have to do with physically joining things together, but only <u>cemented</u> can also be used metaphorically in this way. It means something like <u>locked in</u> or <u>solidified</u>.

#19 — Answer = B

Style — Diction. Do the best you can. Hopefully the correct answer sounded better than the others. There's no real rule here. You just need to trust your instincts.

#20 — Answer = A

Grammar — Pronouns. Once again, the choices give it away that we need to think about singular and plural pronouns. The concessions were not liked by <u>both slave and free states</u>, which is plural, so we use the plural pronoun <u>they</u>.

#21 — Answer = B

Ideas — Transitions. Try to make dumb summaries of the surrounding sentences. The sentence before is negative (<u>not popular</u>, <u>did not like</u>), but the sentence with the transition is positive (relieved, crisis averted). Use a contrast word to show the transition from negative to positive.

#22 — Answer = A

Ideas — Sentence Placement. Look for "anchor words" in sentence 3. There's not much, but it implies that the issue has been discussed before. Keeping the sentence where it is now is best because it follows the discussion of problems solved by the compromise. We're also able to connect sentence 2 to sentence 4, which would skip from the compromise to slavery very quickly. Sentence 3 smooths that transition.

#23 — Answer = D

Ideas — Accomplish the Goal. Read the paragraph! It says a lot of nice things about Clay (reputation, heroic, celebrated). Choice D also says nice things about Clay (respected). It's that simple.

#24 — Answer = C

Grammar — Apostrophes. Use apostrophes to show possession. Clay possesses the achievements, but the achievements don't possess anything. So Clay needs an apostrophe, but achievements does not.

#25 — Answer = C

Grammar — Verb Agreement. This looks like it's about tenses, but you should always look at singular or plural verbs first. Choices A and B are plural, Choice C is singular, and Choice D is neither (plus it sounds bad). The subject of the verb is reputation because as one of early America's most heroic figures is extra information. You can also turn the verb into a question: what was dimmed? Clay's reputation, which is singular.

#26 — Answer = B

Ideas — Accomplish the Goal. Don't over-think it. The previous example talks about studying Americans from wars, and Choice B talks about studying Americans during times of peace. It maintains the rhythm of the sentence.

Line Reference lesson

The Basics

Line Reference questions represent the most basic Reading question. They NARROW YOUR FOCUS to just a few lines, and you need to pick the choice that captures what's going on in those lines. But obviously there's more to it, or everybody would always get them right!

Example 1

The question asks about the first paragraph, so you should read the entire paragraph. Pay particular attention to the first sentence, since that's where main ideas are typically sketched out.

For each answer choice, you are looking for words or phrases that don't match with the text. Train your brain to notice problem words by showing your work and underlining them. This is a crucial part of Process of Elimination (POE)!

The first thing you should eliminate is Choice D. Do they talk about food chains? Of course. But they don't show how they function. Food chains are complex, and a full explanation would be very scientific and probably much longer than these twelve lines. This is why POE is so important — how is not a word that you'd normally pay attention to, but POE forces you to think critically about words that you might ignore.

Choice C is wrong because they aren't really talking about the origins of anything. But also, what would be the emerging area of scientific inquiry? They're studying fish. Is that really a new area of inquiry? And what are the origins of studying fish? They aren't talking about someone conducting an experiment or founding a research institute. This choice has a lot of science-heavy buzzwords, but it doesn't match with the passage.

Choice B is the most commonly chosen wrong answer because it feels true. We all believe that conservation is important, so it's easy for us to agree with this choice. But the paragraph also talks a lot about <u>pollution</u> and <u>harmful chemicals</u>, which makes us think that <u>conservation</u> is probably a good way to solve those problems. And the SAT throws in one final trick: they copy/paste the phrase <u>coastal waters</u> from line 5 into the choice. It's a unique phrase that makes the choice feel more right because it's also in the passage, but that's one of the SAT's most common traps. This passage is not arguing for <u>conservation</u>. It's complaining about <u>pollution</u>, but that's not the same thing.

Choice A is correct because there are a lot of ideas in the choice that match with words in the passage. They certainly discuss <u>certain types of fish</u> when they specifically mention <u>tuna</u> and <u>swordfish</u> and more generally talk about fish that are <u>long-lived and high on the food chain</u>. And they say explicitly that these fish are <u>great candidates for research</u>, which matches nicely with <u>chosen as the basis of a study</u>. Since both of these matches are in the first sentence of the paragraph, we can be even more confident that we're describing the main idea. A good writer (like those who write the SAT passages) will typically start each paragraph with a topic sentence that sets up the main ideas of the paragraph. When you're confused, topic sentences are great places to look for a concise summary.

Line Reference — The Basics

Use the QLC Method:
1. Question
2. Line Reference
3. Choices

Do not simply pick the answer that "feels" best. Use Process of Elimination to examine the individual words and phrases in the answer choices.

Beware choices that simply copy/paste unique phrases from the passage. You want to match the ideas, not necessarily the words.

Use the topic sentence at the beginning of the paragraph to help you understand the paragraph's purpose. But this does not always help, so you should also look for ideas that are repeated throughout the paragraph.

The Twists

When the line reference is more narrow, you need to expand beyond the lines by following the +1 Sentence Rule. The SAT likes to ask about the purpose of a few lines, which might not be clear just from those lines. But good writers make sure that each sentence flows into the next one, so if you read an extra sentence on either side of your line reference, you're more likely to understand the purpose of the lines.

Example 2

They're asking about a weird English saying that you might not understand, but that's why we use the +1 Sentence Rule! The surrounding ideas should put the line reference in context. You can even underline the ideas that stand out, which is a way of making a **dumb summary**: <u>pollutants</u>, <u>predators</u>, <u>humans</u>, and <u>food chain</u> seem to carry a lot of weight. You could try to find the choice that seems to cover those topics.

Or you could use POE! Ask yes/no questions to help you understand the lines better. Many tutors encourage their students to write out summaries of the lines, the paragraph, or the entire passage, but I do not think this is a good use of time. Frequently, your summary won't matter for the question, or you'll be too confused by the text to summarize in the first place. How can you summarize something you barely understand?

Asking yes/no questions is a way around this. For example, you might not be able to summarize reaping what we sow or the surrounding lines very well. But you could probably turn Choice A into a few yes/no questions: what are the methods? Are they measuring chemical concentrations? You might not know what the passage is about, but you probably know what it's not about. It doesn't seem like they're measuring anything. And I don't think they're using any new methods. That's enough to eliminate Choice A.

Choice D is the next easiest to eliminate, but only if you're an SAT POE pro. Remember that you have to be careful of Strong Words that go beyond what the lines are saying. A lot of Strong Words have to do with quantity. In this case, the entire choice can be quickly eliminated just because of the word most. Does agricultural runoff cause pollution? Sure, at least according to line 5. Do scientists blame the runoff? Probably, since they're the ones studying it. But do the scientists say most of the pollution is caused by runoff? No way. Or at least they don't say that in this passage. Most is a word with a very specific meaning — "more than half". This passage never quantifies where the pollution is coming from, so we have no evidence that more than half of it is from runoff. If you can get good at noticing Strong Words in the answer choices, you will do significantly better on the SAT Reading section. Sometimes the only problem with a choice is that it includes a very Strong Word.

Of the two choices that are left — B and C — do you notice any other Strong Words? Anything else about quantity? Choice B talks about pollutants entering the environment, which the passage also discusses. But the passage never discusses the rate

at which these pollutants enter the environment. What's more, they never say that the pollutants are increasing. This is a very tempting choice because we probably know from current events that the oceans are indeed becoming more polluted, but we must base our answers only on the evidence in the passage. And that paragraph never says anything about the rate of pollution, so increasing rate is another Strong Word.

That leaves Choice C, which is correct. We can also ask yes/no questions to prove it right. Does the author mention negative consequences? Yes, he talks about dangerous levels. Does he say humans are susceptible? Well, not explicitly, but it's strongly implied. He says that humans are the top of the food chain and that predators absorb pollution, so Choice B is basically connecting the dots. But you don't even need to understand it on that level to confidently pick Choice C. For one, we've confidently eliminated everything else. But we've also matched a lot of the ideas from Choice C with our dumb summary: pollutants = negative consequences; predators = species; humans = humans; food chain = susceptible? The last one is a stretch, but 3 out of 4 matches is good enough!

Line Reference — The Twists

Use the +1 Sentence Rule to gain context. Always read 1 sentence before and 1 sentence after the specified line reference when it's in the question.

Ask yes/no questions to better understand the choices and the line references. It's difficult to accurately summarize a line. It's easy to ask if a line is about something specific.

Look out for Strong Words. If you can get good at spotting these, you'll do significantly better on the SAT Reading. Often, the only problem word in a choice is a Strong Word that you'd normally ignore on other kinds of tests.

> Words that discuss quantity are often too strong: most, increasing, majority, consensus, all, many, widely believed, few... the list goes on!

Answers: Line Reference

#1 — Answer = D

Choice A is wrong because the researchers aren't <u>skeptical</u>. They're simply asking a question. Choice B is wrong because <u>need</u> is a Strong Word. The question in the line reference doesn't seem essential. It's just about reading numbers. Choice C is wrong because it never says that the method is <u>unlikely to succeed</u>. There's nothing really negative about these lines. Choice D is correct because of the +1 Sentence Rule. Right after the questions, the passage says that these scientists <u>devised an experiment to answer that very question</u>, which pretty clearly matches with <u>an area of study discussed in the passage</u>. Notice how we do not need the entire passage to make a confident guess about what the passage is about.

#2 — Answer = C

Choices B and D are pretty clearly wrong because there is no <u>contrast</u> and no <u>remedy</u>. Some people pick Choice A because the overall group of lines seems to talk about a <u>formula</u>, but they don't go into detail to <u>describe</u> it. We'd expect to see more about the variables and equations. Choice C is correct because the question is asking about just the lines between the two dashes. What term do they explain? <u>Gross Domestic Product</u>. Notice how we can turn the choice into a short question that is fairly easy to answer using the text. That's a great sign!

#3 — Answer = C

You can probably stick to the immediate area around the two lines with <u>deeds</u>, but it can't hurt to read the entire paragraph if you're confused. What ideas are repeated? Choice A is wrong because <u>need</u> is a Strong Word, and Roosevelt seems to suggest that <u>planning</u> is not a good thing. Choice B is wrong because <u>war</u> is not the main idea, and there doesn't seem to be anything <u>controversial</u>. (You don't need to find all of the problem words when you use POE, and there may be others that I don't even notice!) Choices C and D are both about <u>action</u>, which seems

to match closely with some of the words in the passage: <u>arena</u>, <u>strives</u>, <u>effort</u>, <u>strive</u>, <u>devotions</u>, <u>worthy cause</u>, <u>triumph</u>, <u>achievement</u>, and <u>daring</u>, just to name a few. The best way to decide between the choices is to turn them into questions. Is action <u>important</u>? Seems so. All of the words we listed seem to suggest Roosevelt thinks so. Does Roosevelt think action is <u>commendable</u>? Yes, for sure. A dumb summary of these lines would at least note that Roosevelt has a positive tone. Does Roosevelt reference a <u>specific</u> action? Not that I can see. He talks generally about action, but he never specifies one action in particular. As a whole, Choice D is too strong, whereas Choice C is conveniently vague. Notice that Choice C doesn't get into <u>why</u> action is important. Those kinds of vague answers are frequently right on the SAT.

#4 — Answer = B

Dumb summaries help a lot here, since we don't have the full passage but the choices mention it. If this were on the test, you could always read more, but the purpose of this exercise is to show you that NARROWING YOUR FOCUS to just a few lines isn't as risky as it seems. Use connotations to guide you. The first paragraph is clearly negative (<u>shrinking</u>, <u>alarming</u>, <u>worse</u>, <u>drought</u>, <u>strain</u>). The +1 Sentence in the next paragraph is clearly positive (<u>leading</u>, <u>new</u>, <u>energy efficient</u>, <u>drinkable</u>). So look for choices that sound like they're transitioning from negative to positive. Choice A sounds like the opposite: a <u>theory</u> (maybe positive?) is <u>undermined</u> (definitely negative). Plus, what's the <u>theory</u>? They never give one, so Choice A is wrong. Choice B sounds like the correct transition: a <u>problem</u> (negative) is <u>alleviated</u> (positive). Keep it in. Choice C also sounds like the opposite: a <u>consensus</u> (positive) is <u>challenged</u> (negative). But even more important, <u>consensus</u> is a very Strong Word. A <u>consensus</u> occurs when the vast majority of people agree on something. This passage only gives us Nancy Flenderson's opinion, so we do not know what the majority of people believe. Choice D is a better fit with our dumb summary: a <u>hypothesis</u> (neutral?) is <u>supported and refined</u> (positive). If you have to pick between Choices B and D, you should go with the answer that better matches your dumb summary. Furthermore, what's the <u>hypothesis</u> mentioned in Choice D? The first paragraph isn't really a hypothesis, like you'd use to design an experiment. It's more a statement of fact.

#5 — Answer = A

This one is really hard to understand! It's a great question for practicing POE and really focusing on the words in the choices, instead of worrying about what the passage says. Choice C is probably the most obviously wrong because they never get into the mathematical formulas. Choice D includes the easy-to-miss Strong Word how. Do they say that locomotion (movement) affects the bubbles? Yes, in lines 11-13. Do they say how the movement affects the bubbles? No, they never get into that much detail. They also never specifically say that it affects the size of the bubbles. Choice B is trap. The phrase repeating units matches with several words in the passage: symmetrical, uniform, and geometry. But Choice B says the opposite of what the passage is arguing. The lines say that the actual bubbles are more varied than the uniform/repeating fur. In other words, the theory says the bubbles should be repeating, but the actual fur is complicated. This matches closely with Choice A. Notice that, like question #3, the correct answer is pretty vague. Choice A says that the bubbles differ, but it never goes into how the bubbles differ. That's such an important distinction!

#6 — Answer = C

POE works very well here. Choice A is wrong because they never mention studying for exams. Choice B is wrong because responsibility is a Strong Word. And Choice D is wrong because primary is a very Strong Word (and one that the SAT uses a lot). You could confidently pick Choice C based only on the problems with the other answers, but it also matches nicely with the +1 Sentence before the line reference. They say there's a new experiment and the choice talks about more research. That's a great match!

#7 — Answer = B

Once again, the answer choices seem to reference the rest of a passage that we don't have. But also once again, it doesn't matter! You could read more, but you do not need to. Use dumb summaries to understand how the paragraphs transition. The main paragraph in the middle is clearly negative (anything but enjoyable, tedious struggle, boring, frustration, do not resonate, look nothing like, have trouble). Even with just one sentence, we can tell that the paragraph before is positive (a good number, still appear). And the paragraph after is also positive (easier to digest). So look for a choice that suggests a negative paragraph surrounded by positive ideas. Choice A is wrong because that would not be a change from positive to negative. If the main paragraph were a continuation of the argument in the previous paragraph, we'd expect both to be positive or both to be negative. That's not the case here, so we can eliminate Choice A. Choice C doesn't have a transition either. It suggests that the entire passage is negative, but we've got positive paragraphs surrounding this one. Choices B and D both suggest a negative idea surrounded by positive ones. But Choice D talks about a policy, and we don't really have evidence of that. On the other hand, Choice B talks about something valued by the author (which is suggested by the surrounding positive paragraphs) that has some flaws (which is suggested by the negative words in the main paragraph). To put it more simply, Choice B is more vague than Choice D, so it's the safer choice.

Answers: LR Short Passage

#1 — Answer = C

With old-timey passages, you can usually read between difficult words and phrases to understand the main idea. Here, Washington is using more words than he needs to make his point. Choice C is correct because period matches with date and not far distant matches with approaching. The other choices are too strong. Choice A is wrong because prohibited is not supported by the lines. Choice B is wrong because people did not want is not supported. We don't know what they wanted. Choice D is wrong because trust in the executive branch is not really the main point. But notice that they are copy/pasting from lines 3 and 7.

#2 — Answer = A

Read around the line reference and you'll see that Washington is speaking positively (no diminution of zeal, future interest, grateful respect, past kindness). Choice A is also positive. Choice B says the opposite (lacked respect). Choice C actually contradicts the next paragraph. Choice D contains the Strong Word wide praise.

#3 — Answer = C

This question is essentially telling you to read the entire paragraph. You could easily turn most of these choices into questions. Why does Washington prefer democracy? The paragraph doesn't say. What is Washington's political philosophy? Doesn't say. Choice D is wrong because he's not seeking reelection. We've established this through the other questions. Is Washington hesitant to serve as president? Yes. The paragraph talks about how he had previously been reluctantly drawn from his retirement. He only served as president because of duty and the people's desire.

#4 — Answer = D

The final paragraph is positive (rejoice, persuaded, you will not disapprove). Choice D is also positive (hope, sympathy). Choice A is negative because of controversial, which is also a Strong Word. Choice B is wrong because a counterargument is never brought up. Choice C is wrong because this paragraph is not a list of steps to achieve a goal. It's also unclear what his proposal would be.

No Line Reference lesson

The Basics

Do not neglect the Chronology Rule! It is such a helpful tool if you understand it and remember to use it on the test. If you use the No Reading Strategy, the Chronology Rule is essential for finding the line references when they aren't given in the question. But even if you read, the Chronology Rule can help you narrow down your options when you have an Evidence Pair.

Example 1

Where would you expect to find the answers to each of these questions?

1. The question says lines 1-12, but with the +1 Sentence Rule, you'd probably end up reading **lines 1-14**.

2. No Line Reference. But since #1 is about lines 1-12 and #3 is about line 19, you should start by reading **lines 12-19**.

3. You still need to read the full sentence, so you're probably reading **lines 18-20**.

4. No Line Reference. Because of #3 and #5, you would expect to find this answer in **lines 19-27**.

5. Again, read the full sentence, which probably covers **lines 26-28**.

6. Even though the question is only mentioning two specific lines, you probably need to read the entire paragraph, which is approximately **lines 30-45**.

7. No Line Reference. This is the last question, so we can only use #6 to guide us. You should expect the answer to be **after line 42**.

No Line Reference — The Basics

If you're using the No Reading Strategy, you must understand and apply the Chronology Rule to find answers when there is No Line Reference.

Chronology Rule — SAT Reading questions are generally in the order they appear in the passage. When there's no line reference, use the line references from the surrounding questions to estimate a line reference to read.

The Twists

Most reading passages will not be as straightforward as Example 1, but if you get comfortable with the Chronology Rule, it won't matter. In fact, Evidence Pairs fit into the chronology just like any other question.

Example 2

Where would you expect to find the answers?

8. This is a Whole Passage question, so you should **save it for last**. The answer won't be in a specific line. You'll need to understand the main ideas that are repeated throughout the passage.

9. No Line Reference. The question suggests that there is a definitive answer, and that they aren't asking about main ideas. You should expect there to be a line somewhere that defines a habit loop. Whenever you don't have a line reference, you must look to the next question for guidance. Unfortunately, #10 is also a No Line Reference question! That's okay. Just look to #11. According to the Chronology Rule, the answer to #9 should be somewhere **before line 23**.

10. No Line Reference. According to the Chronology Rule, the answer should be **before line 23 but after the line with the answer to #9**. This one would also be easy to skim for the lines about the burn reflex.

11. You should read the full sentence, so you're probably reading **lines 22-24**.

12. There's no line reference in the question, but skipping ahead to #13, we see that we have an Evidence Pair. We can still use the Chronology Rule, though! **The answer to #12 will depend on the answer to #13**.

13. You can sort through these line reference choices using the Chronology Rule. Based on the references for #11 and #14, we would expect the correct line reference choice to be **between line 23 and line 47**. If it's a little off, that's okay too, so don't eliminate a choice that says line 22 or 48.

14. Based on the +1 Sentence Rule, we should expect to find the answer approximately in **lines 45-50**.

Hopefully these examples showed you how the Chronology Rule can be used to NARROW YOUR FOCUS. But remember that the Chronology Rule is sometimes broken by the SAT. So if you are very sure that the answer is somewhere else, then break the rule! And remember that the Chronology Rule is meant to be a starting point so that you read the lines that are most likely to contain the answer. You can always read more if you want to.

No Line Reference — The Twists

The Chronology Rule also applies to Evidence Pairs. Use the questions surrounding the Evidence Pair to estimate a possible line reference range for Part 2. Line References that aren't in that range are unlikely to be correct. You should still read every line reference just to be sure.

Since the Chronology Rule works for the correct evidence choice only, you might have difficulty estimating line references if you've gotten an Evidence Pair wrong. Be flexible.

Whole Passage questions are not the same as No Line Reference questions. Whole Passage questions are about the entire passage, so there won't be a specific line that contains the answer. No Line Reference questions ask about a specific line without telling you the line. If you can tell the difference between these two question types, you'll be more confident using the No Reading Strategy.

The Chronology Rule is occasionally broken, so read more if necessary. Unpaired Evidence questions, in particular, tend to break the rule. Be flexible.

Answers: No Line Reference

#1 — Answer = D
No Line Reference. The question seems to be asking about a very specific piece of information, not a summary of the entire passage. For this reason, you

should <u>not</u> treat this like a Whole Passage question. Answer it now by trusting the Chronology Rule. We'd expect to find the answer before line 7 (because of #2). We can quote line 2 to get our dumb summary — the study is <u>extensive</u>. Choice A is wrong because they never mention the specific people on the team. Choice B is wrong because they do not talk about the harshness of the <u>environment</u>. You may know that the Arctic is extreme, but the passage needs to provide the evidence. Choice C is wrong because they do not talk about the <u>instruments</u>. Choice D is correct because <u>wide scope</u> matches nicely with <u>extensive</u>.

#2 — Answer = D
Reading Vocab. It's tricky to come up with a guess for this one. Something like <u>create</u>? The best match is Choice D because they are causing doubt. Choices B and C seem to suggest the opposite — that doubt is going away. And Choice A doesn't make sense if you put it back in the sentence.

#3 — Answer = B
No Line Reference. Since the next question doesn't have a line reference either, we need to look at #5 to help us estimate. We should expect the answer to be somewhere between line 7 and line 19. Read with purpose by underlining key words in the question: you want to know why the scientists believed the <u>tusks were for dominance</u>. Lines 10-17 basically give it away. Choice A is wrong because <u>closely related</u> is too strong — there's no evidence that narwhals are genetically related to other horned animals. Choice C is wrong because this fact is not related to the rubbing behavior. Choice D is wrong because <u>nerve endings</u> aren't mentioned here. <u>Observed</u> in Choice B matches perfectly with <u>witnessed</u> in line 14.

#4 — Answer = C
No Line Reference. According to the Chronology Rule, we'd expect the answer to be somewhere between lines 17 and 19. Notice that we're using the location of our answer to #3 to help us find #4. But always be flexible when applying the Chronology Rule. In this case, the passage discusses <u>sexual dimorphism</u> through line 21, so it's okay to read that even though it goes beyond our prediction. The passage suggests that <u>sexual dimorphism</u> has

something to do with <u>males and females</u>. Only Choice C talks about <u>males and females</u>, so it's the best option.

#5 — Answer = D

Line Reference. Use the +1 Sentence Rule to gain more context, but we've read most of this already for previous questions. Choice A is wrong because there's no <u>method</u>. Choice B is wrong because there's no <u>hypothesis</u>. Choice C is wrong because the parenthetical is not <u>defining</u> anything. Sexual dimorphism was defined before those lines, not in them, which is an important distinction. Choice D is correct because they're backtracking a bit on the definition. They're saying that <u>some females</u> have the tusk, so it's not perfectly true that <u>only males</u> have the tusk.

#6 — Answer = A

Evidence Pair Part 1. With no line reference in the question, we have to look to the next question on the next page. Sure enough, it's an Evidence Pair. The SAT loves to split Evidence Pairs over two pages, so get in the habit of checking! Look to #7 below for an explanation on sorting through the line references, but once you do, you still need to sort through the choices for #6. Choice A talks about a <u>difficulty</u>, which could be construed to match with the <u>limited data</u> mentioned in Line Reference C, so keep this choice for now. Choice B is wrong because <u>local fishermen</u> are not mentioned. Choice C is wrong because they never go into detail about the specific <u>factors</u> that affect <u>narwhal diet</u>. Choice D matches with Line Reference D because they both talk about <u>sonar</u>, but this isn't a great match with the other ideas in the line reference. They never talk about <u>areas</u> where they found narwhals, nor did they talk about <u>past studies</u>. Choice A is vague, which is why it matched better than the others.

#7 — Answer = C

Evidence Pair Part 2. Line References A and B would break the Chronology Rule, so they're unlikely to be correct. However, we should still read them. Neither reference talks about an advantage of Jacobsen's methods. Line Reference C has both a negative and positive connotation. They suggest that <u>data would be limited</u>, so Jacobsen did a <u>comparative study</u> to

solve the problem. That sounds like it could match with the question in #6, so keep it in the mix. Line Reference D seems like a fact about narwhals, not about Jacobsen's methods. But you can also keep it in if you're not sure. Still, Line Reference D would break the Chronology Rule, since it's before #8's reference to line 41. Ultimately, Line Reference C matches with Choice A in #6.

#8 — Answer = A

Reading Vocab. This one is also difficult to come up with a guess for. Maybe something like <u>about</u>? But none of the wrong answers make any sense in the sentence, so Choice A is correct because it's left over.

#9 — Answer = B

No Line Reference. We should still look to the next question for a line reference, and #10 looks like the second part of an Evidence Pair. However, you must still read the question to #10. You'll see that it's actually an Unpaired Evidence question, so #9 stands alone. You could do #10 first to get a better sense of where to look for #9, though. The question asks for something that undermines Jacobsen's theory, so we need to read with purpose to better understand Jacobsen's theory. The word <u>speculated</u> in line 54 matches nicely with <u>theory</u>, and a dumb summary of this paragraph would be that sound is involved (<u>echolocation</u>, <u>sonar</u>, <u>sound</u>, <u>vocal</u>, <u>talkativeness</u>). Choice A is probably wrong because they never talk about what narwhals <u>prefer eating</u>. Choice C is probably wrong because they never talk about the <u>population</u> of narwhals. Choice D is probably wrong because they don't talk about the <u>salinity</u> here or <u>other animals with tusks</u>. Choice B is about <u>echolocation</u>, which matches our dumb summary. You don't really need to understand why this choice works to get this question right. This is why dumb summaries are better than long, complicated summaries.

#10 — Answer = C

Unpaired Evidence. Read with purpose for lines about <u>belugas</u> and <u>eating</u>. Line Reference A is a "what" choice, in that it tells us that <u>belugas eat</u> but not anything about identifying their prey. Line Reference B also fails to talk about identifying prey. Line Reference C does seem to discuss identifying prey (not know the type of prey). Even though it seems like the opposite of what we want, we should still keep it. Line Reference D is about narwhals, not belugas, so you can eliminate it. Line Reference C is correct because it answers the question: belugas have some ability to identify their prey because they don't know the type until they are within close proximity. So even though the lines are saying the belugas normally can't identify the prey, they still imply that the belugas eventually know what they're hunting when they get close.

#11 — Answer = B

No Line Reference. Once again, we should trust that Whole Passage questions occur at the beginning, and that this question will have a specific line where we can find the answer. Based on the Chronology Rule and #10, we'd expect the answer to come after lines 59-61. In lines 77-78, the passage matches the question, saying what Jacobsen believes. Choice A is wrong because the Strong Word primarily goes beyond what the lines are saying. Tusk rubbing may be one way narwhals communicate, but we do not know for sure that it's the primary way. Choice C is wrong because the lines do not compare the past beliefs to the present ones. There's nothing to suggest that they had any theories about the complexity. Choice D is wrong because earlier in the passage, they say that narwhals aren't talkative at all. Plus, these lines aren't about this. Choice B is correct because past experiences matches with information about where they have been in the lines. Choice B is also weak, in that there is evidence leaves some room that the hypothesis could be wrong.

Whole Passage lesson

The Basics

Remember that the Whole Passage question strategy applies no matter what, regardless of whether you use the No Reading Strategy. Always save Whole Passage questions for last.

Example 1

Obviously, you'd be able to compare your answer to the rest of the passage on the test. But the purpose of this example is to show you that you don't always need to understand everything that a passage says. There are a lot of ways to figure out the main idea. The title can sometimes be one of them! In this case:

- Choice A is wrong because widely held is one of the SAT's favorite Strong Words. We don't get any information from the title that a belief is widely held, and the passage is unlikely to provide that evidence. My confidence eliminating this choice comes from experience. I've seen thousands of SAT questions at this point, and phrases like widely held are a recurring feature of wrong answers. The more you practice, the better you'll get at immediately noticing Strong Words.

- Choice B has some words that we'd need to verify with the passage, like study, but it has other words that seem to match with the title, such as origins with how and evolutionary trait with long neck.

- Choice C is probably wrong because the title does not mention extinct species. Of course, the passage could mention them as it talks about giraffes, but the title seems to keep the focus of the passage on the giraffes themselves.

- Choice D has a similar problem. The title does not talk about different animals. Again, the passage might bring up other animals, but those examples probably won't be the main idea of the passage. This is why focusing on the title can be helpful: just because something is mentioned in the passage doesn't mean it's the main idea. The passage will make small arguments along the way, but Whole Passage questions are asking about the main argument — the repeated ideas.

Even without the passage to verify, I'd be fairly confident that Choice B is the correct answer. To be clear, you should <u>not</u> try to do this on the actual SAT. Use the passage and the other questions to better understand the main ideas. The point of this example is to show you that the title can be another piece of evidence that you use to decide on the main idea. The title can also be a tiebreaker if you're having trouble deciding between two choices.

Whole Passage — The Basics

Save Whole Passage questions for last, regardless of whether you use the No Reading Strategy.

As always, use POE to find Strong Words that take the ideas of the passage too far. With practice, certain Strong Words will start to stand out, making some choices much easier to eliminate.

Main ideas are repeated throughout the passage, so don't focus on one paragraph or sentence. Just because the passage includes an idea doesn't mean that idea is the main topic of the passage.

The title can help you identify main ideas, especially on the Science passages. Don't forget about the blurb!

The Twists

This cannot be stressed enough — main ideas are repeated ideas. The entire No Reading strategy rests on this premise. No good writer (and certainly not the SAT) will hide a main idea in some small piece of an obscure sentence.

Example 2

This experiment is meant to show you that you don't need to understand every single word or sentence to still have a pretty good guess at the main idea of a passage. You should never actually read a passage like this, but this example should feel a bit like those old-timey passages where you can barely understand what they're saying. Instead of reading,

try to <u>absorb</u> the main idea. What ideas are repeated?

You can also use POE to turn the answer choices into questions. This is a very useful tool because it's hard to summarize a passage you barely understood. It's much easier to ask yourself if the passage was about something more specific:

- Choice A seems pretty good. Is there a dangerous situation? A lot of words seem to suggest it: <u>rolls</u>, <u>worse</u>, <u>swinging</u>, <u>swell</u>, <u>jerky</u>, <u>stir</u>, <u>movement</u>. Is another character calm? This one is harder to answer, but we should see a few clues. The end seems to be saying "what's <u>the matter?</u>" But also the Captain is <u>reading</u>, <u>not lying</u> down, and simply <u>holding on</u> to something. Notice how we're guessing at some of the covered words, which is also what we do when there are big words we don't know the definitions of. We guess! So far, we have some good matches with these ideas, but it's certainly not enough to confidently pick Choice A, so you still need to try the other choices.

- Choice B has ideas that are harder to confirm based on the passage. Does something <u>unexpected</u> happen? I'd like to see a few words that have to do with surprise, but I don't see any. Does a character <u>not want to be</u> <u>disturbed</u>? Again, I don't see anything to suggest that. It's possible those words are covered, but the odds are slim we'd miss all of them. Choice B is not better than Choice A.

- Choice C is a bit better. Is there a <u>problem</u>? Seems that way. All of the words we noticed for Choice A could easily indicate a problem — the boat is rolling in the waves. But is there <u>disagreement</u>? I don't see anything to suggest the characters are fighting or arguing.

- Choice D also has a match with <u>risky behavior</u>, which could be sailing in a storm. But is there evidence that <u>a lifelong goal</u> is involved? Not that I can see. Again, maybe we could imagine a situation where these characters are driven by a goal, but we just don't have the evidence for it in the lines. As much as possible, you want the passage — not your own experiences — to supply the evidence for your answers.

Choice A is the best guess because it is the most easily justifiable with the lines that we see and understand. Often, you will have to pick answers that you're not 100% sure are correct. There's nothing you can do about that! Just get over your need to completely understand everything. The SAT doesn't lend itself to perfectionism.

Plus, your brain is pretty good at picking up repeated ideas on its own. You may want to find an exact match in the text, but that won't always be possible. First, it takes a lot of time. But it's also limited by your vocabulary and comprehension. Unless you frequently read 250-year-old texts, you probably won't have a perfect idea of what the old-timey passages are saying.

Whole Passage — The Twists

Accept the fact that you won't always understand everything. You'll need to take guesses. Use POE to eliminate the choices that are obviously wrong, and then guess from what's left.

Try to absorb ideas, rather than fully reading them. In other words, notice which ideas are repeated. This is especially helpful on old-timey passages where the vocabulary can prevent you from reading and understanding every sentence. Dumb summaries can also keep things simple.

Whole Passage questions are not the same as No Line Reference questions. Look for phrases like "main idea" and "central claim". These questions should be saved until the end, after you've answered everything else. But if the question is about a specific idea, you can probably use the Chronology Rule to estimate a line reference that contains the answer.

Answers: Whole Passage

#1 — Answer = C

Whole Passage. Choice D is the most obviously wrong because the narrator <u>is</u> the main character. For the other three choices, the best thing to do is use a dumb summary. What's this passage about? A kid in winter. With that, Choice A is wrong because it's not about a specific <u>day</u>. This seems to be more about the entire experience of winter. Choice B is wrong because it's about the kid, not <u>the residents</u>. Choice C is vague and matches with the main ideas: winter is the <u>period</u>, and most of the passage seems like <u>memories</u>.

#2 — Answer = B

Whole Passage. You should wait until the end to answer this one. But a dumb summary would be that light starts out as a negative but becomes a positive. Choice D is the opposite (positive to negative), so you can eliminate it. Choice C is wrong because they never talk about <u>knowledge</u>. Choices A and B both match the dumb summary, but Choice A is too specific. The light isn't <u>a source of entertainment</u> because they're not playing with light. And while you might feel <u>lonely</u> in this situation, we don't have any lines to suggest the narrator does. We have much more evidence that <u>winter is bleak</u>, and then the well-lit rooms give the narrator a sense of happiness.

#3 — Answer = A

Whole Passage. We have to save this for the end because it's asking about the author's overall technique. There's no one line that will prove these answers. Choice B contains the Strong Word <u>precise</u>, and there's no way you could draw a <u>map</u> based on this passage. Choice C is wrong because we've already said that this passage isn't about the other <u>characters</u>. It's about the narrator as a kid. I also don't remember much about <u>teaching lessons</u>. Choice D is wrong because <u>historical context</u> would include information about what else was going on in the world at the time. This is very much about one particular child. Choice A is nice and vague. The passage frequently used similes and metaphors, which are examples of <u>figurative language</u>. And of course it's the narrator's <u>understanding of the world</u> — who else's would it be?

#4 — Answer = A

No Line Reference. This question seems to be asking about the setting, which is often discussed in the first paragraph or two. In fact, #5 references lines 19-23, so we could look for this answer before then. Since the first word of the passage is winter, we have a pretty good sense that the answer will be found in a few specific lines near the beginning, instead of being a repeated idea throughout the whole passage. Our dumb summary should be that winter is negative. That eliminates Choices B and D, which suggest something positive (cozy and beauty). Choice C might be true based on your own experiences with winter, but the beginning of the passage is about the kid, not the other citizens. More important, Choice C contains the Strong Word most, which should scare us away from this choice. There is no evidence that most people do anything in particular, even though we get occasional examples of what some people do. Choice A matches with light of truth and this is reality in lines 14 and 19.

#5 — Answer = D

Line Reference. Follow the +1 Sentence Rule to gain context. Right after the quote, he says that winter makes him feel punished. That matches nicely with resentment in Choice D. Choice A sounds like something you'd hear in English class in school, but this is not about some high-minded idea about life and death in nature. It's about a kid in winter! Choice B is wrong because Antonia is not speaking — the wind is. Choice C is wrong because the narrator does not say that winter isn't harsh. He seems to be pretty miserable.

#6 — Answer = B

Evidence Pair Part 1. Once you've sorted through the Line References in #7, you can use POE to narrow down these answers. Choice A is wrong because hunger isn't mentioned. Choice D is wrong because faked is too strong, and nobody cares how tough they are. Choice C seems to match with Line Reference C, but you really need to be careful because there's a very Strong Word here. Unexplainable means that something cannot be explained, which is not the same as not knowing the explanation. Line Reference C contains the phrase

without knowing why, which seems to match with unexplainable, but it's not quite perfect. Line Reference D actually offers an explanation: the glass held us there. So maybe the characters and narrator didn't know back then why they were standing in the cold, but the narrator clearly has an explanation right now. That's enough to make Choice C wrong. Line Reference D matches with Choice B because the color of the glass is the reason they stay out in the cold.

#7 — Answer = D

Evidence Pair Part 2. Focus on the question in #6. You want lines that have something to do with people's tolerance for the cold. Line Reference A is about people not tolerating the cold as they hurry toward a fire. Maybe keep it? It doesn't seem to be saying much, though. Line Reference B is similarly about people running in the cold. Again, it doesn't seem to be saying much besides what we already know: it's cold out. Line Reference C talks about people lingering outside, even though they're very cold. That sounds like they're tolerating the cold. Line Reference D is basically about the same thing, even though it isn't as specific. This is a good example where a little context can help: when they say held us there, it's a good idea to ask yourself where there is. It's outside in the cold! There's no real way to get an answer to this without #6. You need to find the best overall match.

#8 — Answer = A

Reading Vocab. The next sentence suggests the narrator wants to go inside the Harlings' home. We should guess that drew means something like "welcomed" or "pulled". Choice A matches.

#9 — Answer = B

No Line Reference. Based on the Chronology Rule, we'd expect to find the answer between lines 56 and 70. They explicitly say that he would be disappointed (line 66) when Mr. Harling was at home (lines 60-61).

#10 — Answer = C

Reading Vocab. This one is hard to come up with a guess. Maybe something like "be"? Choice B is wrong because it's not like a factory that's manufacturing dancers. Choices A and D could make sense, but the sentence isn't supporting the idea. It actually says that Frances is doing the teaching, so maybe Frances is creating or appointing the best dancer. But Antonia seems to be the student, not the teacher, so she would become the best dancer. In a way, we're using the Strong Words idea here, trying our best to pick choices that are supported by the text and that don't go beyond what's explicitly written.

Both Passages lesson

The Basics

Don't panic. The double passage isn't that much different than the others. The worst part is that the two passages are usually old-timey passages, so the vocabulary and sentence structure might make the passages hard to understand.

Example 1

Always read the blurb! This one strongly suggests that **the passages will disagree**. For one, that's the typical relationship anyway. But also the blurb includes the word debate, which suggests that they have different opinions. We'll see the choices for this question later in the Exercise, so remember your dumb summary!

Both Passages — The Basics

Always read the blurb. The relationship between the double passages is often revealed in the blurb.

If it's a debate, it probably means there's a disagreement.

If the second passage is "a response to" the first, then it's also probably a disagreement.

The Twists

All of the advice about dumb summaries and basing your answers on the passage is worth keeping in mind. But I also want to stress that you can still use the No Reading Strategy on the double passage. However, if you're struggling, this is a place where some students decide to read anyway. The individual passages are shorter, so it's easier to keep track of the main ideas. There also might not be a lot of line references in the questions, making it difficult to use the Chronology Rule.

If you decide to read the double passage before you answer the questions, make sure you follow the strategy outlined in The Twists. It's easier on your brain to treat it like two passages. Only reading Passage 1 lets you answer the Passage 1 questions without clogging your brain with unhelpful information about Passage 2.

Both Passages — The Twists

Use dumb summaries to help you understand the old-timey passages.

If you decide to read, treat the passages as separate from each other at first:
1. read passage 1
2. answer passage 1 questions
3. read passage 2
4. answer passage 2 questions
5. answer Both Passages questions

Answers: Both Passages

#1 — Answer = D
Reading Vocab. It's fairly easy to come up with a guess here. You should see that the author means something like obeying or following the decision. That matches with Choice D.

#2 — Answer = B
Evidence Pair Part 1. You should go to #3 first and sort through the line references, but it's very difficult to eliminate any. You might need to use dumb summaries so that you can make matches more easily as you use POE on these answer choices. Choice A seems to match with Line Reference A, but shared equally is a Strong Word. Equally means that they have exactly the same amount of power, but that's going beyond what the lines say. Choice D is wrong

because it's positive about the federal government, but the line references all seem pretty negative. If nothing else, Choice C is probably wrong because essential is a very Strong Word. The taxes aspect seems to match with Line Reference D, but the lines don't go so far as to say that the federal government is essential for anything. In fact, this choice also seems positive, even though we're looking for something negative. This leaves Choice B, which we'd love to be able to match with ideas in one of the line references to boost our confidence in the answer. There are a lot of matching ideas with Line Reference B: cannot be constrained = Government without limitation; states = States; unconstitutional laws = barriers of the Constitution shall be overleaped. Notice that Line Reference B was initially very difficult to understand, but NARROWING OUR FOCUS to individual words and phrases in the choice helped us make sense of the lines. That's a perfectly fine way of answering questions!

#3 — Answer = B

Evidence Pair Part 2. You are looking for line references that are related to the federal government. Unfortunately, they all seem to be related. Line References B and C mention it explicitly, and A and D maybe hint at it. It's hard to understand what many of these lines are saying. That's okay! Our job is not to come up with one answer. We just need to get a quick sense of what's going on. Line Reference A is about the Congress and Supreme Court. Write a little dumb summary next to the choice so you remember. Line Reference B is about limits maybe? Good enough to keep it for now. Line Reference C is about the federal government being bad. Line Reference D is about taxes, which is sort of about the government, so maybe keep this one too. You'll need to use the choices for #2 to better understand these lines and find the best match.

#4 — Answer = C

Line Reference. A dumb summary of this paragraph would be that it's about principles. Choice A is wrong because it does not outline anything. An outline is basically a list, and they don't get into the specific conditions when people can rebel. Choice B is wrong because compromise isn't really the main idea, and they don't get into how likely it is. Choices C and D

are very similar. The paragraph is definitely using a historical example and citing an authority. But Choice D takes it too far. Hampden does not agree with Hayne's argument. If you read the footnote, you'll see that Hampden was alive only until 1643. The blurb tells us this debate occurs in 1830, so Hampden is long dead and, thus, can't possibly know Hayne's argument. Choice C is much more vague. Hayne is creating an analogy. Notice that the choice doesn't get into the specifics about what the analogy is doing. That's the hallmark of a correct SAT answer.

#5 — Answer = B

No Line Reference. If you save this until the end, that's okay, but the question is specific enough that we should at least try to use the Chronology Rule to help us find the answer. We should read up to line 65 in Passage 2 to start (we can always read more). Sure enough, it says a lot about the Constitution and revolution. Choice A is wrong for a similar reason as Choice A in #4. We do not see a list of anything. Choice B is very strong because of only, so you might eliminate it. Choice C is wrong because the paragraph never says that the Constitution allows for revolution. That's crazy! Of course it doesn't allow for revolution. Choice D, however, is wrong for the opposite reason. The lines don't say that the Constitution prohibits revolution either. Instead, the lines say that revolution is above the Constitution. We have a problem because we might have eliminated every single choice — this happens sometimes! That's okay. Just go back and see if you can actually prove any of the Strong Words using the text. In this case, Webster is saying that revolution is okay, but only when the people are leading it, not the states. So Choice B is strong, but it passes the test. Occasionally, Strong Words will be okay because the text proves them.

#6 — Answer = C

Reading Vocab. It can be hard to find a guess here, but reading to the end of the sentence gives us a word we can steal: circumstance. Choices A and B definitely don't match with circumstance. Plugging the words back into the sentence, Choice C makes the most sense.

#7 — Answer = A

Both Passages. Remember our dumb summary from the example under The Basics: the passages disagree. Which choice best matches with that? It's Choice A and it's not even close. What historical context? What ideas were merely implied in one passage? What solutions were proposed? Hayne says the states can overrule the federal government. Webster attacks that assumption, saying that only the people can rebel.

#8 — Answer = D

Evidence Pair Part 1. This is still essentially a Both Passages question, but strategy-wise, we're following the Evidence Pair rules. Start by reading the line reference in this question to get a sense of what Webster is saying. A dumb summary is that there's no middle course between submission and rebellion. Now go to #9 to sort through the line references. Once you do, you can return to the choices for #8 and use POE to find the best match. Choice A is wrong because nothing says that the People have chosen to submit. Choice B is wrong because Southern morality is not mentioned anywhere. Choice C is wrong because they don't talk about using the courts, and we don't get any sense of what the states intend. Choice D matches with Line Reference B, which talks about resistance as a good thing that also preserves the Union. This is a middle course. Hayne is saying that you can simultaneously resist and preserve, whereas Webster thinks that's ridiculous.

#9 — Answer = B

Evidence Pair Part 2. Line Reference A has nothing to do with resistance or submission. Line Reference B has a lot of those ideas, so we should keep it. Line Reference C seems random. Cross it out. Line Reference D maybe is about resisting something. It's hard to tell. You can keep it if you're unsure. Once you go back to the choices in #8, you'll be able to match more ideas and confidently realize that Line Reference B is the best answer. Notice that we are not considering the Chronology Rule here. The Both Passages questions will be all over the place, so don't expect the lines to stay in order.

#10 — Answer = B

Both Passages. This is a very common double passage question. Even when the passages disagree, they like to ask what they agree on. As a general rule of thumb, the passages tend to agree on the "problem" and disagree on the "solution". In this case, they both agree that there are times when resistance is justified, but they disagree on who is able to resist (the states or the people). Choice B matches with that idea, but you can also use POE to eliminate the others. Choice A is too strong because Passage 1 does not believe that the people have sole authority to resist — the states do as well. Choice C is wrong because businesses are never mentioned. Choice D is wrong because equally is too strong, and Passage 2 believes the opposite.

#11 — Answer = A

Both Passages. Dumb summaries help here. Go to the lines to get a better sense of what's going on. Hayne is saying that the states should be able to disagree with the federal government, otherwise the states aren't independent. We know from our earlier dumb summaries that Webster disagrees with this. That helps us eliminate Choice B, which is a positive reaction to Hayne when we want a negative reaction. Choice C is very strong with words like ensure and victim. Webster doesn't want to give the states too much freedom, but he's not predicting the end of the world. Choice D is wrong because Webster doesn't really talk about taxes. At the end of Passage 2, Webster talks about the absurdity of letting the federal government take orders from four-and-twenty masters (lines 85-90). He's saying that the government would get conflicting instructions from the states. You might need to read more to get this question right with certainty, but it's okay to eliminate the clearly wrong answers and pick Choice A because it's the only thing left.

Unpaired Evidence lesson

The Basics

The copy/paste idea is one of the SAT's favorite tricks. They know your brain can't help itself. It sees a strange phrase in the passage and the question/

choice, so it locks onto it and can't let go. Remember that the ideas need to match, not necessarily the words.

Example 1

You should underline key words from the question so you know the ideas you're looking for in the lines: human health effects, poorly understood.

- Line Reference A tells me what I already know. I know that microplastics are bad, but the question wants a reference that talks about our knowledge of the effects. This isn't enough.

- Line Reference B seems random.

- Line Reference C has a great match: very little is known matches with poorly understood. It's also clearly about the effect on our bodies, or living tissue.

- Line Reference D copy/pastes the phrase human health from the question, but it doesn't actually answer the question. We really want a match for the idea that the effects are poorly understood, and there isn't one here.

Line Reference C is correct because it matches with the most ideas from the question. In fact, it's best to think of Unpaired Evidence questions as actually a series of smaller questions. You want the line reference that covers as many of those small questions as possible.

Unpaired Evidence — The Basics

Underline key concepts from the question so that you're reading with purpose.

Be careful of line references that simply copy/paste weird phrases from the question. This applies on all sorts of Reading questions.

Be careful of choices that only answer part of the question. Correct answers will include multiple ideas from the question.

The Twists

Example 2

This question can be divided into three smaller ones: 1) does it talk about soil? 2) does it talk about remote areas? 3) does it explain how microplastics enter the soil?

- Line Reference A tells us what we already know. We know that microplastics are in soil miles from urban centers. The question wants to know how/why they ended up there.

- Line Reference B also tells us that microplastics are in remote landscapes, but it once again fails to explain how they got there.

- Line Reference C talks about microplastics that are hundreds of miles from where'd you'd expect to find them. It also explains why they're there — trade winds. This line reference adds in the how portion of the question.

- Line Reference D is random.

The answer is Line Reference C because it matches with all the parts of our original question. Most important, it explains how the microplastics ended up in remote areas. Just like in the POE chapter, we're being forced to think about words that we would normally ignore. This time, though, the Strong Words are in the question, not the answer choices. In a way, Evidence questions are like regular Reading questions in reverse: you're given the answer, and you're looking for the proof that it's correct.

Unpaired Evidence — The Twists

Learn to distinguish between what choices and why choices.

What choices tend to repeat information from the question without elaborating or explaining. The question will often want to know why something happens. The line reference should explain why.

Unpaired Evidence questions occasionally break the Chronology Rule. If you're confident that an out-of-order line reference answers the question, then break the rule and pick it!

Answers: Unpaired Evidence

#1 — Answer = A
The question wants us to link populism to centralization. Line Reference A mentions these movements, which we can assume is populism, but we would normally have the full passage to check for sure. It also talks about nationalization and new social programs, which are clues that they're talking about centralization. This is enough to keep this choice. Line Reference B doesn't seem to talk about either populism or centralization. Line Reference C talks about populism, but not centralization. Line Reference D also talks about populism only. That's good enough to pick Line Reference A, even without the full context of these movements.

#2 — Answer = B
The question gives us a few goals: something unpleasant and something about Mrs. Reed. Line Reference A talks about Mrs. Reed, but it doesn't get into any past relationship. Line Reference B talks about former days, which suggests a history with Mrs. Reed. It also talks about chastisement or reprimand, which are negative things, suggesting that the history was unpleasant. Line Reference C is random. Line Reference D is positive, which doesn't match with unpleasant.

#3 — Answer = C
Only one choice includes anything that hints an Bobby being uncomfortable. Line Reference C says he is afraid to join in. Now, we don't know for sure that they're talking about Bobby or his coworkers, but we would normally be able to read a little extra to be sure. Still, none of the other line references talk about discomfort.

#4 — Answer = A
You need to find out more about the critics, so go to line 17 first. In this case, the relevant lines are included below the question. You can create a dumb summary to make things easier: the critics think mapping is one of many strategies for making memories. There's a lot of science-y words in these line references, so keep going back to your dumb summary. Does Line Reference A suggest mapping isn't the only way? It seems like color is also used, assuming grid-based tests are about mapping in some way. Line Reference B doesn't specify what the control group did or what the test was about. We could read more to understand the line reference better, but it's not a good sign that we haven't found anything that relates to our dumb summary. Line Reference C seems to suggest the opposite of our dumb summary. It says that the spatial component helped, but we want something that suggests that location-based memories are not the only way. Line Reference D is a what choice. It says that location mattered, but it doesn't say why or how. Line Reference A ends up being our best guess, and a little extra context might make us even more confident in the answer.

Evidence Pairs lesson

The Basics

You need to be comfortable with the strategy for Evidence Pairs. You're still following the QLC Method, but it's split over two different questions. It's a long and annoying process, but it's absolutely the best process for these questions.

Evidence Pairs — The Basics

Follow the QLC Method:
1. Question (from Part 1)
2. Line References (from Part 2)
3. Choices (from Part 1)

Underline key words in the question, line references, and choices. You're going to have to keep track of a lot of information. Underlining can boil it down to simpler pieces that are easy to find again if you need to re-read.

Dumb summaries can help you capture the essence of complicated line references, even when you don't fully understand what they're saying.

Stick to the line references in Part 2. You should only read extra if you need to understand a pronoun or quotation. Remember that the line itself needs to support your answer, so you want to focus on the line.

You do not need to choose one correct Line Reference at first. You can eliminate the ones that are completely irrelevant and keep the ones that sort of fit. You'll narrow them down even more once you look at the answer choices in Part 1.

Use POE. Strong Words still matter.

The Chronology Rule can help you get rid of line references that are out of order from the rest of the passage. But if you're confident that an out-of-order line reference is correct, then break the rule!

The Twists

Example 1

Start with the question. We're looking for a problem with future research. Notice how I'm kind of ignoring the weird science term. That's because the science won't usually matter much. We're more interested in the structure of the passage and what they say about the science. Don't get intimidated by

complicated science vocab. Focus on what you do understand.

Now go to the line references. Line Reference A is a what choice. It tells us that there are problems, but it doesn't get into the specifics. We can eliminate Line Reference A. The rest of the line references do mention problems, so write dumb summaries next to each so you remember what they're about:

- Line Reference B — unusable
- Line Reference C — money
- Line Reference D — hurt butterflies

That's good enough for now. We'll use POE to sort through the choices and find a good match.

- Choice A is nice and vague with the word could, but it doesn't immediately match with our dumb summaries. Though, I remember reading that the money couldn't be spent on other research in Line Reference C. Maybe that's enough to keep Choice A for now.

- Choice B talks about a long timeframe, which was also mentioned in the passage in line 47. But there's no match in the line references, so this can't be right. The SAT does this occasionally, which is why you always want to do Part 2 first. You don't want to accidentally pick an answer to Part 1 that doesn't have support in the line references from Part 2.

- Choice C is wrong because the passage does not say that there are not enough butterflies. Line Reference D suggests that butterflies could be hurt in the future, but that's not the same thing as having too few butterflies right now.

- Choice D is wrong because executives are not mentioned. Nobody is blocking anything either.

This leaves us with Choice A and Line Reference C. It's not an obvious match, but we're more confident in it because we took the time to sort through everything else. This is they key not only for

Evidence Pairs in particular but also the entire SAT Reading section. Process of Elimination and the QLC Method are all about using a formal process to sort through everything. Our instincts may help us on easy questions where the right answers also "feel" right. But we won't improve our scores without a process that helps us overcome our bad instincts on the hard questions.

Evidence Pairs — The Twists

Be careful of <u>what</u> choices that merely repeat the question without adding on an answer. You usually want to know <u>why</u> something is true.

Trust the process. The SAT is trying to lure you into wrong answers by making them sound mostly right. But there's a big difference between mostly right and totally correct. POE and the QLC Method force you to pay attention to words that you'd normally ignore. The process may take longer at first, but once you're used to it, you'll be able to move more quickly — and more accurately — through the passages and questions.

Answers: Evidence Pairs

#1 — Answer = B
Whole Passage. You should save this for last. A dumb summary would be that the passage seems pretty negative about Babbitt. It seems like Babbitt hates fun and likes a guy (Littlefield) who is not portrayed nicely in the last paragraph. That would eliminate Choices C and D, which are positive. Choice A is a little true because he seems <u>curious</u> about the car at the beginning. But that's just one part of the entire passage. We have a lot more instances of Babbitt <u>judging</u> other people. He judges Doppelbrau negatively and Littlefield positively.

#2 — Answer = C
Unpaired Evidence. Make sure you actually read the question. Some people assume this is Part 2 of an Evidence Pair with #1, but it's not. It's a completely separate question! We're looking for something about the <u>ideology</u> of the <u>men</u>. Line Reference A is the only choice that fits the Chronology Rule, but it

seems pretty random. What do <u>pirate ships</u> have to do with <u>ideology</u>? The randomness of this choice, plus the fact that it's an Unpaired Evidence question, both suggest that we're going to need to break the Chronology Rule. Line Reference B also feels random. Line Reference C has a few matches. <u>System of industry and manners</u> could be an <u>ideology</u>. And <u>instinct</u> matches with <u>assumptions</u> from the question. Line Reference D seems like a random description, so Line Reference C is the best match. This is a case where we can confidently break the Chronology Rule.

#3 — Answer = A
Reading Vocab. The sentence gives a helpful clue word. We should guess that <u>brush</u> means something like the <u>bruisings</u> mentioned later in the sentence. Clearly something is bumping into something else, which matches best with Choice A.

#4 — Answer = C
Evidence Pair Part 1. You could read all of lines 1-20 if you want, but the line references in #5 are all included in that range. Those specific fragments are where we'll need to find our match. Once you do #5, you'll most likely have two line reference left. It's very tempting to pair Choice A with Line Reference B because they both suggest something negative. However, Choice A has the very Strong Word <u>unanticipated</u>, which directly contradicts the line reference. It says something bad happened to the car <u>each day</u>. Furthermore, Line Reference C says that he was <u>prepared</u> to find a problem with the car. If it were <u>unanticipated</u>, he'd be surprised. Choice B is wrong because we don't read anything about <u>maintenance</u>. And Choice D is wrong because the <u>neighbors</u> idea is only briefly mentioned at the end. As crazy as it may seem to you, Babbitt actually likes his car problems! In Line Reference C, he felt <u>belittled</u> when there was no problem. If he's unhappy when there's no problem, then we'd expect him to be happy when there is a problem. Line Reference C, therefore, supports Choice C. This is a great example of why you can't use your own assumptions and beliefs to answer the questions. You must use the evidence in the passage. You might think a car problem is an obstacle, but the question isn't about you!

#5 — Answer = C

Evidence Pair Part 2. Line Reference A feels like nonsense that isn't related to a problem with Babbitt's car. Line Reference D is similarly random. Line Reference B says it's a crisis, and Line Reference C says Babbitt is belittled when the engine starts. Both are related to the car's performance, so you should keep them. When you go back to Part 1, you'll need to make sure you're finding a match based on the passage, not your own assumptions.

#6 — Answer = D

Line Reference. Use the +1 Sentence Rule to get the context. Line 28 says Babbitt disapproved of the Doppelbraus. That's a good enough dumb summary to eliminate Choices B and C because they're positive. Choice A is negative, but how can a house be disrespectful? Choice D is negative, and it makes much more sense for a house to be unsightly, which means ugly.

#7 — Answer = A

Evidence Pair Part 1. Always flip to the next page to see if the questions are linked. The SAT loves to split Evidence Pairs over two pages. This is a very difficult pair, and sorting through the line references won't eliminate much. Remember that the question wants to know about the statistics. Choice C is true, but not based on this passage. We never read about the legislators using other information. Choice D is also wrong because we don't really know that few people have time for research. Few is a Strong Word that frequently causes problems in choices. Similarly, Choice B includes the Strong Words more eloquently. We definitely know that Littlefield is impressive, but they're not really comparing him to any experts, at least not in how eloquent he is. This may seem like nitpicking, but that's exactly why POE is so useful. It gets us to focus on words we would normally ignore. Choice A is actually supportable with Line Reference B because they say that Littlefield argues that some policy will simultaneously increase rental values and lower rents. Those are contradictory things!

#8 — Answer = B

Evidence Pair Part 2. If it's unrelated to statistics, get rid of it. Line Reference A talks about figures, so we have to keep it. Line Reference B is only part of a sentence, so we should read a little extra to make sure we know what they're talking about. It's actually part of the same sentence as Line Reference A, so we know that both are talking about how Littlefield uses figures. Line Reference C is about all sorts of trivia, but I guess you could say it includes statistics. Line Reference D also mentions figures, so we also need to keep it. We haven't confidently eliminated a single line reference. This happens sometimes! It's still okay because we have a rough understanding of what's happening, and we'll be able to use the choices in #7 to find some matches.

#9 — Answer = D

No Line Reference. We want to use the Chronology Rule, but it's difficult when we're surrounded by Evidence Pairs. We could answer #10 and #11 first to see what reference we'll use, but we don't have to. We can also just get a rough estimate that the answer to #9 is probably in the 50s or 60s. The problem with using the Chronology Rule around Evidence Pairs is that the chronology is based upon the correct line reference. In other words, if we got #8 wrong, we might estimate the lines for #9 incorrectly. The best way to handle this is to just be flexible. In this case, reading the 50s and 60s doesn't give me a clear sense of the answer. Most of those lines are about Littlefield, not Babbitt. But line 70 starts to compare Littlefield to Babbitt. Choice C is definitely wrong because education is not really mentioned. Choice B is also wrong because intolerant is pretty strong. Maybe he's intolerant of the Doppelbrau's, but he seems to like Littlefield. Choice A is very tempting because we read in line 63 that Babbitt is awed by Littlefield's knowledge. But that's not quite the same as being fascinated by numbers. Is he fascinated by Littlefield? Sure. But it's not really the numbers that the narrator is talking about. Choice D is correct because lines 69-71 say that he is a strict and firm believer in his religion and his politics. This puts us on the edge of the line references for #11, which is fine. It means that Line Reference D in #11 is more likely to be correct, but it's also close enough to Line Reference C that I'd say the Chronology Rule wouldn't be broken.

#10 — Answer = B

Evidence Pair Part 1. We've already read a lot of lines that talk about Littlefield, but you should still go to #11 first. Choice A is wrong because there's nothing about Littlefield <u>hosting parties</u>. Choice C is wrong because <u>public service</u> isn't really mentioned. Choice D is way too strong. His daughter is mentioned very briefly, and we have no evidence that he's <u>completely devoted</u> to her. Choice B matches nicely with Line Reference D, which fits the Chronology Rule too (see #9). Both Line References C and D mention <u>faith</u> and <u>beliefs</u>, but Line Reference D also matches <u>convinces</u> with <u>confirmed</u>. The more matching ideas, the better.

#11 — Answer = D

Evidence Pair Part 2. The question in #10 says we want information about Babbitt and Littlefield. Line Reference A can be eliminated because <u>they</u> refers to the Doppelbraus if we just read back a little bit. The rest of the Line References seem to talk about both Littlefield and Babbitt, or at least they talk about Littlefield in a positive light that could be seen as Babbitt's view. Keep B, C, and D, but keep in mind that Line Reference B would be very out-of-order from the other questions. If possible, we'd prefer to stick to the Chronology Rule.

#12 — Answer = C

Reading Vocab. Your guess here is probably something like <u>except</u> anyway, so this one shouldn't be too hard.

Reading Vocab lesson

The Basics

It's very important that you continue to follow the QLC Method. The SAT is trying to trick you with the choices, so you need to read the line reference first. You don't want to bias yourself with the answer choices. Coming up with your own guess is the best way to avoid the traps.

Reading Vocab — The Basics

Follow the QLC Method:
1. Question
2. Line Reference — come up with your own guess
3. Choices — match your guess

When you read the line reference, pretend the vocab word is a blank. Your job is to fill in the blank with a word that captures the meaning. It doesn't need to be an academic word or one of the answer choices.

If you need to, physically cover the answer choices with your hand so that you aren't tempted to look at them before you read the line reference.

Do not eliminate hard words that you don't know. If you find a good match for your guess, then pick it. If not, then don't be afraid to pick a word you don't know.

The Twists

Example 1

If you don't read the line reference, you'd probably pick Choice A or D, but that's not what the word means in this context. The lines suggest that she found the food <u>bad</u>. That's a perfectly valid guess! It doesn't need to sound eloquent. Your job is to capture the meaning.

The only choice that's also negative is Choice C. And this is a valid definition of "wanting". Look it up!

Example 2

The language is much harder to understand in this passage, but the clue words are much more helpful. Notice that the sentence is structured to repeat itself: <u>security being the true design and —— of government</u>. They're hinting very strongly that the meaning of the vocab word is <u>design</u>. It's great when you can "steal" words from other parts of the sentence.

The best match for <u>design</u> is Choice D. Even if you're not quite sure what <u>intention</u> means, you know that the other words don't work. Don't be afraid to pick harder words when the easier ones are wrong.

Reading Vocab — The Twists

When you can, use words that are already in the sentence to help you come up with your guess.

Dumb summaries can help you figure out the connotation when you're confused about the exact meaning.

Answers: Reading Vocab 1

#1 — Answer = C
It's unlikely the SAT would ask for such a specific and unusual definition, but this question highlights the problem you're up against. You have spent years building your vocabulary, and you know what words typically mean. But on the SAT, you'll sometimes need to fight your instincts. They're clearly talking about numbers here, so it makes perfect sense that Choice C would be right. But if you can't fight your instincts, you'll pick one of the other answers simply because it feels safer.

#2 — Answer = B
Use the sentence to come up with your guess: <u>conceived</u> should mean something like <u>brought forth</u>, which we're stealing from the sentence itself. Choice B matches.

#3 — Answer = B
It's harder to find a clue word here, but you can probably guess that <u>proposition</u> means something like <u>idea</u>. And that's a choice! Sometimes you get lucky.

#4 — Answer = A
The sentence says that they're at war, so a good guess would be something like <u>fighting</u> or <u>participating</u>. Choice A is a little weaker, but it captures the same meaning.

#5 — Answer = D
<u>Civil</u> normally means polite, but that's clearly not what Lincoln means when he's talking about a war. In this case, you might have to pick a word you're not normally familiar with. <u>Domestic</u> means "having to do with your own country". For example, a <u>domestic</u> flight is between airports in the same country. We know that the Civil War was between the northern and southern states.

Answers: Reading Vocab 2

#6 — Answer = B
He's clearly talking about <u>a long time</u>. It's okay that I'm still using the vocab word. There aren't many rules when you come up with your guesses. You just want to better understand the meaning of the word. Choice B captures the meaning.

#7 — Answer = D
You could use the next sentence to guide you since they're phrased in a similar way. Our guess should be something like <u>come</u> or <u>come together</u>. That matches best with Choice D. Choice C also means <u>come together</u>, but it's used to describe fusing objects together, like metals. The Reading Vocab questions don't usually hinge on these kinds of usage differences, but you might see them once in a while. Usage differences are more common on Writing Vocab questions.

#8 — Answer = A
Our guess should be something like <u>honor</u>. That doesn't match with Choices B, C, or D. You may not know what <u>sanctify</u> means, but it's the only thing left.

#9 — Answer = B
Your guess should be something like <u>part</u>. That matches exactly with Choice B. Choices A and C are close, but not quite right. Just plug them back into the sentence. It would be weird to talk about a <u>serving</u> of a field or a <u>quantity</u> of a field.

#10 — Answer = D
The soldiers <u>sacrificed</u> their lives. It's a perfect match with Choice D.

#11 — Answer = B

Once again, the sentence gives us a very helpful clue by repeating itself: <u>fitting</u> and <u>proper</u>. Choice B matches with <u>proper</u>.

#12 — Answer = C

It's hard to come up with a guess for this one. Maybe something like <u>way</u>? Once you look at the choices, you'll see that most don't fit with the sentence. Lincoln's talking about ideas again, so <u>understanding</u> is good enough.

#13 — Answer = A

This one should be easy. Lincoln is talking about a <u>battlefield</u>, so that should be your guess. It matches with Choice A.

#14 — Answer = D

This one is meant to be easy! But it's also meant to show you how we can sometimes "steal" clue words from the sentence, even when they mean the opposite of the vocab word. Compare this question to #11. In that case, we saw <u>fitting and proper</u> as a repetition of the same idea. This time, we know that <u>living and dead</u> is meant to be opposites. Context will tell you when the author is listing synonyms or opposites. We know that we want something that means <u>not living</u>, and Choice D is the match. You should know what <u>deceased</u> means, but you should at least know that the other choices don't have the right meaning.

#15 — Answer = B

Our guess can be vague, and I thought the word should mean something like <u>bad</u>. All of the words are negative, but only <u>inadequate</u> makes sense when talking about power.

Answers: Reading Vocab 3

#16 — Answer = B

We can steal from this sentence. Our guess should be something like <u>remember</u>. Choice A is too specific. Choice B is more general, and thus a better fit.

#17 — Answer = A

Lincoln's been talking about the living and the dead, so our guess should be pretty straightforward: <u>not dead</u>. That clearly matches with Choice A. Sometimes they're easy!

#18 — Answer = C

It's hard to come up with a guess for this one, but if you need to look at the choices, only one will make sense when plugged back into the sentence. They're <u>committed</u> to the unfinished work.

#19 — Answer = A

Our guess should be something like <u>job</u> or <u>task</u> (stolen from the next sentence). It's not a <u>chore</u> because that implies that it's something Lincoln doesn't want to do. <u>Project</u> is the more neutral fit.

#20 — Answer = A

There's a positive connotation here. Our guess should be something like <u>helped</u>. Choice A is also positive and fits the sentence. As a side note, this definition of the word <u>advanced</u> is worth remembering. It sometimes comes up on other Reading questions.

#21 — Answer = C

You might be able to use the opposites in this sentence to come up with a guess. The dead <u>gave</u> devotion, so we <u>get</u> devotion? It's good enough to match with Choice C. The other answers don't make sense in the sentence.

#22 — Answer = D

Just like #19, we can steal from other lines to guess <u>task</u>. That matches with <u>objective</u>.

#23 — Answer = D

You might get lucky and guess <u>amount</u> here just based on the sentence. But if you have trouble, you can plug the words back into the sentence. It's weird to think of devotion as something that you can have <u>amounts</u> of, but Lincoln is being metaphorical here.

#24 — Answer = A

You should be able to guess something like <u>decide</u>, and that's a perfect fit with Choice A.

#25 — Answer = B

Lincoln is saying that the dead will inspire the living to keep fighting. If they died <u>in vain</u>, then they died <u>for nothing</u>. That matches with Choice B. None of the other answers would make sense if plugged back into the sentence.

Reading Figures lesson

The Basics

You can't let the graphs intimidate you. Don't cut corners and you'll be fine.

Example 1

The question is directing you to the <u>insulated flasks</u>, so stick to the right side of the graph. Since the y-axis is labeled <u>temperature differential</u>, we know that we're looking at the right thing. Choices C and D are clearly wrong because the graph says nothing about <u>boiling points</u> or <u>density</u>.

Choice A is tempting, but the question is specifically directing you to the <u>insulated flasks</u>. Why would the <u>uninsulated flasks</u> have any effect on the insulated ones? A better question is why are the bars different heights? According to the legend, it's because the flasks have different <u>volumes</u>. **That matches with Choice B.**

Reading Figures — The Basics

Read everything — the title, the axis labels, the legend... everything!

Use POE to find ideas that aren't mentioned in the figure.

Some choices might be factually untrue based on the data, so be prepared to eliminate them.

The Twists

Notice that we never bothered to understand the experiment in the previous Example. It's irrelevant. They probably discuss it in the passage, but the question is asking about the graph, so we should stick to the graph.

There may be times where the question directs you to the passage, but it's almost always a hurdle you need to deal with, not the main point of the question. If the question says the graph needs to serve as evidence, then the graph had better support your answer choice.

Example 2

This question looks like an Unpaired Evidence question, but our focus should still be the graph. The line references would force you to go back to the passage, but your decision about the correct answer will be based on the figure.

- Line Reference A just talks about a conference. Who cares?

- Line Reference B says that insulation is <u>beneficial</u>, which may be true. However, the graph doesn't make a value judgement about the insulation. In other words, the graph doesn't say whether the insulation is good or bad.

- Line Reference C uses different words, but it basically summarizes the graph. <u>Coating the flask</u> (insulating it) definitely <u>reduced the difference</u> (the insulated bars are closer together than the uninsulated bars) <u>in heat loss</u> (probably temperature differential) between the <u>two sizes</u> (200ml and 1,000ml).

- Line Reference D doesn't say anything about the graph.

Line Reference C directly references the ideas in the graph, so it's the best answer. Notice how we didn't need anything beyond those limited line references to answer the question.

Example 3

Again, we don't have the passage, but let's see if it matters.

- Choice A is wrong because the graph doesn't say anything about <u>error</u>.

- Choice B is very vague. The insulation decreased the temperature differential for the 200ml flask, but it increased the temperature differential for the 1,000ml flask. That sounds pretty <u>variable</u> to me.

- Choice C is wrong because we do not know from the graph what scientists <u>favor</u>. Again, the graph doesn't make a value judgement. It merely presents the data in a neutral way.

- Choice D is wrong because <u>safety</u> is not on the graph anywhere.

Choice B is correct because it matches with the graph. Some of these other choices may be true based on the passage or our own experience, but it doesn't matter. We need to base our answers on the figure.

Reading Figures — The Twists

Even when the question makes you read or think about the passage, your focus should still be on the figure. The figure needs to be your evidence.

Most figures don't make value judgements. Data doesn't have an opinion. Avoid choices that have a positive or negative connotation, unless the figure somehow shows other people's positive and negative opinions.

Answers: Reading Figures

#1 — Answer = C
Just look at the numbers! Strawberries have 15.6 prictose and 8.4 biofin. It's probably worth noting that these are both made up compounds. In fact, this entire chart is made up nonsense. That's a good reminder that all the science they throw at you doesn't really matter. You don't need to understand any outside information to answer the questions.

#2 — Answer = C
What's a <u>hexagonal compound</u>? That seems like outside information! But if we trust the strategies, we should remember that all the information we need should be given to us. And since <u>hexagonal compound</u> is a unique phrase, it should be easy to skim the passage for it. To make things easier, I gave you the relevant sentence in the bottom right: <u>prictose is hexagonal</u>. Go to the rows for <u>grapes and plums</u>. The numbers are 9.5 and 13.4.

#3 — Answer = A
Focus on the "becauses" first. There are only two different "becauses", and one of them is factually inaccurate. A quick glance at the fruits will show that <u>nuclide is not double prictose</u>, which eliminates Choices B and D. At least you have a 50/50 shot right now. But once again, it seems like we're missing some information. What was the <u>author's conclusion</u>? the passage should help us, and we'd probably be able to find information about the conclusion near the end. (More often, we would have already read about the conclusion to answer other questions from the passage, so we'd remember where they talked about it.) The box at the bottom right says there will be <u>twice as much nuclide as biofin</u>. That is exactly what Choice A says, so the data supports the conclusion.

#4 — Answer = D
Just go to the right row and columns for pineapple. It's not exact, but 28.7 is approximately double 14.3.

#5 — Answer = B
This time, we don't need the passage at all, so there's no need to go back to these line references. Use POE! Choice A is wrong because the chart doesn't say anything about <u>acidity</u> or <u>sweetness</u>. Choice C is wrong because the chart doesn't show <u>organic reactions</u>. Choice D is wrong because the <u>theories</u> aren't mentioned in the chart. Choice B is right because the <u>chemical content</u> (prictose, biofin, and

nuclide) <u>varies</u> from one <u>species</u> of fruit to the next. The numbers are different!

Accomplish the Goal lesson

The Basics

Example 1 — Answer Choices

I've deliberately left out the question. Can you guess an answer with only the choices? What are you using to decide?

Some people pick Choice A because they seem to be talking about different places, so Nepal fits in. Or maybe it's Choice D because they were talking about violins. Regardless, you probably don't feel great about your answer. You're hoping one choice feels right, but nothing should feel obviously correct.

Hmm… what should we do?

Accomplish the Goal — The Basics

Ideas questions are not about grammar or style. You need to pick the answer that includes the most relevant ideas.

Sometimes the passage will give you clues about what's right. But without the question, it can be very hard to tell. Always read the question!

The Twists

Let's follow that advice and read the question.

Example 1 — Question

The question makes this much easier. They give you a goal, and it's your job to accomplish it. Do what they want, not what you would write if you were in charge. The SAT does not care about your opinion.

In this case, we need a choice that talks about <u>the sarangi's physical and musical characteristics</u>. Only

Choices B and C do. So how do we decide which one is better?

Again, don't use your instincts. Accomplish the stated goal. They want a choice that has <u>the most specific information</u>. Choice B is too vague: <u>medium-sized</u> and <u>unforgettable</u>. Choice C is much more specific: <u>two feet long</u> and <u>sounds like a human voice</u>. Personally, I think that Choice C is a little weird, but my opinion is irrelevant. **The SAT wanted the most specific information, so I do as I'm told and pick Choice C.**

Example 2

When the goal isn't specific, you need to use more of the passage. There are still objectives you need to accomplish, though. In this case, focus on the <u>previous sentence</u>. If you don't read it, you won't be able to get this right!

The sentence before the 2 talks about the sarangi as a <u>dying art-form</u>. We're looking for a choice that matches with that idea somehow. **Only Choice D includes anything relevant** — the sarangi has <u>seen a resurgence</u>, meaning it's coming back.

Goal questions sometimes feel subjective, but there's always a good reason why the right answer is right. The more you understand the goal, the more confident you'll be when you find an answer that accomplishes it.

If the goal is specifically stated in the question, then follow it exactly.

If the goal is more vague, you will probably need to rely more on other parts of the passage.

Use dumb summaries to capture the main ideas of sentences and paragraphs. Repeated ideas are main ideas.

Pay attention to words that you'd normally ignore, like "establishes" and "supports". A choice that establishes the main idea will be a general topic sentence that summarizes a paragraph. A choice that supports the main idea will be a relevant, narrow fact that repeats a main idea that's already stated. The SAT will include both types in the choices to confuse you.

Answers: Accomplish the Goal

#1 — Answer = D

This question has three goals: 1) Narayan, 2) the sarangi, and 3) a contrast. Choice A is wrong because it does not mention the sarangi. Choice B is wrong because it does not mention Narayan. Choice C is wrong because it does not mention the sarangi. Choice D mentions Narayan, the sarangi, and creates a contrast. The first part of the sentence talks about fame in the world, and Choice D is about fame in India. The word but is also a helpful contrast word.

#2 — Answer = A

This goal is more vague, but it's essentially telling us to read the surrounding sentences. We'll look for ideas that match with key ideas in the choices. Choices B, C, and D don't really contain any ideas at all. They kind of seem like rambling extra clauses. Of course Narayan's father is from the same place as Narayan! Of course the father paid for a tutor! These ideas don't add anything. Choice A builds upon the ideas in the passage. At first, the father was reluctant, but he eventually relented.

#3 — Answer = B

The biggest mistake students make on this question is they stop reading. The goal is to establish the main idea. You can't do that if you don't know what the main idea is. And you won't know the main idea if you don't read the full paragraph! It talks about his education, then his first job, a little failure, and then success. If you read everything, your dumb summary will match perfectly with Choice B. Choice A supports the main idea, but it does not establish it. They're not asking for the first chapter of Narayan's story. They want a summary of his story.

#4 — Answer = B

This is a weird question. The goal is vague, so we'll need to figure out for ourselves which ideas we need. Make sure you read around the underlined portion so that you understand the context. Here's a dumb summary of the story: Narayan applied for a job as a singer; he didn't get the job; the manager saw his fingernails; the manager hired him for a job as a sarangi player. Something is missing from this story! How does he get a completely different job because of his fingernails? We need to fill in the gap in this story. The only choice that explains this is Choice B. The information is relevant because it tells the reader why Narayan's fingernails would get him a job playing the sarangi. The other choices might be true information, but they don't connect the dots in the story.

#5 — Answer = B

The goal is very clear in this question. Independent success matches perfectly with solo career. And tried matches with several failed attempts. You have to get questions like this correct!

#6 — Answer = A

This one is tricky! There's one obvious goal: promoting sarangi music. Choice A accomplishes that goal because a scholarship would certainly promote the music. But Choices B and C could also promote the music because Narayan is playing the sarangi in places that wouldn't normally know about it. Plus, Choices B and C fit better with the sentence that comes before this one (Narayan performs internationally). So then what makes Choice A better? It comes down to the second goal, which is not as obvious. The question says the writer wants another example, which means we cannot repeat the same information from the first sentence. Since Choices B and C continue the idea of performing internationally, they do not provide another example. Choice A is correct because it's a new example, not a repetition of the first one. If you were unsure as you answered this, that's actually a good sign that you're missing something. Most Accomplish the Goal questions will be fairly straightforward once you find and understand the goal. If you're having trouble, read the question again more carefully. See if there are secondary goals like in this question.

#7 — Answer = D

This question also has multiple goals. They want us to recall an earlier claim, which could mean referencing any part of the passage. That's a difficult goal to check for, so it's best to focus on the easier goal first: a hopeful conclusion. You can use dumb summaries to figure out the connotation of each choice. Choice A is wrong because it's introducing a new character in the very last line, which is completely irrelevant to Narayan. Choice B is wrong because eclipse has a negative connotation. Choice C is wrong because being dominated by other instruments isn't hopeful for the sarangi. Choice D is hopeful because it includes a lot of positive words, like promote, talented, dedicated, and pick up the torch. And it accomplishes the goal of recalling an earlier claim because talking about the 21st century parallels the references to the 12th and 20th centuries on the first page.

Add or Delete lesson

The Basics

The goal is in the answer choices. Make sure you read the "becauses"!

Add or Delete — The Basics

You need to add or delete the information based on good reasons. The "becauses" are like the goals, and you need to make sure adding or deleting the information accomplishes the goal/because.

Use POE to help you sort through the choices. Strong Words might be a problem, just like in the Reading section.

The Twists

It's okay to have a hunch, but you need to test it by reading the becauses. Make sure you read the becauses!

Add or Delete — The Twists

It's okay to have a hunch that the information needs to be added or deleted. But you must read the becauses to make sure your hunch is correct.

You might find that you'd prefer to delete some information, but the becauses won't make sense. Don't force it. You may need to add the information, simply because the choices provide better reasons for adding it. Be flexible!

Answers: Add or Delete

#1 — Answer = A

Is this really necessary? It could go either way. But Choice D is clearly wrong because the information is not provided later. Choice B is clearly wrong because it's not an example of a dying art-form. You might think that the information detracts from the paragraph, but the "because" is incorrect — the paragraph is not focused only on Narayan. The paragraph talks about the sarangi too, so it's okay to keep the information as a way to define the sarangi.

#2 — Answer = D

Who cares? This information is unrelated to Narayan or the sarangi. We should definitely delete it, and

Choice D has the better "because". Choice C is wrong because we simply don't care about other instruments. Including more information would make this sentence worse, not better.

#3 — Answer = C

They're trying to trick you by adding a sentence about Lahore right next to the sentence that mentions Lahore. But the passage isn't about the history of India and Pakistan. It's about Narayan and the sarangi. Choice C is correct because it's the weaker of the two delete choices. Choice D includes the Strong Word undermine, which means to attack or to weaken. In this case, the sentence isn't attacking or contradicting the passage. It's just a random fact that we don't need.

#4 — Answer = A

Personally, I don't have a strong feeling about this sentence. It feels like a random fact that I wouldn't want to include, so we might lean toward Choices C or D. However, the becauses don't make sense. Choice D is wrong because the paragraph is not about Narayan's teaching roles. That's just one small part of it. And Choice C is wrong because the idea is clearly explained. What's confusing about it? Narayan got an award for doing something good. That's pretty clear. Choice B is wrong because the sentence is not a counterargument. That leaves Choice A, which makes sense. The previous sentence is about how Narayan helped promote the sarangi, so it's logical that he'd receive an award for his work.

Transitions lesson

The Basics

It's important to note that Transitions questions don't look like the other Ideas questions. They are the only Ideas questions that don't explicitly ask a question. They only include the answer choices, so they look more like Grammar and Style questions. Still, Transitions questions are easy to recognize because the answer choices will be transition words!

Example 1

Always read the sentence before and the sentence that contains the underlined transition word. Use dumb summaries to capture the meaning in the simplest terms possible. You can always get a more complicated summary if you need to.

In this case, the first sentence is positive (trying to remove). The second sentence is clearly negative (too late). So we need a transition that gets us from a positive to a negative. In other words, we need a contrast word. **Choice D serves that purpose.** In fact, however is the most common answer choice on Transition questions. It's correct more than any other transition word, but it's also incorrect more than any other. Luckily you know its meaning and contrasting sentences are relatively easy to notice.

Transitions — The Basics

Read the sentence before the transition and the sentence that contains the transition.

Use dumb summaries to capture the meaning of each sentence.

Don't forget that Transition questions are not about Grammar or Style. They test the Ideas in the sentences and how you should connect them.

The Twists

If the relationship isn't obvious, don't panic. There are some strategies that can help you. But also, don't be afraid to pick a weird transition word if none of the more common ones work.

Example 2

Once again, we'll use dumb summaries to help us understand the relationship between the two sentences. The first sentence seems positive (achieved, greater fame). The second sentence also seems positive (popular, admirers). That eliminates Choice C because despite this is a contrast transition.

From here, it can be hard to tell the difference between the choices. But luckily, if we know the categories that these transition words belong to, we can easily find the correct answer. If you look to the right, you'll see that both therefore and thus belong to the category of "so" words. In fact, there is no difference between these two transition words. So if they mean the same thing, then how could one be right but not the other? That's not possible. If Choices A and B can't both be right, then they must both be wrong.

That leaves us with Choice C, which probably isn't a word that most of us use in our daily lives. Indeed is used to add emphasis, so it makes sense that both sentences would be positive. To go beyond our dumb summary, the first sentence is telling us how famous Kahlo is, and the second sentence is giving even more evidence of that fame. The second sentence is emphasizing the point made in the first sentence.

It would be great if we always knew which transition word works best, but we sometimes need to use Process of Elimination. This is a great reminder that the SAT operates under different rules from normal tests. The right answer won't always jump off the page. You need to reason your way through the choices. The categories give you an easy way to sort through everything.

Transitions — The Twists

If the dumb summary isn't enough to know the correct transition, use the categories to simplify the choices.

If two choices have the exact same meaning, then it's highly unlikely that those answers are correct. You can cross them both out. Looking at the two remaining choices is usually an easier task.

Categories

These categories are meant to get you started as you try to learn the transition words. Most of the words on the left side of the dashed line (the first two columns) have the same or similar definitions. The words on the right (the third column) still fit into the category, but they might have a slightly more nuanced definition. Here's a bit more about each box:

But words create a contrast. They can either transition from positive to negative or negative to positive ($+ \rightarrow -$ or $- \rightarrow +$). However is the most common **but** word. Words like regardless can also be used dismissively, as a way to create a contrast and imply that the point in the first sentence isn't relevant.

And words continue an idea. They usually don't transition at all, continuing the positive or negative thought that came before ($+ \rightarrow +$ or $- \rightarrow -$). Often, **and** words will be correct because everything else is wrong. Similarly and likewise are very common wrong answers. There just aren't a lot of circumstances where you'd correctly use those words. Essentially, they both are used when you want to create an analogy or comparison between two similar things.

So words suggest a cause and effect. They also continue the connotation of the previous sentence ($+ \rightarrow +$ or $- \rightarrow -$). The key is that the second sentence contains an idea that somehow follows from the first. The words in the third column are a little weaker. They suggest chronology, but don't necessarily have to be used for cause and effect. They can simply say that the first sentence happened before the second sentence.

For example words are self-explanatory. They give an example. The best way to think of it is as a big, general idea to a small, specific example ($+ \rightarrow {}_+$). If you use in short, the second sentence had better be a shorter version of the first sentence. Basically, it's used to restate the same ideas in a more concise way.

Emphasis words are a little harder. Sometimes they can be used for a contrast. But more often, they're used to show that the second sentence expands or highlights an idea in the first sentence. You might think of **emphasis** words as the reverse of the example words (${}_+ \rightarrow +$).

Answers: Transitions

#1 — Answer = D

Find key words that can help you make a dumb summary. The first sentence is about a simple past (once, simply), and the second sentence is about a complicated present (is, modern, science, chemistry, understanding). Choice A is wrong because the second sentence is not an effect of the first sentence. Choice C is wrong because the second sentence is not a more specific version of the first sentence — they're about different things. Choice B is tempting, but it implies that we're dismissing the first sentence as if it didn't matter. We do want to make a contrast, but it's a contrast about time. Choice D makes it clear that we're comparing the past to the present. This word wasn't in our Category boxes, but it's okay. Use the boxes as much as you can, but don't be afraid to pick a new word if it's a better fit.

#2 — Answer = C

There's a clear contrast here. The first sentence says that there's a link to the past, but the second sentence says it's actually quite different. Choice C is a **but** word that makes the contrast.

#3 — Answer = A

The first sentence is positive (leading, advanced). The second sentence is also positive (philanthropist, donated, promote). That eliminates Choices B and C, which are both **but** words. (They also mean the same thing, which is a good sign we can cross them out.) Choice D is wrong because the second sentence is not a shorter version of the first. That leaves Choice A, which is an **and** word that continues the previous idea.

#4 — Answer = C

Dumb summaries can be tricky here. The first sentence is about what the conservationists recommend, and the second sentence is about what the organizations encourage. These seem like similar ideas, so Choices B and D are probably wrong because they're **but** words. You might not know what Choice C means, but Choice A is in the **so** category box. In fact, subsequently is just a fancy word for next. Time isn't passing between these two

sentences. They aren't talking about events that happen in some order. That leaves Choice C, which we should pick because we know the others don't work. But it's also important that you know what to this end means, since the SAT has used it before. In this case, end means goal. Think of the phrase "the ends justify the means". We say this when we want to talk about how the ends (our goals) are good enough to justify some questionable means (the methods we use to achieve our goals). In this question, to this end is a great transition because the organizations are encouraging certain behaviors to accomplish the goals that were recommended in the first sentence.

#5 — Answer = D

This time, the transition word is in the middle of the second sentence, but the overall strategy hasn't changed. We still need to see how the first sentence relates to the second. A dumb summary should be easy here. The first sentence is negative (apocalypse), and the second sentence is positive (robust). We need a **but** word, and Choice D is the only one.

#6 — Answer = D

Both sentences are positive (famously, attract millions). Choices A and B are both **but** words, so they won't work. And Choice C is self-explanatory. The second sentence is not a more basic version of the first sentence. If we can find a transition word that works, we should not choose to delete the underlined portion. But if none of the transitions fit, then it's okay to avoid the transition altogether.

#7 — Answer = A

Both sentences are positive (essential, on behalf, increased funding). That eliminates Choices C and D because they're both **but** words. Choice B is an **and** word, but it's almost never correct. We're not comparing two situations. Choice A is correct because it's a **so** word, and we have a cause and effect relationship: Mr. Rogers believed programming was good, so he asked for more funding.

#8 — Answer = A

This one is tricky because both Choices A and B would be considered **but** words. We might want to cross them both out since they are in the same category, but this is the rare case where they don't have the exact same meaning. The answer is Choice A because we're contrasting Gray and Bell. Choice B would be used if one person had two options: Gray filed a caveat; <u>alternatively</u>, he could have filed a patent.

Combine Sentences lesson

The Basics

It's okay if you hate Combine Sentences questions. They're complicated, and there's usually a lot to read. Just remember that Grammar and Style are secondary to Ideas.

Example 1

Notice that the original version of these two sentences repeats some phrasing: <u>technology companies</u>. If possible, we'd love to shorten everything by cutting out the extra words.

Choices A and B both repeat <u>technology companies</u>, so they're probably not right. In Choice B, the <u>by which</u> also sounds a little strange. In fact, you would probably eliminate both of these choices simply because they sound weird. That's okay!

Choice C is short, but there's an Ideas problem. Without a comma after <u>notice</u>, the sentence seems to suggest that <u>the people</u> are <u>creating products</u>. That's not what the original sentences say. We want the <u>technology companies to get users to log in</u>. **Choice D accomplishes this goal by treating the <u>which</u> clause like an extra part of the sentence.** The commas on both sides let us remove that clause from the sentence.

If that explanation doesn't make sense, don't worry about it. The simpler explanation is that Choice D is shorter, and shorter is better when possible.

Combine Sentences — The Basics

The main goal of the question is to connect the Ideas. You might need to consider Grammar and Style, but you should generally assume that all of the choices are grammatically correct.

When in doubt, pick the shortest choice (unless it has a big problem).

The Twists

Example 2

It can be hard to know which choice is shortest when all of the sentence is underlined. You can sometimes "hear" the best choice, but you should also be aware of some of the potential traps.

- Choice A sounds fine, and it's grammatically correct. However, our goal is to combine the sentences <u>and</u> the Ideas. A semicolon is used to join two sentences, but a semicolon is basically still a period, so the sentences are weakly combined. In general, semicolon answers will <u>not</u> be correct for Combine Sentences questions.

- Choice B suffers from a similar problem as Choice A. <u>And</u> is a weak connection. It's still treating the two ideas like they're unrelated. Choice B also repeats the phrase <u>harmful chemicals</u>, which makes it a bit too wordy.

- Choice C might sound a little off. It's hard to pinpoint the problem, but you don't need to if you think Choice D is better. Still, it's worth talking about the word <u>being</u>. It's normally a word you want to avoid on the SAT. Unfortunately, <u>being</u> is in every single one of these choices, so we can't completely avoid it for this question. However, it's the second instance of <u>being</u> that is the real problem in Choice C. Narrow your focus to the second clause: <u>the effect being that they cause health problems</u>. How does that sound to you? It might sound better if we said the effect is that they cause health problems. The problem with being is that it makes sentences sound a little backwards. If you're stuck between two choices, go with the one without being.

- **Choice D is correct because it actually combines the Ideas.** A simple comma and which was all we needed to make the second sentence "flow" from the first. As much as possible, you want to avoid breaks in your sentence, but commas are shorter breaks than a semicolon or an and. It's clear in Choice D that the chemicals cause health problems.

Combine Sentences — The Twists

When the underlined portions and choices are long, you won't easily be able to pick the shortest choice.

Think about how the ideas "flow" through the sentence.

Avoid hard breaks that stop you mid-sentence.

Wrong answers will generally include:
- semicolons
- weak transitions, like and
- being
- lots of interruption clauses

When in doubt, go with the choice that sounds best.

Answers: Combine Sentences

#1 — Answer = A
As we've said, shorter is better. Choice D has the hard stop of a semicolon, which prevents the Ideas from flowing. Choice C includes the word being, which isn't a great sign. Choice B is short, but it probably sounds a little strange. Do you often use the phrase such that when you write? You probably don't use dashes all that much either, but you should. In this case, the dash is acting like a colon. It indicates that the second part of the sentence explains or answers something that's brought up in the first part. Opponents claim the opposite. What's the opposite? That the bags are actually worse. In the Punctuation chapter, we'll talk more about how dashes and colons work.

#2 — Answer = B
Choice A is wrong because the first which clause is right in the middle of the sentence, interrupting the flow of the Ideas. Avoid choices with lots of comma clauses. Choice C uses the word while, which suggests that the two ideas are opposites. That's not true, though. The original sentences are trying to make a comparison, not a contrast. Choice D includes being, but it also sounds pretty bad. It's hard to understand what the sentences are even saying. Choice B is best because it only includes one transition by the comma. The ideas are much easier to follow.

#3 — Answer = C
Choice A is weird because in effect doesn't really do anything. Choice B uses the semicolon and repeats Roosevelt. It's not a strong connection. Choice D uses likewise, which is another word that is rarely correct on the SAT (see the Transitions packet). Choice C use and, which is normally too weak to be the right answer, but it's okay here because it's the best option. This is a common issue on Combine Sentence questions — you'll often need to adjust your expectations to deal with unique situations.

#4 — Answer = C
Choice A is wordy, and it's probably because it adds the word being for no good reason. Choice B includes the weak connector and. Choice D turns the first sentence into an interruption that makes it very difficult to follow the ideas in the sentence. Notice how the comma clause is cutting the idea about access right in half! Choice C is best because the ideas flow, and the colon is an effective connector. Remember that the colon is used to explain or answer something brought up in the first part. Why is the policy controversial? Because law enforcement has unrestricted access.

Sentence Placement lesson

The Basics

It's very inefficient to read the entire paragraph four times, trying to "hear" where the sentence should go. Instead, NARROW YOUR FOCUS to a few pieces of the sentence at a time. "Anchor words" focus your attention onto the structure of the sentence and any transitions that will relate the sentence to others in the paragraph.

In this first sentence, but and the task can serve as anchors. But tells us that we're looking to contrast our sentence with whatever is supposed to come before it. We should look out for a sentence that's negative since this one is positive (enthusiasm). The task is also important because it suggests that the task has already been mentioned earlier in the paragraph. We need to introduce the task before we can talk about it in this sentence.

The second sentence has one very obvious anchor phrase: these concerns. This is hugely important because it tells us that our sentence needs to follow some sort of introduction into what the concerns are. This sentence is clearly referencing concerns that have already been discussed. Pronouns are a great way to find the right place for a sentence.

This third sentence doesn't give us much, but we'd expect Jansen to have been introduced before. It also sounds like this sentence is one step in an experiment of some kind. We'd want to anchor this sentence so that the chronology makes sense with the rest of the experiment.

This final sentence makes it sound like the exhibit has been introduced already. It also provides us with an introduction to scrimshaw, which can definitely help us place it. We want to make sure this sentence is placed before any other references to scrimshaw.

Once you've found some anchor words, you can read the paragraph — without reading the sentence we're moving — to "hear" if there are any gaps that need to be filled. Your anchor words should help you

confirm that your sentence makes sense in its new location.

But before you circle your answer, make sure that placing the sentence somewhere new doesn't also create new problems. For example, you may want to place it after sentence 5 because of some anchor words, but you also need to make sure that you're not breaking up sentences 5 and 6. They might need to go together for other reasons. Sentence Placement questions are tricky because there's a lot to think about. But luckily there are only around two of them per test.

Sentence Placement — The Basics

Find anchor words that can help you place the sentence within the paragraph. Pronouns and transitions are the best anchor words.

Read the paragraph without the sentence that you're placing. Try to listen for any gaps that need to be filled.

Double check to make sure that you didn't place your sentence somewhere that breaks up other ideas that need to stick together.

The Twists

Example 1

First, look for anchor words in sentence 5. The most obvious is today, which suggests that there's going to be some sort of contrast over time. If that's the only anchor word you can find, that's okay!

Next, read the paragraph without sentence 5. The first sentence is talking about the past, which would make a great contrast with sentence 5. Choice C would let us transition from 1984 to today.

But wait! Let's make sure that we're not disrupting the flow of other ideas in the paragraph. Sentence 2 is also about the past (was), so we wouldn't want to jump back and forth from the past to the present and back to the past. We should group similar ideas together. Keep sentences 1 and 2 together, since they're both about the past. Sentence 5 can come after sentence 2 because it transitions into the present, which is also the topic of sentence 3 (is).

Choice D uses our anchor words as a guide, but then keeps similar ideas together. Once we place sentence 5 after sentence 2, we might also see that there's another anchor idea that confirms our decision. Sentence 2 talks about the <u>fishing industry</u>, which contrasts with how the bay is <u>protected</u> today.

Sentence Placement — The Twists

It's okay if you don't find many anchor words at first. Sometimes the connections between the ideas will reveal themselves after you've placed the sentence in a new location.

Answers: Sentence Placement

#1 — Answer = D
Sentence 4 is clearly negative (<u>problem</u>). We can make dumb summaries of the other sentences to better understand the flow of the ideas. Sentence 3 is positive (<u>showcase</u>, <u>unique</u>). Sentence 5 is also positive (<u>envisioned</u>, <u>huge</u>). But sentence 6 is negative (<u>challenge</u>). Ideally, we'd be able to keep the two positive sentences together and the two negative sentences together. Choice D lets us do that by moving sentence 4 so that 3 and 5 are next to each other and 4 and 6 are next to each other.

#2 — Answer = C
Sentence 3 has the very helpful anchor phrase <u>all that pumping</u>. It strongly suggests the <u>pumping</u> has been mentioned before. Only sentence 5 mentions <u>pumping</u>, so we should place sentence 3 after sentence 5. We also have the added connection of <u>night</u> flowing into <u>day</u>. You might be tempted to delete the sentence entirely, but you shouldn't delete unless you're absolutely sure the sentence can't fit anywhere. In fact, it will be obvious if you need to delete the sentence because it'll be completely unrelated to the paragraph.

#3 — Answer = D
This time the sentence isn't in the paragraph at all, but that doesn't change the strategy. There are some anchor words in the sentence: <u>massive windows</u> and <u>viewed from two levels</u>. Where else do they talk about the windows? The first three sentences are all about small windows, but sentence 4 shifts the ideas to the big windows that the aquarium wanted to <u>immerse visitors</u>. Our sentence belongs after this shift.

Writing Figures lesson

The Basics

Example 1

These are not much different than Reading Figures questions. Start by checking the accuracy of the choices.

- Choice A is inaccurate because <u>cattle feed</u> is approximately 2 billion, but <u>food processing</u> is close to 1.5 billion. 2 is not double 1.5.

- Choice B is inaccurate because the bar for <u>distilling</u> is actually shorter than the bar for <u>food processing</u>.

- Choice C is accurate because <u>ethanol</u> is clearly the tallest bar.

- Choice D is inaccurate because <u>exports</u> is not the tallest bar, so it cannot be the <u>majority</u> of corn usage.

This example only had one accurate answer choice, so Choice C must be correct. This actually happens on the SAT!

Writing Figures — The Basics

Check the answer choices for accuracy. If the statement doesn't match the data, cross off the choice.

The Twists

Example 2

Start as we did before by checking the accuracy of the choices.

- Choice A is not accurate because the y-axis says that <u>food production</u> actually uses close to 1.5 <u>billion</u> bushels. Just like in Reading and Math, always check the axis labels and scales!

- Choice B is accurate because adding up the bars for <u>cattle, hogs, and poultry</u> would be much higher than the bar for <u>food processing</u>.

- Choice C is inaccurate because the figure says absolutely nothing about the <u>cost</u> of any corn usage.

- Choice D is accurate because <u>ethanol</u> does account for around 3.5 billion bushels of corn.

If you're wondering how we knew that <u>ethanol</u> was related to <u>gas tanks</u>, then you're already thinking about the other part of Writing Figures questions — relevance. The rest of the paragraph talks about <u>ethanol</u> and <u>fuel</u>. Without the context, we'd have no idea that Choice D matches with the figure.

And since Choices B and D are both accurate, we need to go beyond the figure to find the correct answer. Which choice is a better fit with the main idea of the paragraph. As always, a dumb summary can help us. The paragraph repeatedly talks about <u>ethanol</u> and <u>fuel</u>, so it would make sense to pick Choice D because it's also about <u>fuel</u> and <u>gas</u>. Looking even closer, Choice D matches <u>hungry families</u> with <u>starvation</u> in the previous sentence. Choice B, on the other hand, brings up feeding animals, which isn't talked about elsewhere in the paragraph. **Choice D is the only relevant answer.**

Writing Figures — The Twists

After you've checked for accuracy, see which of the remaining choices is most relevant to the ideas in the paragraph.

Use dumb summaries to better understand the main ideas of the choice and the paragraph.

Answers: Writing Figures

#1 — Answer = A

Choice B is inaccurate because the graph does not show the number of <u>downloads</u>. It shows the <u>dollar sales</u>. Choice C is inaccurate because <u>digital entertainment</u> is the dotted line, not the solid line. Choice D is inaccurate because <u>3 out of 12 sales</u> is not the correct way to read the graph. Choice A is correct because the dashed line for <u>digital entertainment</u> is close to $3 billion in 2009.

#2 — Answer = D

Choice A is not accurate because we have no evidence that digital sales <u>did not exist</u> before 2009. Just because the graph doesn't start until 2009 doesn't mean that there were no sales in 2008. Choice B is not accurate because the dashed line for <u>digital sales</u> does not <u>level off</u> in 2012. It continues to increase. Choice C is accurate, but not relevant. The main idea of the sentence is that <u>digital sales have grown</u> and now <u>dominate</u>. Choice C does not really support that idea. Choice D is both accurate and relevant. There were small increases in digital sales before 2011, but the lines go up much more quickly after that, which matches with <u>took off</u>.

#3 — Answer = C

First check for accuracy. Once again, the SAT is trying to trick us by messing with the units. The figure talks about the <u>sales in billions of dollars</u>. The sentence talks about 15 billion <u>total sales</u>. Those are not the same! Do not confuse the cost of the sales with the number of sales. Choice C is correct because the sentence misinterprets the graph.

General Comma Rules lesson

The Basics

`Example 1`

Even though this sentence is long, it doesn't need any commas. First, Choices A and B are wrong because they're trying to put commas before prepositional phrases. As you'll see in the Verb Agreement packet, prepositional phrases are extra clauses that could be deleted from the sentence. Usually, extra information is perfect for a comma or two, but not with prepositional phrases like <u>for combatting climate change</u> and <u>on remote islands</u>.

Choice D is also trying to trick you by using a comma in a place that sometimes gets one. You probably know that <u>or</u> sometimes gets a comma, usually when it's part of a list of three or more items. Occasionally <u>or</u> gets a comma because it's helping to redefine something in the sentence, essentially an extra clause that further explains something. But in this case, <u>or in populated</u> is not an extra clause. It's just part of the description of the <u>coastal cities</u>.

If you read the sentence out loud, you'll hopefully hear that there isn't really a significant pause anywhere in this sentence. **That's a good sign that you don't need any commas, and Choice C has none.**

`Example 2`

Once again, they're trying to lure you into some traps. The SAT knows you're a little iffy on comma rules, so it puts them in places where you might think they would belong.

The word <u>that</u> almost never gets a comma. The similar word <u>which</u> usually gets one, so they're trying to confuse you between the two. We can eliminate Choices A and B because they include an unnecessary comma with <u>that</u>.

You also might remember that commas go before quotations. The rule is that they must go directly before the quotation, so Choice C isn't quite right. **Choice D is correct because we only need a comma after <u>said</u> to lead us into the quote.**

General Comma Rules — The Basics

A comma usually indicates a pause. If there's no need for a pause, there's probably no need for a comma.

Do not use commas with prepositional phrases.

Do not use commas with <u>that</u>.

Use commas before quotations.

The Twists

`Example 3`

To truly understand commas, you want to start thinking about the **structure of the sentences**. Commas usually indicate a pause because we tend to pause when sentences shift their structure. We use commas to mark off clauses so that our eyes can easily follow the structure of the sentence.

This sentence needs a comma after <u>embarrassing</u> because <u>while</u> tells us that we're in a dependent clause, which is an extra piece of a sentence that helps out the main sentence by explaining or elaborating. Dependent clauses cannot exist on their own. They are not complete sentences. Try reading the main sentence out loud: <u>this habit has been shown to relieve stress and increase happiness</u>. That sounds like a complete thought! The <u>while</u> part helps us understand the main sentence, but it sounds incomplete if we read the dependent clause alone. **Choice A places a comma where the structure of the sentence shifts from the dependent clause to the main core of the sentence.**

Choice B places a comma in the middle of an idea, which you can probably hear is wrong. Choices C and D are trying to trick you because you sometimes use commas with <u>and</u>. This is not one of those cases because <u>and</u> is used to list only two ideas.

Example 4

Sentences get more complex as we include more and more extra clauses. In your own writing, you should use commas to help you mark the shifts in the structure and ideas of the sentence. In this example, it's hard to know what the sentence is saying because we're missing some punctuation.

The easiest choices to eliminate are Choices B and C. A semicolon is used to join two complete sentences, so it's exactly the same as a period (for the SAT, at least). In other words, Choices B and C are functionally identical, so we can eliminate them both.

If we try out Choice D, we can hopefully see how the sentence is supposed to sound. The <u>experts say</u> part is extra. It interrupts the main sentence, so we should use two commas to show that it's a separate clause. You can see that it's extra by reading the sentence without it: <u>If nothing changes in the next ten years, then the supply of oil will eventually fail to meet the demand.</u>

General Comma Rules — The Twists

Think about the structure of the sentence. Commas are used to separate different clauses from each other in a sentence.

Dependent clauses would not be able to stand alone as a full sentence. They only make sense when they're attached to a full sentence. Use commas to connect dependent clauses to the main sentence.

Clauses that interrupt a sentence need two commas to show when you're leaving the main sentence and returning to it. If you can read the sentence without a clause and it still makes sense, then the clause was probably an unnecessary interruption.

Answers: General Comma Rules

#1 — Answer = A
There's no need for a comma here. Reading it aloud, you shouldn't need to pause after <u>waited</u>. The SAT is trying to get you to use a comma with the prepositional phrase that begins with <u>for</u>, but remember that prepositional phrases do not typically get commas.

#2 — Answer = B
The middle of this sentence is an unnecessary clause that describes L'Enfant. The clause begins with <u>who</u>, which also has a comma before it to show that the sentence structure is changing. Since the <u>1790s</u> portion is part of the description of L'Enfant, the comma should come after it to show that we're returning to the main sentence. We could have used two dashes instead, but since we didn't use a dash at the beginning, we can't switch to a dash at the end, so Choice D is wrong.

#3 — Answer = D
<u>While</u> doesn't always get a comma, but this sentence clearly has two parts, and the change in ideas occurs at the <u>while</u>. A comma shows the change. You can also get this right by eliminating everything else. Choice A is wrong because there's no need for a comma before <u>and</u> because this is only a list of two things. Choice B is wrong because <u>that</u> clauses do not get commas. Choice C is wrong for the same reason.

#4 — Answer = B
The sentence starts with an introductory clause (<u>During the speech</u>), and the comma shows that it's separate from the main sentence. You don't absolutely need a comma after <u>speech</u>, but all of the other answers use commas incorrectly. Choice A is wrong because prepositional phrases don't get commas, and <u>with</u> is a preposition. Choice C is wrong for the same reason. Choice D is wrong because <u>and</u> does not get a comma when the list only has two things (<u>chants and slogans</u>).

#5 — Answer = C
Choices A and D are essentially the same, since a semicolon joins two complete sentences. That's a

good sign you can eliminate both choices. Choice B is grammatically correct, but it sounds bad. There's no need to break up these two ideas that dramatically. Choice C is shorter, and it turns the second idea into an Appositive (next lesson).

#6 — Answer = C

This one is tricky because we don't typically write our own sentences in this way. The middle piece is an interruption, so we need two commas to show that we're leaving and returning to the main sentence: <u>Many people believe that Southern California is heaven on Earth.</u> Choice A is wrong because it only uses one comma, and it's not even after the correct word. Choice B is wrong because colons can only be used when the part that comes before the colon is a complete sentence. Choice D is wrong because it starts the interruption clause in the wrong place.

#7 — Answer = A

Similar to #4, this sentence starts with a brief introductory clause, so we should put a comma after <u>2000s</u>. It's not absolutely necessary, but all the other choices use commas incorrectly. Choice B puts a comma after <u>brief</u> for no good reason. Choice C puts one after <u>videos</u>, also for no reason that makes sense. Choice D uses the dash incorrectly. We sometimes uses a dash instead of a comma to mark off an extra clause at the end of a sentence. But we don't really want to use a dash to mark off an extra clause at the beginning of a sentence. It's just not done.

#8 — Answer = B

The <u>who</u> starts a descriptive clause that gives more information about <u>Jackson</u>. We should use two commas to separate the extra clause from the rest of the sentence. The extra information ends with <u>presidency</u>. The main sentence is <u>Early exit polls showed that Congressman Jackson had pulled into second place.</u>

Appositives lesson

The Basics

You probably know what an Appositive is, even if you've never heard the word before. I don't care if you ever learn it. Just understand when and why we need commas.

The most common example involves a brief description of something in the sentence. The description is typically extra information, so we use two commas to separate the clause from the main sentence. In this case, <u>the junior senator from Arizona</u> is the appositive. It provides extra information about Barry Goldwater. You might also think of an appositive as a second way of defining or identifying the noun that comes before it.

The main sentence is <u>Barry Goldwater received the Republican nomination in 1964</u>. Notice how removing the appositive doesn't really affect the main sentence — it still sounds like a complete sentence. That will be important later.

Example 1

In this example, the appositive is <u>the mountain peak</u> because it provides a second way of describing <u>the most difficult part of their journey</u>. **We should use two commas to indicate that it's an extra clause, so Choice C is the answer.** Notice that crossing out the appositive wouldn't cause any problems for the main sentence. It would still sound like a complete sentence: <u>The hikers could see the most difficult part of their journey directly ahead of them.</u>

Example 2

This time, things aren't so simple. You are probably drawn to Choice B because it looks a lot like the correct answers we've seen so far. However, there's a problem. Is <u>Charles Dickens</u> really extra information? What if we crossed it out? How would the main sentence sound? <u>Famed novelist was paid to write by the word.</u>

(Notice that when we look at the "main sentence" we still cut out extra clauses in other places. The <u>which</u> clause is extra information too, so I'm ignoring it so we can NARROW OUR FOCUS to the smallest version of the sentence we can.)

Something doesn't sound right about the main sentence without <u>Charles Dickens</u>. It feels like it's missing something. That's a sign that we have an appositive that is not extra — it's essential. In those cases, we would not use commas because we do not want to separate the words out from the main sentence. **In fact, there's no need for any commas here, so Choice D is the answer.** More on this in The Twists…

Appositives — The Basics

An appositive is typically a second way of defining or describing something in the sentence.

Use two commas to show that the appositive is extra information that is not necessary to the main sentence.

The Twists

Example 2 showed us something that the SAT will absolutely do. They know that you know the rule about appositives, so they'll try to trick you into using it when you're not supposed to.

Look at how the first "Right" sentence is nearly identical to the "Right" sentence we used in The Basics. Yet no commas! That's because appositives are sometimes essential to the sentence. It all comes down to how the sentence is put together. Looking at the wrong version, you can see that it would be wrong to use commas for this version of the sentence. Apply the "cross out" test. If we crossed out <u>Barry Goldwater</u>, we'd be left with another sentence that sounds incomplete like in Example 2: <u>Arizona senator received the Republican nomination in 1964.</u> Maybe if we said <u>The Arizona senator…</u> or <u>An Arizona senator…</u>, but it doesn't sound right without the appositive.

Try the cross out test on the second set of sentences. Crossing out the appositive would give us <u>Arizona senator platform was the most conservative in history.</u> It sounds like the senator's name is Platform! When there's an apostrophe, there's a good chance that the appositive is essential to the sentence, so it shouldn't get commas.

The cross out test will help us in other packets as the punctuation rules get even harder. In general, if you can cross something out, it's not essential to the sentence, which means it probably needs some sort of punctuation to separate it from the rest of the sentence. But there are definitely exceptions! We already talked about how prepositional phrases don't get commas in the General Comma Rules lesson.

Example 3

This example is getting into rules that we'll see at the end of this chapter. **The correct answer is Choice D because it turns the second idea into an appositive that describes <u>Erica Willoughby</u>.** As written, the sentence doesn't actually sound bad. But it's grammatically incorrect because it's a run-on sentence. Choice B would create a run-on, too.

Run-on sentences occur when you join two complete sentences together with only a comma. There are many ways to fix run-ons, but Appositives have the benefit of shortening things a little.

Appositives — The Twists

The SAT likes to give you situations that seem very similar to the appositives that you're used to, so you'll be tempted to always use two commas. Unfortunately, it's more complicated than that.

Use the **cross out test** to see if the appositive is essential to the sentence (no commas) or extra information (usually two commas).

Appositives can also help you fix run-on sentences.

Answers: Appositives

#1 — Answer = C
<u>The head of the university's engineering department</u> is extra information about <u>Bill Marshall</u>. You could delete it from the sentence, so we should use two commas to show that it's a separate clause. Choice D is missing both commas. Choice A is missing the

second comma. Choice B is missing the second comma but also has a random comma after <u>head</u>.

#2 — Answer = A

This is one of my favorite questions! The magician's name is so weird that it's very difficult to "hear" whether the sentence needs commas or not. You should at least know that Choices B and C are wrong because they each only have one comma. Since the appositive would be in the middle of the sentence, this is pretty much a two commas or zero commas situation. It's a perfect opportunity to use the cross out test. If you cross out <u>The Amazing Hubert's</u>, you'd get a very strange sentence: <u>I couldn't wait to see magician latest illusion.</u> Like the examples in The Twists, this sentence loses something essential when we cross out the appositive. It may also sound strange with the magician's name, but that's only because he has a strange name. We also saw in The Twists that apostrophes often signal that information is not extra and so cannot be separated with commas. This question is a great example of how your instincts can deceive you, yet the rules can be applied nonetheless to find the correct answer.

#3 — Answer = D

What's an <u>ablution</u>? Probably a <u>ritual washing</u>. Appositives sometimes literally define words for us. They might be essential for understanding the difficult word, but they're not grammatically essential. Just be careful because all of these choices have commas very close to each other. Use the cross out test to make sure you don't accidentally put the comma in the wrong place. The actual extra clause is <u>or ritual washing</u>.

#4 — Answer = C

This is a very mean question. Obviously, the SAT is trying to get you to think about appositive rules. In this case, we cannot use commas to separate <u>Jamie Oliver</u> from <u>celebrity chef</u>. The title is kind of like a part of his name. The cross out test would give us a weird sentence: <u>Celebrity chef owns several restaurants.</u> That should eliminate Choice B. But we still need a comma here because the sentence also has an unnecessary introductory clause: <u>Known for his knowledge of Italian cuisine</u>. That clause needs a

comma to show that it's being added to the main sentence.

#5 — Answer = D

This one is also tricky because it seems like there might be two appositives. In fact, <u>diarist Mary Chesnut</u> is the full appositive that we could cross out if we wanted to. We should put a comma on both sides of it. The main sentence would be something like, <u>The woman who wrote it is still credited for her account.</u>

#6 — Answer = A

This one is easy. <u>A sculpture</u> is the appositive that describes <u>the artist's first commissioned work</u>. It's not necessary, so we should use two commas to separate it. The semicolon and colon require a complete sentence before the punctuation mark, which is not the case here.

#7 — Answer = B

The comma before <u>impeachment</u> is necessary because the sentence starts with a short introductory clause. This comma has no impact on the rest of the sentence. Right after <u>impeachment</u>, we get a definition of the word that is not grammatically necessary. Using the cross out test, the main sentence is <u>impeachment can be the only way to stop the abuse of power</u>. Don't let the quotation marks distract you from the appositive rules.

#8 — Answer = A

If you're not tech-savvy, you might think that <u>a podcast</u> is a definition of <u>a blog</u>, but I'm hoping you know better. These are two different things, so <u>or a podcast</u> is not extra information — it's an essential part of the list. This question shows why the SAT can be so tricky with punctuation rules. There are so many possibilities in the English language that you can't really say that you always use commas with certain words. Punctuation isn't really about the words being used. It's more about the structure of the sentence. Sometimes <u>or</u> gets a comma, sometimes it doesn't. You should always pay attention to how sentences are put together to see where a punctuation mark might help the reader more easily see a shift in ideas.

Lessons and Answers   197

Lists & Examples lesson

The Basics

Example 1

Don't overthink this. When you're making a list of 3 or more things, you use a comma before the <u>and</u> (or the <u>or</u>). **Choice B places the comma exactly where you've always placed the comma, so it's correct.**

This is sometimes called an "Oxford comma" and people have a lot of strong opinions about it. In some countries, the Oxford comma is not used. But the SAT is made in America, and we use the Oxford comma pretty regularly. I have never seen an SAT question without the Oxford comma. But I also doubt that they'd make it a choice. Notice how the answers to this example include punctuation in lots of weird places. In general, if a comma is optional, the SAT is probably testing something else in the sentence in addition to the optional comma. You'll see what I mean in Example 2...

Example 2

Your instincts hopefully tell you not to use a comma here. **Choice A is correct because that's how most people would punctuate this sentence.**

But it's not the only way. In English, we can use commas when we have multiple adjectives describing the same thing: "the sticky, sweet dessert". But this rule is sometimes open to interpretation. For example, when we write about "the deep, blue sea", are we really saying that the sea is both deep and blue? Or is the sea just the color "deep blue", in which case we wouldn't want to use a comma. Ugh. This is why grammar can be so hard — sometimes we have choices!

In Example 2, we could make the case that the comma after <u>brilliant</u> is helpful because we're describing the <u>accents</u> as both <u>brilliant</u> and <u>gold</u> — one noun, two adjectives But we could also argue that we're just describing <u>gold accents</u> as <u>brilliant</u> —

one compound noun, one adjective. So if both are right, then how could we know the correct answer? The SAT will never have multiple correct answers, so there must be something else going on in the question. The real issue isn't the comma after <u>brilliant</u>, it's the comma after <u>accents</u>. We don't need it because <u>and</u> is used for a list of only 2 things here, which means we do not put a comma like we did in Example 1.

If this confuses you, don't worry about it. This is a very minor point about comma usage. The big picture idea is that you might have a question where a comma or other punctuation mark seems optional. Just look at other parts of the answer choices — there may be another punctuation mark that isn't optional. The SAT frequently tests multiple grammar rules in one question, so try to break the choices down into multiple questions that you ask yourself.

Lists & Examples — The Basics

For lists of 3 or more things, use a comma before <u>and</u> or <u>or</u>.

For lists of 2 things, do not use a comma with <u>and</u> or <u>or</u>.

When multiple adjectives describe the same noun, you might be able to use a comma to separate the adjectives. See what else is going on in the choices first, though. There might be other rules involved.

The Twists

Example 3

Even though you probably don't use colons a lot in your own writing, you still know a little about how to use them. Colons are for lists! Since <u>bananas, kiwis, and guavas</u> is a list of <u>tropical fruits</u>, we would use a colon to indicate the start of the list. **So Choice B is correct.**

Remember that Choice A is wrong because a semicolon must have a complete sentence before the semicolon and a complete sentence after the semicolon. Choice C is wrong because the comma would suggest that tropical fruits is a member of the list, but we want to make it clear that it's the topic of the list.

Example 4

Once again, we have a list, so it seems that we should use another colon. Nope! Once again, the SAT knows that you associate colons with lists, so it's going to give you situations that are very similar to each other but aren't identical. In this case, we would not use a colon, so Choices A and B are wrong.

But why can't we use a colon here? Like semicolons, colons have a strict rule that we can apply to "test" whether we should use the colon. **The part before the colon <u>must</u> be a complete sentence. The part after the colon could be a list, but it could also be a full sentence or just one word.** Generally, the part after the colon should be an explanation of or answer to a "question" that's raised in the part before the colon (more on this in the Advanced Punctuation lesson).

Let's apply the "complete sentence test" to the part before the colon: <u>Many families use their attics to store items they no longer need but don't want to part with, such as.</u> That's definitely not a complete sentence. The <u>such as</u> makes us think that we're going to continue the idea, but the colon would indicate that the idea is complete. In other words, the list is essential once we used the <u>such as</u>. We can't separate it from the main sentence with a colon.

We should, however, separate the entire list from the main sentence with a comma. The <u>such as</u> starts the list, so it's part of the same clause. We should put the comma before the <u>such as</u>, which makes sense because we could end the sentence there if we wanted to: <u>Many families use their attics to store items they no longer need but don't want to part with.</u> **Choice D puts the comma where the extra clause begins, so it's the best answer.**

Another way to think about it is to see the colon as redundant. Colons start lists. <u>Such as</u> also starts

lists. So we wouldn't want to use two list-starting things in one sentence. Pick one or the other. Choices A and B are wrong because they use both.

Lists & Examples — The Twists

Colons are frequently used to start lists.

The part before a colon must be a complete sentence. The part after a colon can be a list, a complete sentence, or just one word.

Other phrases are also used to start lists (<u>such as</u>, <u>including</u>, <u>like</u>), so you should not use a colon with those phrases.

Answers: Lists & Examples

#1 — Answer = C
This is a list of 3 things, so you need a comma before the <u>and</u>.

#2 — Answer = C
<u>Not only… but also</u> is a strange sentence construction, but the SAT really likes it for some reason. In this case, you should get to Choice C by eliminating everything else. Choices A and B are wrong because the part before the colon would not be a complete sentence. Choice D is wrong because neither part would be a complete sentence.

#3 — Answer = B
There are a lot of commas here! First, Choice C is wrong because we shouldn't use a colon with <u>such as</u>. Choice D is wrong because we should really put the comma before the <u>such as</u>, not after it. But actually, we don't need the comma before the <u>such as</u> at all. You could get away with omitting it. The main issue is the comma after <u>elasticity</u>, which we do need. The <u>which</u> starts an unnecessary clause that adds extra description to the sentence. But immediately after <u>which</u>, there's an interruption within our interruption. The word <u>partly</u> starts another unnecessary clause that ends with <u>elasticity</u>, so we need commas on both ends to indicate that we're leaving and returning to the <u>which</u> clause. It's the second comma that forces us into Choice B. This is

an extremely complex sentence with multiple layers. Commas are the tool writers use to show the layers in their sentences.

#4 — Answer = D

Choice A is wrong because this is not a list of 3 things. There are two things that the writer is thankful for. The colon lets us list those things at the end of the main sentence. Cross them out and you'd still have a complete sentence before the colon.

#5 — Answer = B

This one is tricky because the part before the colon is indeed a complete sentence. However, the sentence picks up again after the list, which means we can't use a colon. Essentially, a colon must come after a complete sentence, and we cannot return to that sentence again once we're done with the list that the colon starts. In this case, we can separate the list from the sentence using two dashes. We'll see more of this in the Advanced Punctuation lesson.

#6 — Answer = C

Choice D is wrong because we shouldn't use a colon with such as. Choice C is correct because the such as is essentially part of the list, so the comma should come before that entire clause.

#7 — Answer = A

We need a comma before and because this is a list of 3 things. But we also need a comma after tone because all of which is attaching a clause to the main sentence. The semicolon is wrong because the second part is not a complete sentence.

#8 — Answer = D

This question is similar to #5. Since the list is in the middle of the sentence, we can't use a colon. The two dashes accomplish the same goal, separating the list from the main sentence while still allowing us to return to the main sentence when we're done with the list.

Apostrophes lesson

The Basics

For some reason, students really struggle with apostrophes. When I read students' essays, I frequently see students leave them out of their writing completely. One problem might be that you misunderstand the purpose of an apostrophe. Sometimes they're used for contractions, but in formal writing you'd really only see apostrophes used this way on contractions involving pronouns. Yet when we speak, we often use them to shorten the word is. You probably say:

Becky's going to the store.

…which actually means:

Becky is going to the store.

The SAT will almost never use apostrophes like this. When apostrophes appear on a noun or a name, they indicate possession:

Becky's friend is going to the store.

The apostrophe tells us that Becky has a friend. She owns, or possesses, her friend (in the grammatical sense).

All of these examples about the dogs are meant to show you how apostrophes can get confusing. First, apostrophes sound the same whether we're talking about a singular or plural noun. But we also have to contend with multiple possessive phrases in one sentence. In the "multiple possessives" section, the five sentences mean the following:

- one dog has one owner, who has one house
- multiple dogs have one owner, who has one house
- one dog has multiple owners, who have one house
- multiple dogs have multiple owners, who have one house

- multiple dogs have multiple owners, who have multiple houses

Yeah. It's not just you. It's confusing.

Example 1

Luckily, the SAT gives us answer choices, which can help us figure out what the sentence is trying to say. Sometimes we don't need an apostrophe at all, so don't let the choices trick you into using one.

In this example, you can ask yourself, "do the beaches own anything?" Not really. It's just multiple beaches that are being eroded. **There's no need for an apostrophe here, so Choice A is correct.**

Apostrophes — The Basics

Apostrophes generally indicate possession.

When the noun is singular, the apostrophe usually goes before the S.

When the noun is plural, the apostrophe usually goes after the S.

There are a lot of exceptions to the above rules, so be flexible. Pay attention to each situation, and ask whether anything is owned or possessed.

You can create multiple possessives, showing multiple layers of possession.

The Twists

The biggest exception to the possession rule is pronouns. Possessive pronouns do <u>not</u> get apostrophes. You know this fact for certain possessive pronouns, like <u>his</u>, but it's easy to forget the rule when you're taking an SAT. The first column shows the possessive pronouns, none of which have apostrophes.

The second column shows the words that are frequently confused for the possessive pronouns. All of these words are contractions, meaning that they

are a shortened version of two words. You hopefully know that <u>it's</u> is actually <u>it is</u>. You might not have known that <u>who's</u> is <u>who is</u>, but you should remember it because it could come up on a hard question.

Lastly, the SAT sometimes tries to trick you by including choices with apostrophes that are never correct. <u>Its'</u> is never correct. You're more likely to make this mistake with words that you don't use frequently, like <u>ours</u>. Just remember that possessive pronouns are special and do not get apostrophes. Any pronoun with an apostrophe is a contraction.

Example 2

This is actually a Pronoun question from the Consistency chapter, but it's worth talking about the wrong answers here. Choice C is wrong because that version of <u>its</u> does not exist. Choice A is wrong because that's really <u>it is</u>. You should at least be able to eliminate those choices on most Pronoun questions.

Choice B is the answer because the pronoun is referring to <u>the battalion</u>, which is a singular noun. Try to think about what possesses the <u>instructions</u>. The <u>battalion</u> does. They're the <u>battalion's</u> <u>instructions</u>. Since it's only one <u>battalion</u>, we would use the singular pronoun <u>its</u>. (More on this in the Pronouns packet.)

Example 3

This question is very hard, and it's unlikely to appear on the SAT. Still, it can't hurt to be prepared just in case.

We're dealing with a weird word here because <u>women</u> is already plural, even though it doesn't end in S like most plural nouns do. **Choice C is the answer because we would need to add the S to make it possessive.** We wouldn't want to pick Choice A because <u>womens</u> is not the plural version of <u>woman</u>. Basically, we add the apostrophe-S when the word does not already end in S. When it does end in S, we would usually just add the apostrophe, but there's also differing opinions on that rule. The SAT would not ask you to use an apostrophe that professional writers can't agree on, so if you find yourself in that situation, there's probably something else going on in the question. Look for other punctuation rules.

Apostrophes — The Twists

Possessive pronouns do <u>not</u> have apostrophes.

Contractions are shortened versions of two words, and they do get apostrophes.

<u>its</u> = possessive pronoun (The dog wags its tail.)

<u>it's</u> = contraction for <u>it is</u> (It's a cute dog!)

Irregular plural nouns will usually get an apostrophe-S like regular singular nouns.

Answers: Apostrophes

#1 — Answer = C
The <u>nation</u> possesses the <u>scientists</u>, so we need an apostrophe on <u>nation's</u>. That rules out Choice A. Choice B involves multiple <u>nations</u>, which could be correct. But the bigger issue is that the <u>scientists</u> don't possess anything, so we should not use an apostrophe. That eliminates Choices B and D, leaving us with Choice C.

#2 — Answer = B
The <u>tourists</u> don't own anything, so there's no reason for an apostrophe. Choice C sounds bad, so Choice B must be right.

#3 — Answer = D
Even if you're confused about <u>edges</u>, you can still get this right by focusing on <u>its</u>. Choice B includes the always-wrong <u>its'</u>. And Choices A and C actually say <u>it is</u>, which is not correct. That leaves Choice D, which make sense since the <u>edges</u> don't possess anything.

#4 — Answer = B
This is tricky because <u>United States</u> already has an S at the end. We wouldn't want to separate that S from the rest of the word, so Choice D is wrong (it's not <u>United State</u>). Choice C is wrong because <u>the United States</u> possess the <u>economy</u>, so we need an

apostrophe on <u>States'</u>. (Another way to look at it is that the <u>economy</u> belongs to <u>the United States</u>). Choice A is wrong because the <u>market</u> does not own the <u>economy</u>. In fact, it's supposed to be one noun — a <u>market economy</u>. If you are confused by this one, don't worry. It's unlikely that the SAT will test this version of the rule.

#5 — Answer = A
This one is also very difficult. Choice C is wrong because it's only one <u>coworker</u>, but the apostrophe after the S means that they're talking about multiple <u>coworkers</u>. Choice D is wrong because it sounds bad. Choices A and B both involve acceptable apostrophe usage. However, Choice B would create another punctuation problem. When we have a quotation at the end of a sentence like this, we want to introduce it by saying something like "he said" or "she replied". Essentially, we want a verb just before the quote. Choice B would change the meaning to make <u>comment</u> a noun, not a verb. To do that, we would need a different punctuation mark before the quote, most likely a colon, instead of the comma. Choice A preserves <u>comment</u> as a verb. This is a very weird situation that does not come up often on the SAT or in general writing.

#6 — Answer = D
The <u>astronauts</u> don't possess anything, so there's no need for an apostrophe. This eliminates Choices A and C. Choice B is wrong because it would create a run-on sentence. The dash in Choice D would let us connect these two complete sentences. The dash is a very versatile punctuation mark that can replace almost every other punctuation mark. In this case, it's acting like a colon or semicolon. (More on dashes in the Advanced Punctuation packet). And just so you're aware, Choice A and the colon would be correct if the apostrophe weren't there.

#7 — Answer = A
Narrow your focus to one word at a time. First, <u>Rose</u> has a <u>son</u>, so we need an apostrophe on <u>Rose</u>. That eliminates Choices C and D. Next, the <u>son</u> has a <u>dog</u>, so we need an apostrophe on <u>son</u>. That gives us Choice A. It's worth noting that the sentence doesn't give us enough information to know for sure whether Rose has one son or multiple sons. If she has multiple

sons, then the apostrophe in Choice D could be correct with <u>sons'</u>. Luckily, we didn't need to decide how many sons Rose has because the other apostrophes led us to the correct answer.

#8 — Answer = B
Remember that <u>ours</u> should not have an apostrophe because possessive pronouns do not get apostrophes. That eliminates all of the wrong answers!

Advanced Punctuation lesson

The Basics

Example 1

Many questions that look like they involve advanced punctuation actually don't. The answer choices in this example might make you think that you need to know the rules for semicolons and colons, but **most people would naturally put a comma after <u>determination</u> and pick Choice B.** The beginning of the sentence is an introductory clause, which we would separate from the main sentence with a comma.

Example 2

But sometimes you do need to know the more complicated punctuation marks. In this example, the comma would not be correct. While we could use two commas to separate out this interruption clause, the sentence already uses a dash to start the interruption. **We need a second dash to finish the interruption and return to the main sentence, so Choice C is correct.** The SAT really likes the double dash as a way to interrupt sentences. I use it a lot too!

Advanced Punctuation — The Basics

Don't get scared by semicolons, colons, and dashes. If a comma works, use a comma.

The **dash** can sometimes replace commas. Dashes provide a more "dramatic" way to separate extra clauses from the main sentence.

For the sake of symmetry, if you start an extra clause with a dash, you need to end it with a dash. Similarly, if you use a comma to start the extra clause, you should end it with a comma too.

In general, double dashes are preferred when the extra information is a list because they're visually different from the commas that make up the list.

The Twists

Example 3

Sometimes you need to be very comfortable with the rules for the advanced punctuation marks. First, remember that semicolons must separate two complete sentences. The second part is not a complete sentence, so Choice C is wrong.

We should also eliminate Choice A because we obviously need some sort of pause after <u>developed</u>. You can hear it when you read the sentence.

That leaves the colon and the dash, which can actually be used interchangeably in many cases, including this one. Remember that the part before a colon must be a complete sentence, and this example passes that test: <u>Its most popular attraction is also its least developed.</u> That could stand alone if we wanted it to. We associate colons with lists, so you might be inclined to eliminate Choice D because <u>Moran State Park</u> is only one thing. But colons are actually used for more than just lists.

A colon is used when the second part explains or answers a "question" that's implied by the first part. Let's test this out. We could turn the part before the colon into a question: What's the <u>most popular</u>

attraction? The answer follows the colon: <u>Moran State Park</u>. **Choice D is correct because it is an acceptable use of the colon.**

But the dash would actually be correct too! Dashes can replace pretty much every other punctuation mark, so the dash in Choice B would be a perfectly good substitute for a colon. But if we look closely, we can see that Choice B has the incorrect <u>it's</u>. We don't want to say <u>it is</u>. That's the only reason Choice B is wrong. In fact, if Choice B had said <u>its least developed—</u>, we'd have no way to know whether Choice B or Choice D were right. There would be no difference! This is a good reminder that when two punctuation answers seem like they could be correct, there's probably something else going on in the choices.

Example 4

This sentence is crazy long. It's very easy to get lost. Try to NARROW YOUR FOCUS as best you can, and apply the rules for each punctuation mark.

Choice D is, hopefully, the most obviously wrong answer. It's a run-on sentence. There are two long ideas here, and we need more than just a comma to break them apart. Since the first complete sentence ends with <u>source</u>, we need a hard stop before the next idea. A colon, period, semicolon, or dash would all be acceptable "long pauses". A comma is a "short pause", which is not enough to break the sentences apart.

Choice C is wrong because the dash inserts a long pause for no good reason. We want to just continue reading without pausing at that spot.

Choice B is wrong because the colon is used incorrectly. We'd want to complete the first idea before the colon, but the second idea is a continuation of the first idea. It's an unnecessary clause that tells us more about what happened with the pig. Another way to see it is that we want a short pause here so that the second idea flows from the first idea. A colon after <u>Island</u> would be too big of a break.

• **Choice A is correct, even if you think it's still too long of a sentence.** The colon is a hard stop, so we are allowed to use it to end the first sentence after <u>source</u>. We're also allowed to use a colon to separate two complete sentences, just like a semicolon. We'd just want to make sure that the second sentence answers or explains an implied question from the first sentence. Here's how I apply the colon test. The sentence says <u>a new conflict arose from the most unlikely source</u>. What was the source? <u>An American farmer shot an Irishman's pig</u>. The first sentence isn't literally a question, but it leaves us wanting more. The second part satisfies that curiosity.

Advanced Punctuation — The Twists

Semicolons join two complete sentences. The part before the semicolon <u>must</u> be a complete sentence, and the part after the semicolon <u>must</u> be a complete sentence.

Colons are used to answer or explain. The part before the colon <u>must</u> be a complete sentence. The part after a colon answers a question that is implied by the first part.

Colons can be followed by a full sentence, a list, or just one word.

Dashes are very versatile. They can replace pretty much every other punctuation mark. There will be exceptions where a dash cannot be used, but be open-minded about dashes.

There may be two answer choices that both use acceptable punctuation marks for a certain situation. If so, then there must be something else going on in the choices that makes one right and one wrong. Look for other punctuation or word choices that might force you to pick one answer over the other.

Answers: Advanced Punctuation

#1 — Answer = D
The middle part of the sentence is an extra clause that interrupts the main sentence. We could use two commas or two dashes to show where the

interruption starts and ends. Since the sentence already uses a comma before <u>especially</u> to start, we should be symmetrical and use a comma after <u>music</u> to end.

#2 — Answer = C

This question is all about the structure of the sentence. There are a lot of ways that <u>for example</u> could be used in a sentence, and each one would use different punctuation. In this case, <u>for example</u> is interrupting the main sentence. We could use the cross out test to remove it from the sentence to see if everything else still makes sense, and it does: <u>The pinot gris variety grows in cool climates, and other grapes are well-suited to inland soils.</u> That's a good sign that two commas would be okay. We can also look at the other choices. The colon and semicolon aren't right because the <u>and</u> is connecting two ideas that need to stay closer together. The colon and semicolon would create a hard break in the ideas. This is kind of like in the Lists & Examples packet when we couldn't use a colon because we were already using <u>such as</u>. In this question, the <u>and</u> is already showing that we're connecting two sentences. Using a colon or semicolon to do that too would be redundant.

#3 — Answer = C

The opening of this sentence is an unnecessary introductory clause. We should use a comma to connect it to the main sentence. Don't forget that Choices A and B are essentially the same because semicolons separate two complete sentences, just like periods. Choice D is wrong because we would not want to use a dash to separate an introductory clause, even if it's unnecessary.

#4 — Answer = D

The dash is behaving like a colon here. The part before the dash is a complete sentence, and the part after the dash is answering a question that's implied by the first part. What's the <u>situation</u>? <u>Escaping reform schools</u>. Be careful with Choice A. The dash is fine, but we do not want a comma after <u>escaping</u>. We use one after <u>dirty</u> because we're using multiple adjectives. Choice C is wrong because the part after the semicolon is not a complete sentence.

#5 — Answer = A

This is such a great use of the colon. The part before the colon is a complete sentence. The part after answers a question implied by the first part. What would <u>save the project</u>? <u>Larger windows</u>. This sentence shows that the colon does not need to start a list of multiple items. It's perfectly okay to use a colon to name one item. As an aside, a dash would also be acceptable here.

#6 — Answer = C

The double dash. This is why you should always read the full sentence. If you stop halfway through, you might want to use a comma because this extra clause is an appositive. But since there's a dash at the end of the clause, we should use a dash at the beginning for symmetry.

#7 — Answer = B

If you read this sentence aloud, you won't pause after <u>know</u>. That's a good sign that you don't need any punctuation. But it's worth noting how the SAT is trying to trick you here. You almost always use a comma when you use the word <u>which</u>. The SAT is trying to get you to follow your habit without thinking about the context. But in this case, <u>which</u> is not introducing an extra clause. It's an essential part of the sentence! We would never say <u>Records allow biologists to know</u>. To know what? This sentence doesn't end there. This is a great reminder that punctuation isn't really about certain words that get commas. It's about the structure of the sentence. For every comma rule we've covered in this guide, there is almost certainly a situation where you'd break it. Pay attention to the way sentences are constructed! What's essential and what's extra?

#8 — Answer = B

This is another case where the SAT is trying to trick you. They want you to see the word <u>ask</u> and immediately pick one of the choices with the question mark. But read the sentence aloud. It's not actually a question! It's a statement of what might be asked. You should be able to hear the difference between the choices, since question marks make sentences sound different.

Fragments & Run-ons

The Basics

We've talked a lot about sentence structure, essential information, and extra clauses. FRO questions are where you can really prove whether you're a grammar master.

Remember that the main strategy for the Writing section is to predict the topic of the question as you go so that your brain knows what to look for as it reads. Punctuation questions are usually very easy to identify because all of the choices will have the exact same wording, but the punctuation marks will be different. FRO questions may not look like that. Their answer choices may vary the punctuation, but they may also vary the wording very slightly. You may think you're dealing with a Style question, where you can just pick the shortest choice. But FRO questions are almost always trying to trick you, so the shortest choice may actually create a run-on sentence or some other structural problem.

Example 1

For this question, I'd know to worry about run-ons because the choices seems to center around a comma/period. That's a good sign that we're changing the structure of the sentence. It also means that multiple choices might sound correct because run-on sentences will not sound bad. They'll sound like two complete sentences! The problem isn't the wording — it's the punctuation.

- Choice A is wrong because it creates a run-on sentence. This is a favorite of students and teachers alike could stand alone as a sentence, so we can't use only a comma to join it to the first sentence. This choice sounds correct, though, so you have to be careful.

- Choice B is wrong because A favorite of students and teachers alike is not a complete sentence. It's a fragment of a sentence, so we cannot use a period.

- Choice C is correct because it takes the second clause and turns it into an appositive. Essentially, it's describing Pride and Prejudice. Since it's an unnecessary clause with extra information, we are allowed to use just a comma to attach it to the main sentence.

- Choice D is wrong because this makes it a run-on sentence. Hopefully, you also think that being sounds really bad.

Choice C might also seem correct because it's the shortest choice. That's more an added benefit than a solid reason to pick Choice C. As we'll see, the shortest choice might not be right if it creates a run-on sentence.

Example 2

This question doesn't initially look like a punctuation question at all. There's no punctuation in any of the choices! But a grammar master would notice that the underlined portion is directly after a comma — a sign that we might need to think about the structure of the sentence.

If you're only going by how the sentence sounds, you might have a lot of trouble with this question. All of the choices sound fine to me! But all of the choices with pronouns — Choices A, B, and D — create a run-on sentence. A pronoun is essentially a new subject, which creates a new sentence by introducing a new idea. The word which has a special power to turn separate ideas into unnecessary clauses (fragments) that we can attach to the main sentence with a comma. **Choice C is the only one that lets us connect these ideas with just a comma.**

If this is getting grammatically confusing, you can use a shortcut to get most of these questions right. In general, the best way to fix run-on sentences is to replace a pronoun with which. There are definitely exceptions, but they come up so rarely that this rule should work most of the time.

Fragments & Run-ons — The Basics

A run-on sentence occurs when two complete sentences that could stand alone are joined with only a comma.

There are many ways to fix run-on sentences:
- turn the second sentence into an unnecessary clause, like an appositive
- replace the pronoun with which
- replace the comma with a semicolon, colon, or dash
- rephrase something so that one of the parts is not a complete sentence

The Twists

Example 3

The SAT is going to try to trick you. None of these choices sound great. You might not even think about run-on sentences if you saw this question on an SAT. But notice that the underlined portion is right next to a comma — that's a big clue that sentence structure is important!

Choices C and D probably sound the best, but both would create run-on sentences. Just read the second part aloud with Choice C: Both of them are polling in the single digits. Doesn't that sound like a complete thought? There's an action (are polling) and something doing the action (both of them). Even without the them, we'd have a run-on in Choice D.

Choice B seems to follow our "replace pronouns with which" rule. But it's actually not correct. Choice A is essentially using the same rule, but whom is the better word to use, even though it sounds very strange. Basically, whom is the same as which, except that we use whom (and who) for people and which for things. **Since we're talking about candidates, we should use whom, so Choice A is surprisingly correct.**

Fragments & Run-ons — The Twists

Pay attention to the answer choices and the punctuation that's close to the underlined portion. It can be hard to tell when you need to worry about run-ons, but there are usually clues if you know what to look for. Look for commas!

Which is a helpful word to turn sentences into unnecessary clauses and fix run-ons. Occasionally other words will do the same job but for other situations: who/whom is for people, where is for places, and when is for times.

Not Only ... But Also

Example 4

For some reason, the SAT really likes this phrasing. It's a valid way to construct sentences, but you tend to see it on the SAT more often than in your daily life. Just knowing it exists should be enough to eliminate Choices B and C.

Between the two that are left, most people will pick Choice D because it's shorter, and it is indeed correct. But there will be situations where not only... but also is used but the shortest choice is wrong.

In this case, we do not need to repeat it or benefits because those words already appear in the sentence before the start of the not only. I like to think of not only... but also like a math equation with parentheses. Everything before the parentheses gets distributed to the parts inside:

There are benefits (not only for tourists but also for local residents.)

Since benefits is before the parenthesis, it gets "distributed" to both the not only part and the but also part.

But you can also write a version of this sentence where it doesn't get distributed, in which case you'd need to repeat yourself:

(Not only are there benefits for tourists but there are also benefits for local residents.)

Since not only starts the sentence, there's nothing to "distribute". We would need to repeat ourselves to maintain the symmetry of the sentence.

If this is hard to understand, don't worry. You can usually "hear" the correct answer for a not only… but also question, but they're also not as frequently tested on the SAT as other rules.

Just As … So Too

Example 5

The title gives it away. **Choice B is the answer.** I wasn't trying to trick you here. I just wanted you to see a sentence with this construction in case it comes up on your own SAT. The odds that it will are very, very low. Still, I think it's the kind of thing that you might remember if you see it once.

Not Only … But Also & Just As … So Too

Try to think of not only… but also as a set of parentheses. Everything before the not only gets "distributed" to the but also, so you won't have to repeat yourself.

Just as… so too exists, so now you know.

Answers: Fragments & Run-ons

#1 — Answer = C
We would know that this is testing run-ons because the underlined portion is very close to a comma. The correct answer follows our rule: fix run-on sentences by replacing pronouns with which. Notice that all of the other choices would be shorter, but they all create run-on sentences. Some lost 25 percent is a complete thought!

#2 — Answer = C
Here's an example where we have nothing to "distribute" over the not only… but also. We need to

repeat the fireworks display again in the but also part. Luckily, we're still allowed to use pronouns to shorten things a bit.

#3 — Answer = D
We would know this question is testing run-on sentences because the underlined portion is right next to a comma. Choices A and B are run-on sentences. Choice C sounds awful. By deleting the underlined portion, you turn a complete sentence into an unnecessary clause that simply describes Cynthia Rogers.

#4 — Answer = A
This one is a little strange, but Choices B and C would both turn this introductory clause into a complete sentence. Choice D sounds bad. Choice A keeps the clause an incomplete thought (a fragment) that we can attach to the main sentence with a comma.

#5 — Answer = C
We would know this question is testing run-on sentences because the underlined portion is messing with the wording right around a comma. Be very careful with Choice D! Many people read this sentence incorrectly, thinking that the are is also underlined. It's not, so it stays in the sentence no matter what we pick. Choices A and B would be run-on sentences because they create a new complete sentence by following the comma with a pronoun and noun. Choice C lets us continue the thought by making a list of 2 things: The flies and mosquitos are swarming and are biting. It sounds a little strange, but it's grammatically correct.

#6 — Answer = D
This is the rare case where the sentence is a fragment, which is an incomplete sentence that needs to be lengthened to be able to stand on its own. As written, the sentence does not have a subject — there's nobody doing the donating. Choice D is the longest answer, but we need to pick it to add a subject to the sentence.

#7 — Answer = B
We'd know this is testing run-on sentences because it's changing the punctuation in the underlined

portion. Choice C is wrong because the part after the semicolon could not stand alone as a complete sentence. Adding it would make it a complete sentence, but that would create run-ons if we still used a comma. Choice B keeps the comma but fixes the run-on by dropping the pronoun and turning the sentence into an extra clause.

#8 — Answer = A

Again, the underlined portion includes a comma, so we should worry about sentence structure. Choices C and D would create run-on sentences because we need more than just a comma to connect these two ideas. Choices A and B would fix the run-on by using a comma and a conjunction. Conjunctions are sometimes shortened to FANBOYS, which stands for for, and, nor, but, or, yet, so. These words, like which, have a special power that lets them connect two sentences with a comma. They have different meanings, and Choice B would be wrong because the two ideas are not in a cause/effect relationship. Choice A is simple without creating a run-on sentence.

Pronouns lesson

The Basics

A pronoun is a short word that replaces a noun so that you can talk about the noun without constantly repeating yourself. For most Pronoun questions, all you need to remember is:

- its = singular
- their = plural

- it's = it is
- they're = they are
- there = not a pronoun

You know this rule in simple situations:

The dog wagged its tail. (singular)
The dogs wagged their tails. (plural)

In these examples, dog and dogs are called the antecedents because they are the words that the

pronouns replace. Since dog is singular, we use the singular pronoun its to refer back to it. When we use the plural dogs, we need to use the plural pronoun their instead.

Example 1

The SAT is going to complicate things by giving you sentences that include multiple nouns. In this example, many people think that the pronoun its is referring to the menu. But you can turn the sentence into a question to check: what has freshness and cost? Menus aren't fresh, and they don't have a cost. Ingredients, on the other hand, can be fresh and they have a cost. The underlined pronoun refers back to the ingredients. **Since ingredients is plural, we need to use the plural pronoun their, so Choice C is correct.**

For almost every Pronoun question, you should be able to eliminate two choices right away. You're almost done with high school. You should not be confusing its and it's or their, there, and they're. There is no excuse for picking Choices B and D.

Example 2

The main problem with Pronoun questions is that we get this rule wrong so often in our daily lives that we can't trust our instincts. Read the sentence for this example. How does it sound? Most people would say that Choice D is the best answer because it sounds natural. Unfortunately, it's wrong.

The underlined pronoun is referring to the singular a teacher at the beginning of the sentence. Their is a plural pronoun, so we'd be violating the rule if we used it. Choice A is singular, but it would be weird to refer to a person as an it, even if we're talking about a hypothetical person. **Instead, we should use his or her, which makes Choice B correct.**

But would you ever say this sentence with Choice B if you were talking to your friends? I wouldn't! It sounds weird. And this is why it's so important to use the answer choices to predict the question before you start reading. You need to recognize that the SAT is testing Pronouns so that you can actively apply the singular/plural rule. You should <u>not</u> use your instincts to answer Pronoun questions. In some cases, you're so used to getting this rule wrong that the right answer will actually sound wrong. Success on the SAT Writing section comes from learning to recognize when you can trust your instincts and when you need to fight them to apply a strict grammar rule.

Pronouns — The Basics

<u>Its</u> is a singular pronoun.

<u>His or her</u> is a singular pronoun.

<u>Their</u> is a plural pronoun.

Singular pronouns must replace singular nouns, and plural pronouns must replace plural nouns.

Turn the sentence into a question so you can figure out what the pronoun is referring to.

Do <u>not</u> trust your instincts. Always apply the rule. We get the Pronoun rules wrong a lot in our daily lives, so you won't have a good sense of what's right and wrong just based on how the sentence sounds.

The Twists

Example 3

This question isn't technically about pronouns, but you should be able to recognize that it's testing the same rules. Remember, use the answer choices to predict the question. What are the differences between these choices? Some are singular and some are plural. That's a huge clue that you need to match the choice with something else in the sentence that's either singular or plural!

The sentence talks about <u>any civilian</u> and <u>the owner</u>, which are both singular nouns. We should match these words with another singular noun. **Only Choice B is singular, so it must be correct.** Sometimes you can figure out the right answer by playing a game of "one of these things is not like the other". Choices A, C, and D are all plural, which is a

strong clue that Choice B is right because it's the odd one out. Ideally, you'll recognize the rule and apply it without having to guess.

Example 4

This question looks like a typical Pronoun question, so you'd probably just start looking for nouns that <u>they</u> could be referring to. Without looking too hard, you should recognize that <u>the trees</u> are important for preventing erosion.

Except that's not quite right. Looking at the choices, we'd see that maybe it's the <u>tree roots</u> that are important. Someone else might look at these sentences and think that <u>they</u> is actually referring to the <u>scientists</u>. After all, I'm sure a few of those scientists think very highly of themselves. The fact that there are a few different things that <u>they</u> can refer to is a big problem.

Pronouns are helpful tools that let us shorten our sentences, but we always need to know what the pronouns are replacing. As written, the sentence is an example of an ambiguous pronoun, which is a pronoun that has multiple possible meanings. When this happens, we need to ditch the pronoun and say specifically what we're referring to. **Choice C may be the longest answer, but we need to pick it for the sake of clarity.**

The SAT does not test ambiguous pronouns often, but you should be able to recognize when they do test it because the answer choices will include a version that specifies the noun. As a general rule of thumb, if the SAT gives you the option to specify the noun, you should choose that answer. You may be smart enough to know what the sentence is supposed to mean, but we should assume that other people won't be as smart as you!

Pronouns — The Twists

Singular and plural rules also apply to nouns that refer back to other nouns. If you notice that the answer choices are a mixture of singular and plural options, look for something in the sentence that matches. Treat it like a regular Pronoun question.

Avoid ambiguous pronouns. If it's unclear what the pronoun is referring to, you should take the time to write out the specific noun.

If the SAT gives you a choice that includes the noun instead of a pronoun, you should take the offer to specify and be clear.

Answers: Pronouns

#1 — Answer = C

The pronoun refers to the university, which is singular. Even though a university has multiple students and faculty members, it's still a single university.

#2 — Answer = C

The pronoun refers to Ethiopian scholars, which is plural. Choices A and B are both singular. Choice D sounds terrible.

#3 — Answer = D

The pronoun refers to corn, which is singular. (It's not corns.) This sentence is unusual because the pronoun comes before the noun it refers to.

#4 — Answer = C

Since they are never specified in the sentences, we need to get rid of the pronoun and make it clear who they are. We don't actually know until we look at the choices. The it isn't ambiguous because the sentence is referring to the symbol. Choice D is technically shorter, but it hopefully sounds pretty bad to you.

#5 — Answer = B

The pronoun refers to the bookstore, which is singular.

#6 — Answer = D

Once again, the pronoun is ambiguous. You might not think that there's anything wrong with this sentence, but the answer choices are a big clue that we're dealing with an ambiguous pronoun. Remember, if the SAT gives you the option to specify, you should almost always choose that answer. In this case, it's best if we specify that we're referring to the trend.

#7 — Answer = D

The pronoun refers to gold and silver, which is plural. This one is tricky because, individually, gold and silver are both singular. But the and means that we're talking about them together, so we need a plural pronoun. Just think about it logically: two things are getting polished.

#8 — Answer = B

The answer choices strongly suggest that we need to care about singular and plural nouns. Find a matching noun in the sentence. A candidate is singular, so we need another singular noun. Only Choice B is singular.

Verb Agreement lesson

The Basics

Verb Agreement is one of the most complex grammar rules on the SAT. If you can understand this rule, you should be able to get a great score.

Our brains know this rule intuitively — in most cases. Every time we speak, our brain decides whether to use singular or plural verbs without us ever realizing it, and we almost always get it right. We would immediately know something was wrong if we heard The penguins waddles across the ice.

But the SAT isn't going to test the obvious situations. What's more, the very fact that we have four options will make us second guess our instincts, even when the sentence is relatively easy to follow. Like with Pronouns, you should not use your instincts for Verb Agreement questions. Always assume that these questions are difficult and diligently apply the rule.

Example 1

You can probably hear the correct answer for this one. But many people look at these answer choices and assume that the SAT is asking for the correct tense. Actually, the tense of the verb works itself out if you first pay attention to singular and plural.

The subject of the sentence is <u>ways</u>, which is plural. **The only choice with a plural verb is Choice B, so it must be right, regardless of the tense.** Choices A, C, and D are all singular because the verbs end with S. Remember that all singular verbs end with S, which is the opposite of what you'd expect. You usually think of nouns as plural when they end with S, so it can be difficult to change your thinking to accommodate the verbs. If you have trouble, think of simple sentences where the correct verb is obvious, like the two <u>penguin</u> sentences at the beginning. Your brain is very good at knowing the correct verb when the sentences are simple.

Example 1 is unusual because the verb comes before the subject. Still, you can hear the correct answer a little better once you cross off all of the extra pieces to get down to the core of the sentence: <u>There are many ways.</u> We'll see that crossing off extra clauses is the key to mastering Verb Agreement.

Verb Agreement — The Basics

Singular verbs end in S.
- <u>waddles</u>
- <u>drives</u>
- <u>runs</u>
- <u>is</u>
- <u>has</u>
- <u>was</u>

Plural verbs do <u>not</u> end in S.
- <u>waddle</u>
- <u>drive</u>
- <u>run</u>
- <u>are</u>
- <u>have</u>
- <u>were</u>

Singular verbs <u>must</u> be used with singular subjects. Plural verbs <u>must</u> be used with plural subjects.

You can usually hear the correct subject/verb pairing when the sentences are simple. The SAT will always make things more complicated!

The Twists

Example 2

The SAT will usually try to hide the subject by separating it from the verb. The subject is always essential to the sentence. In other words, you can't have a complete sentence without a subject, so the subject won't ever be in extra clauses.

In this example, there's a long descriptive clause that interrupts the main sentence. It's a distraction. Cross it off to better understand the subject of the underlined verb. The main sentence should be easy to hear once you get rid of the interruption: <u>These portraits has not been publicly displayed since 1953.</u> That sounds bad, right? **It should clearly be <u>These portraits have not been displayed</u>, which makes Choice D correct.**

Once you eliminate extra clauses, your brain will usually be able to hear the correct answer. But the SAT is trying to trick you into thinking that another noun is the subject — his wife. First of all, that doesn't really make sense: his wife has not been publicly displayed? That's not what the sentence is trying to say. But notice that wife is singular. The SAT is deliberately putting a noun that's singular next to a verb that's supposed to be plural. They do this a lot! It's super mean, but if you learn to expect this trick, you're more likely to avoid it.

Verb Agreement — The Twists

The subject of a verb is an essential part of the sentence, so it won't be in an unnecessary clause.

Cross out unnecessary clauses so that you can bring the subject closer to the verb.

Be careful of fake subjects that are very close to the verb!

Prepositional Phrases

Example 3

This is the hardest aspect of the Verb Agreement rule, and it's very likely that the SAT will use it to try to trick you.

A preposition is a small word that adds extra information to a sentence in the form of a prepositional phrase. A lot of prepositions indicate location: under, on, over, around, between, in, within... But others are hard to describe or put into a category. They're just small words that we usually ignore: of, for, with, to, from, in, on...

Prepositional phrases give us more information about something in a sentence. But since they're technically extra information, they cannot contain the subject of the sentence. This sounds very similar to the rules we used for Example 2, but it's much harder to apply because we won't have commas telling us where the extra clauses begin. Plus, the information in prepositional phrases often seems essential, so

you'll be less inclined to cross it out. And the worst part is that the SAT is still going to try to trick you by putting the wrong kind of noun next to the verb so that you feel confident in a wrong answer.

Example 3 starts out with an unnecessary introductory clause that we can cross out to find the main sentence, which is the meaning of his tweets is unknown. The SAT wants you to think that we need a plural verb (Choice B) because tweets is plural. However, tweets is part of a prepositional phrase, so it can't be the subject. In fact, we can cross out the entire prepositional phrase: of his tweets. Although it may be very helpful to understand the ideas in the sentence, it's not grammatically necessary.

Now the main sentence has been reduced to the meaning is unknown. That sounds okay! You can try the other choices, and you'll hear that they don't sound good. The meaning are unknown sounds terrible. **Using the Verb Agreement rule, meaning is singular, so we need the singular verb is, which makes Choice A correct.** This example was relatively short, so finding the subject didn't take very long. They're going to get more complicated.

Prepositional Phrases

Prepositional phrases are short unnecessary clauses that can be crossed out of a sentence.

Unlike other unnecessary clauses, prepositional phrases do not usually begin or end with commas, so they're harder to recognize.

Prepositional phrases always start with prepositions, which are short words that we usually ignore. Start looking for them when you're thinking about verbs!

The most common prepositions on the SAT are of, for, from, to, with, in, and on.

The SAT will use prepositional phrases to trick you, putting a plural noun right next to a verb that's supposed to be singular. Assume you're being tricked and plan accordingly!

The prepositional phrase rule only applies to Verb Agreement. Do not cross out prepositional phrases when you're looking at singular and plural pronouns.

Answers: Verb Agreement

#1 — Answer = D

Cross out the prepositional phrases of the various nuances and in Weber's poetry. The main sentence should be An understanding lead to a greater appreciation. If you pronounce lead correctly, this sentence will sound bad. (Remember that as a verb, lead rhymes with seed. The past tense of lead is led, which is given to you in Choice C. Lead only rhymes with bed when you're talking about the metal.) Once you've shortened the sentence, you can apply the Verb Agreement rule. An understanding is singular, so we need the singular verb leads. Don't forget that singular verbs end in S! Choices A, B, and C are all plural.

#2 — Answer = C

The phrase that feed at night is extra, so we can cross it out of the sentence. The subject is animals, which is

plural. We need the plural verb rely to agree. Choices A, B, and D are all singular.

#3 — Answer = B

Cross out the prepositional phrases of the speech and to the delegates. The subject is the last few minutes, which is plural. We need the plural verb feature. Choices A and D are singular. Choice C sounds bad.

#4 — Answer = C

This sentence is very hard to understand without the prepositional phrase of the trophies, but it makes sense with or without it that all is plural. Choices A and B are singular, so we can eliminate them. Choice D sounds bad, which leaves Choice C. Interestingly, represented is neither singular nor plural. It can be both! Just think of two simple sentences: He represented the criminal and They represented the criminal. They both sound fine because represented won't change based on the subject. In fact, verbs are only really singular or plural when they're in the present tense. The exceptions are was/were and has/have. This question is a good example of why you should always check for singular and plural before you worry about tense. The answer choices will make you think that tense matters, but it might not. If you find the correct subject, it's likely that some of the tenses will be eliminated. At the least, it'll be easier to choose the correct tense if you have fewer options.

#5 — Answer = A

Cross out the prepositional phrase of the population showing symptoms. The subject is the portion, which is singular. It might seem plural because it's referencing multiple people, but it's grammatically singular — it's not portions. Choice B is plural, so it can be eliminated. Choice C would make the sentence sound incomplete. Choice D is singular, but other parts of the sentence make it clear that we need the past tense. Choice A is in the past tense, and was is singular.

#6 — Answer = A

Cross out the prepositional phrase at the State University of New Jersey. The subject is students, which is plural. Choices B, C, and D are all singular.

Choice A is correct because all the other choices are wrong.

#7 — Answer = D

It's very important that you cross out the prepositional phrase in sea level. Some people think that the subject is hurricanes, but it's not. The hurricanes are actually the subject of the plural verb cause. This sentence contains multiple subject/verb pairs, which is actually pretty common. Complex sentences can have multiple clauses that are grammatically complete sentences. The subject that we care about is changes, which is plural. So we need to use the plural verb erode. But there's more! Choices C and D both start with the correct verb. The difference is in a second verb at the end. Since we're still talking about the changes, we still need the plural verb threaten. In this case, one subject has two verbs because the changes both erode and threaten.

#8 — Answer = B

Cross out the prepositional phrase to multiple activities and the interruption including sports. The subject is commitment, which is singular. We need the singular verb creates.

Symmetry lesson

The Basics

The key to Symmetry questions is finding matches. For almost every question, you should be able to point to another part of the sentence to prove your answer.

Example 1

Once again, we're given choices that suggest we need to figure out the correct tense. We should check for Verb Agreement, but that won't help us here. So how do we decide the correct tense? It's less about the past, present, or future, and more about the structure of the sentence. Hopefully, you'll notice that this sentence is a list. When we make a list, all of the parts of the list need to be in the same format.

If we cross out some of the extra parts of the list, we'll see that the three components are calls, demands, and prioritizes. That should eliminate Choices B and C easily. All of the verbs need to fit the same format, which is the singular present tense here.

It's a little harder to decide between Choices A and D because both include prioritizes. **In general, we should pick shorter choices, which would correctly bring us to Choice D.** However, this is about more than just shorter answers. We don't need the it because it's already there. Placing it before calls allows us to "distribute" the it to all parts of the list, so it would be redundant to include it.

If we were to include the it, we'd disrupt the symmetry of the list: it calls, demands, and it prioritizes. Since the second part of the list doesn't include an it, we don't want it on the third part either. This wouldn't be efficient, but we could include the it if we attached it to all three parts of the list: it calls, it demands, and it prioritizes. This version might be wordy, but at least it's symmetrical.

Example 2

This sentence doesn't have a list of three things, but you could consider it a list of two. Regardless, the choices are once again hinting that tense matters. You might be able to get the answer just by seeing what feels right, but you should try to follow a process and find a matching word that proves your answer.

In this case, we can break the main sentence down to better understand what's happening. The revolutionary forces are doing two things: they overtook the garrison and began the process. Notice how the two verbs are now in the same past tense. They even sound like they're continuing a rhythm. **Choice D puts the word in the tense that matches with overtook, so we can be pretty confident that it's right.** Choice C is also the past tense, but there's no other had in this sentence, so we don't have a good match for Choice C.

The Twists

This next version of symmetry is a little different. What do you think of the sample sentence? What are they saying? Rebecca has longer hair than Mike does, right? Wrong! This sentence actually says that Rebecca's hair is longer than Mike's entire body. That obviously doesn't make sense, and we probably didn't think that while we read it. That's because our brains are very good at fixing the grammar error in this sentence without us even realizing it. It's a bad comparison.

Without any apostrophes at the end, this sentence isn't comparing what we want to compare. We need to make this comparison symmetrical by matching Rebecca's hair with Mike's hair. And there are three main ways we can fix this sentence:

- Rebecca's hair is longer than Mike's hair.
- Rebecca's hair is longer than Mike's.
- Rebecca's hair is longer than that of Mike.

When we speak, we're much more likely to say the first or second version. The third version sounds very weird, but it's actually how the SAT tends to fix bad symmetry, so you need to get used to it.

Example 3

The word than is a dead giveaway that the sentence includes a comparison. When you see than, you should immediately think about symmetry. The

choices also make it clear that symmetry is the issue, since they all include the second part of the comparison. Match it to the first part!

What is the sentence comparing. It's saying that certain diseases and parasites are more harmful than others. Choice A is very short, but it's wrong because it's not talking about diseases and parasites. It's comparing the diseases and parasites to fruits! Symmetry questions will often violate the Concision Rule, so it's very important that you learn to recognize these questions within the full Writing section.

Choices B and C both fix the bad symmetry so that we're comparing diseases and parasites to other diseases and parasites. The final decision comes down to singular and plural pronouns. Since diseases and parasites is plural, we should use the plural pronoun those. **Choice C fixes the symmetry and uses the correct pronoun.** It still sounds weird, but that's just how we fix bad comparisons on the SAT!

Answers: Symmetry

#1 — Answer = C

Revealed matches with reflected earlier in the sentence. Choice B is wrong because has is singular, but chips and scratches is plural. Choice A is wrong because we have no evidence that we need the had. It's not on reflected, so it's not necessary.

#2 — Answer = C

Choice D would compare the size and layout to the terminals. That's not symmetrical. We want to compare the size and layout at one airport to the size and layout at larger airports. Choices A, B, and C all include the necessary pronoun, but only Choice C includes the plural pronoun necessary to match with the plural size and layout. These is plural, but hopefully Choice B sounds bad to you.

#3 — Answer = C

This sentence is a list. Find the matching verbs: to steal, access, and record. That eliminates Choices A and D. Choice B is wrong because we do not need another to because there's no to on access.

#4 — Answer = A

This one is tricky! Students who aren't paying attention will match accumulating and dispensing and pick Choice B. But that's not correct because it would suggest that the snow can dispense with the symmetrical layout. It's snow. It can't design a church. Instead, we want to say that the design is doing two things: it featured a steep roof and dispensed with the layout. Sometimes you need to use the ideas in the sentence to find the matching verb.

#5 — Answer = B

The sentence contains a list. Keep the rhythm: the petroglyphs are on walls, in ruins, and on rock formations. There's no need to make the last part of the list any longer. It doesn't add useful information. It's preferable to keep the symmetry and keep it short.

#6 — Answer = D

Not only… but also sentences also need to be symmetrical. Since the verb after not only is promotes, we want the verb after but also to be in the same tense. That eliminates Choices B and C. Choice A is wrong because the it is already implied when cultural society is mentioned before the not only. (See the Fragments & Run-ons lesson for more information about not only… but also.)

#7 — Answer = C

The word than tells us we're making a comparison. We want to compare a transformation to a transformation. Choice D would not establish symmetry. Choices A, B, and C all use pronouns to refer to the transformation, but only Choice C uses the correct singular pronoun that.

#8 — Answer = D

Once again, make sure you're finding the correct matching verb in the sentence. Shorten the sentence to help you: it might anger, as well as violate. Choice B is tempting because it matches with sampling, but sampling isn't used as a verb in this sentence. It's actually the noun: sampling might anger and violate.

Modifiers lesson

The Basics

These questions will be hard to recognize because the answer choices will be on the longer side. They'll also be very similar to each other, so you might think it's more about Style than Grammar. But if you can get good at spotting Modifier questions as you go through the Writing section, you'll be able to add on some quick and easy points.

This first sentence might not sound that bad. You probably know what it's trying to say, but it doesn't actually say it. The first sentence suggests that the mailman has a tail. Yikes! We obviously mean that the dog has a tail. The second sentence makes that clear by rearranging the words.

The overall rule is that modifiers must be immediately followed by whatever they're modifying. **A modifier is a descriptive clause, usually at the beginning of the sentence.** Modifiers give a little extra information about something. When we write, we should follow the modifier and comma with whatever we were just talking about. Otherwise, we might confuse our readers or insult our mailman.

A good way to figure out what the modifier is talking about is to turn it into a question: what has a tail that's wagging playfully? The dog does. So we want to follow the comma with the dog. It's okay that we add the adjective happy to it because the main idea right after the comma is still the dog.

Example 1

Who left his job to travel the world? He did. **Only Choice D starts with he, so it's the only option.** You don't really need to bother reading past the first two or three words of the other choices to know that they're wrong. That's why Modifiers questions can be a great way to boost your score. They don't come up that often on the SAT, but when they do, the answer can be found quickly and easily.

Example 2

Who is speaking about his decades of experience? The professor is. That eliminates Choice C for sure, but the others seem okay. In fact, this question involves a common twist — apostrophes. Even though Choice A seems like the professor follows the comma like it's supposed to, it's actually the lecture that we're talking about. Apostrophes basically turn nouns into adjectives, so professor's is really just describing the real topic of the sentence — the lecture. And the lecture is not speaking about anything.

If you can remember the apostrophe twist, you'll be able to confidently eliminate Choices A and D. **That leaves Choice B as the only answer that actually starts with the topic of the modifier — the professor.**

Modifiers — The Basics

Modifiers are usually introductory clauses that provide extra information about something in the main sentence.

Modifiers must be followed by the thing that they modify. In other words, the topic of the clause should be the first topic discussed in the main sentence.

You can quickly answer Modifiers questions by turning the modifier into a question. The answer should be the main idea right after the comma.

The Twists

Example 3

It's very annoying when the SAT underlines the entire sentence. But it usually means that there's a modifier somewhere in the sentence that needs to be placed in the right spot. In this example, the modifier isn't at the beginning of the sentence. The modifier is hidden among the old books, and we can still turn it into a question: what was hidden among the books? The map was. We need to put the modifier near the thing it's modifying. Choices A, B, and D make it sound like the historian is hidden. **Only Choice C puts the modifier near the map.**

Example 4

This example puts another twist on the modifier rules. The which tells us that we're adding extra information about something. Once again, we can turn it into a question: what uses two flags? Semaphore does.

This time, we can't move the modifier, so we need to rearrange the other clause to bring semaphore closer to the definition of it. **Choice B is correct because it places semaphore right next to the which.**

Modifiers — The Twists

The modifier rules still apply when descriptive clauses are in the middle of a sentence. The goal is to bring descriptive clauses close to whatever they're describing.

The shortest choice might not be correct, so always follow the modifier rules.

Answers: Modifiers

#1 — Answer = D
The modifier is covered with symmetrical bumps because it's describing something in the sentence. What's covered with bumps? The salamander. None

of the choices put the modifier directly next to the salamander, but it also makes sense that its skin would be covered in bumps, so Choice D is right. All of the other choices make it sound like the biologist is covered in bumps.

#2 — Answer = A

What's good for both the environment and the economy? Organic food production. It's not an obvious answer to the question, but none of the other choices make sense.

#3 — Answer = B

This sentence has an unusual feature — parentheses. You should get in the habit of noticing unusual things in Writing questions. They're good clues about which rules matter. What is a waxy substance produced by sperm whales? Ambergris is. Choice A is wrong because it makes it seem like the trade is the topic of the parenthetical. Choices C and D suggest luxury goods are the topic. Only Choice B puts ambergris right next to its definition.

#4 — Answer = D

Who had his first catering job? The baker did. Only Choice D starts with the baker. Remember that the apostrophes in Choices B and C make the cake the topic of the sentence.

#5 — Answer = A

What has an emphasis on rules and reasoning? Geometry does. You may think that Choices B, C, and D add some harmless descriptive words, but it's still better to put geometry right after the modifier.

#6 — Answer = B

The modifier is the clause that's between the two dashes. Who is the founder of Impressionism? Monet is. We want Monet to be right up against that first dash, which only happens in Choice B.

#7 — Answer = C

Who has debt piling up? Cindy does. Only Choice C starts with Cindy.

Concision lesson

The Basics

Example 1

Choice D is right because it's shortest. That's the most important Style rule on the SAT — keep it concise! Sometimes there are clear reasons why longer answers are wrong. In this example, all of the other answer choices repeat information for no good reason. We already know that the chameleon is rare. Saying it's uncommon doesn't add anything. We're being redundant.

This rule can be difficult for some students because you're been trained to write more. For every class essay, you have gotten in the habit of padding your sentences with extra words so that you can hit that word count faster. That's a bad habit, not just for the SAT but for life, in general. Good writers don't use unnecessary words.

Example 2

If we know that the SAT prefers shorter choices, we should feel comfortable deleting this underlined portion. **Choice D is correct because the underlined words are a definition of prevaricated.** It may be helpful to know the definition, but the wording of the choices doesn't seem like we're providing an essential definition. It seems like we're just repeating something that the reader is supposed to already know. We have to trust our instincts here and go with the shortest choice.

Concision — The Basics

Short is good on the SAT.

Avoid redundancy. If an idea already appears in the sentence, you don't need to repeat it.

The Concision Rule only applies when there are no actual grammar rules that need to be followed first. If you can't find a grammar rule that applies to the sentence, then you can just pick the shortest answer choice.

If you're ever guessing on a Writing question that tests Grammar or Style (no actual question), then you can just pick the shortest choice.

The Twists

`Example 3`

Don't think that more words or complicated phrases make you sound smarter. Concision and clarity overlap a lot. If you use too many words, your readers will get lost in your ideas. Make your point quickly and efficiently. **Choice A says exactly what we need it to without burdening this sentence with unnecessary words.**

`Example 4`

You can probably hear that Choice A is redundant — we don't need to say identify twice. Choice B isn't as obviously repetitive, but plus and also basically mean the same thing. Choice D sounds weird. **Choice C gets the point across quickly and efficiently.** You should hear that it sounds best!

Concision — The Twists

Writing more words does not make you more smart. When you write your SAT Essay, make sure you obey the Concision Rule. Be clear and concise!

Answers: Concision

#1 — Answer = B
All of these choices say that where you stay and where you eat are not expensive. It's hard to pinpoint exactly what's wrong with each wrong answer. But it's easy to see that Choice B is the shortest, so it's the best.

#2 — Answer = D
We've already said that we're talking about secrets. There's no need to say that they're hidden, undisclosed, or withheld, which all mean that they're secret. Don't be redundant.

#3 — Answer = A
Choice B is wordy because in a manner that is unnecessary. Choice C is redundant because the first sentence says literally the same thing. Choice D is redundant because at a later date was already said with later earlier in the sentence. Choice A is short.

#4 — Answer = D
All of these choices are relatively short, but Choice D is, in fact, the shortest. But you can also probably hear that the other choices sound a little backwards. Trust your instincts.

#5 — Answer = D
Choice A is wrong because inherited conditions would be part of a family medical history. Choice B is wrong because where they live would include environmental factors. Choice C is wrong because personal habits are lifestyle choices. Unless you can say with certainty that this information is essential, you should lean toward deleting it.

#6 — Answer = D
The beginning of the sentence says that it's an annual audit, so we don't need to say that it happens yearly. That's what annual means! Delete the redundancy.

#7 — Answer = C
A substitute is a replacement! Again, don't include extra words unless they're absolutely necessary.

Writing Vocab lesson

The Basics

Reading and Writing test vocabulary in different ways. The Reading Vocab choices will be different words with different definitions. The Writing Vocab choices will have very similar definitions. They won't be exactly the same, but they won't be different enough that the wrong answers will be obviously wrong.

You can use three things to help you find the right word. First, you should still think about the **meaning** of the words. They won't be very different, but there are usually more subtle things that make one word right and another wrong. It might be more of an instinctive response to the words, too. What do you think of when you're asked to compare butterflies and moths? They're basically the same thing, but your brain naturally stores information about them in separate places. Butterflies are pretty, but moths are usually ugly. Butterflies come out during the day, but moths come out at night. Those are very minor differences, but they might matter for a Writing question. Sometimes this is called a word's usage.

You might also end up with words that do have the exact same meaning. In those cases, you want to pick the word that's the best fit for the tone and **difficulty** of the passage. You should avoid words that are too slangy. This would include words you'd use in a text message or a casual conversation with your friends. On the other end of the spectrum, you should avoid words that are too pedantic. These words are what you might use if you were trying to sound smart. In fact, pedantic itself is an educated word for when people are trying to sound educated. Usually, you just end up sounding like you don't know what you're talking about. You should try to use words that are academic. These words are smart enough that you could use them in an essay for school but not so smart that the average reader would have trouble understanding what you mean. And that's an important lesson about good writing — you want to show that you know what you're talking about without making your reader feel lost.

But a lot of Writing Vocab questions are about what feels right. So if you're unsure, **trust your instincts**. Don't overthink it. If you grew up speaking English, then you'll have an innate sense of what words we can use in certain situations. You might not be able to explain why the right word is right, but you'll feel it in your gut. If you're not a native English speaker, then these questions will be hard for you. You can practice your English by reading newspaper articles or even watching American television. Keep exposing yourself to the English language. You'll absorb a lot of it without even realizing!

Example 1

You should be able to eliminate Choice D because it's too slangy. You keep an eye on kids when you babysit. We're talking about icebergs here. **Hopefully your instincts tell you that Choice C is correct because monitor just feels right.** But you can also tell that audit is wrong because we normally associate that word with money, like in a tax audit. And supervise also reminds us of watching children, or at least people. And that provides a good example of how the Writing Vocab questions test the meaning of the words. Both supervise and monitor mean something like watch, but we associate supervising with people, so it's not a good fit for this particular sentence.

Writing Vocab — The Basics

Think about the meaning, difficulty, and sound of the words. When in doubt, trust your instincts.

The answer choices will have similar definitions, but the words won't necessarily be interchangeable. Pay attention to what you associate the word with. What comes to mind?

If a word is too formal or too fancy, then it's probably not right. You want to pick words that are clear and easily understood by most readers.

The Twists

Example 2

This is just one of those things we say — you pump gas. **Choice C is the answer.** There's no good reason why the other choices are wrong, except that we just don't say them. An English textbook might call this an example of "idiom". In other words, pumping gas is just one of those phrases that exists in English through some accident of history. If you've been around cars in an English-speaking country, you've probably heard this phrase before.

Example 3

This is another case where you've either been exposed to this situation or you haven't. **If you have, you probably know instantly that you steep tea, so Choice A is correct.** If you don't drink tea, then you're probably going to feel like you're guessing. That's okay. You might know that pickling has to do with vegetables, marinating has to do with meats, and bathing has to do with people. All of these words are about submerging something in liquid, but only one fits the specific situation in the sentence.

Writing Vocab questions can be frustrating because there aren't really rules involved. You either know it or you don't. There might not be a good way to figure out the right answer. Just do the best you can with the knowledge you have. Hopefully you'll get lucky on the SAT and know all the vocab words. But to improve your score, you should focus on the things you can control — memorize the Grammar rules, follow the instructions in the Ideas questions. Those kinds of questions are much more predictable.

Writing Vocab — The Twists

Do the best you can. When you're unsure, guess and move on to the next question. You can always come back.

If you're struggling with the Writing section, focus instead on Ideas and Grammar questions. There are other rules that you can memorize and practice. Writing Vocab is more about luck than skill.

Answers: Writing Vocab

#1 — Answer = C
Choice A is weird. Choice B is too slangy. Choice D is not the correct definition for the situation — it's not like a boxing match. We're talking about political conflicts. That's a phrase or idea you should have heard in History class at some point.

#2 — Answer = A
Trust your instincts. Choice A should sound like the best answer by far. The crisis occurred in 1820.

#3 — Answer = B
Choice A is wrong because we'd want to say that something outlasts something else. For example, maybe the compromise outlasted Clay. But that's not what's going on here. Only one noun is involved in the action. Choice C is wrong because linger makes me think of a creepy guy, not a compromise. Choice D is wrong because it sounds weird. Sustain is close to the right meaning, but endure is just the better word.

#4 — Answer = A
Choice D is too slangy. Choice C is the wrong use. You would nurture a child, not a balance. Choice B is wrong because it makes no sense. Make sure you read it correctly. It says persevere, not preserve. The states wanted to maintain balance. That sounds like something I've heard before.

#5 — Answer = B
Choice A is wrong because the population growth isn't rough. What would that even mean? It sounds like we're estimating it, but that's not what the sentence is trying to say. Choice C is too pedantic. Plus, capricious means something like moody. Choice D is too slangy as well, even though its meaning is closer to what we're looking for. We want to say that the growth was uneven because the North grew a lot but the South grew a little.

#6 — Answer = D
This might be one where you don't have a strong feeling. The answer is Choice D because that's a way that we can use the word threatened. It's not literally

threatening, like "I'm going to hurt you if you don't become a slave state!" You might have heard someone describe some dark clouds as threatening rain. That's kind of the same way it's being used here. The other choices are typically synonyms of threaten, but they have the wrong usage for this situation.

Diction lesson

The Basics

If you thought the Writing Vocab questions were hard, then you're not going to like Diction. We're still looking at the right word(s) for the situation, but now we won't really be able to decide based on definition. This is pretty much all instinct.

Example 1

Hopefully Choice B sounds the best because it's the correct answer. Choice A is a little too long with phrases like in the expansion. Choices C and D are wrong because they're just not quite right. I wish my explanations could be better, but sometimes in English things are right because it's how we say them. There isn't a good rule we can memorize to help us.

The best I can do here is say that Choice B is the best because it's "active". The princes expanded their territory is more forceful than The princes included in their expansion. We should try to avoid "passive voice", which is a way of writing that sounds a little backwards. Here are two ways of saying the same thing:

- Active — He jumped.
- Passive — The jumping was done by him.

Notice how the second sentence is much longer than the first. It's not technically grammatically wrong, but it's bad Style. It also violates our Concision Rule, and that's a good reason why active sentences are better. They tend to be shorter, and they follow the format "something does something". Passive sentences treat the action like it's a noun, which isn't ideal. If none of this makes sense to you, don't worry. Just go with the choice that sounds best!

Example 2

Choice B is correct. I really don't have much more than that. Notice that it's not the shortest choice. This is just the way we would say this sentence, probably because someone said it this way back in the 1600s and now we're stuck with it.

Diction — The Basics

Trust your instincts. There aren't always good reasons why we choose certain words. Sometimes an answer is right simply because it's the way we've always said it.

The Twists

Example 3

Are you freaking kidding me?! I need to choose between these four tiny words? This is outrageous! Well, hopefully you know which one is right based on your gut. **You prepare for something, so Choice D is right.**

Example 4

If you cross out the extra words in this sentence, you can make it easier to hear: historians attribute [it] to the overextension. **Choice C is correct.** It's not a perfect system, but it might help you hear something that gets lost in a lengthy sentence. As always, trust your instincts.

Diction — The Twists

Try to shorten sentences by crossing out extra words. You never know what may trigger your instincts. It's all about hearing the sentence from a different perspective.

Answers: Diction

#1 — Answer = A

Choices B and C sound weird because role-played is confusing. Choice D is wrong because for is wrong. You play a role in something.

#2 — Answer = B

Choice C is wrong because it doesn't really connect the ideas. Choice D is wrong because it connects them in the wrong way. It seems to suggest that the number of accidents has happened since, or after, people fell asleep at the wheel. It's adding chronology for no reason. Choice B is more concise, so it's better than Choice A.

#3 — Answer = A

Choice A is clear and concise. There's no need to jumble up the words here.

#4 — Answer = D

The correct phrasing is that you show a willingness to do something.

#5 — Answer = B

They're talking about something being noticeable, so we should use the phrase stand out. All of the other answers are other phrases that we use with stand, but they don't apply to this specific situation where we want to say something is identifiable or solely responsible.

#6 — Answer = C

Sometimes we say that we have a reason to be optimistic. But the way this sentence is worded forces us to talk about a reason for optimism.

#7 — Answer = C

Confide means to talk in a secretive or personal way with someone else. So don't be afraid of the difficult word, especially since Choices A and C both sound bad. From there, you hopefully hear that Choice C is better.

#8 — Answer = B

You can cross out some of this sentence to better hear the words. Long periods can leave [them] with permanent damage.

Frequently Confused Words lesson

The Basics

Example 1

This is just a Pronoun question! You cannot ever confuse the possessive pronouns its and their with the similar-sounding it's, there, and they're. Remember that apostrophes on pronouns make contractions.

Beyond that, you still need to decide whether you need a singular or plural pronoun. **Since it was the committee's decision, we need the singular pronoun its, so Choice D is right.** Remember that it's just one committee, even though it's composed of many members.

Example 2

Again, don't confuse their and there. We're referring to college students, so we need the plural pronoun. There is typically used for locations or to point something out.

That gets you down to Choices A and D. Than is used for comparisons, and then is used for time. **We're clearly making a comparison, so Choice D is correct.** You're old enough that you cannot be making this mistake, even outside of the SAT!

Frequently Confused Words — The Basics

<u>its</u> is a singular pronoun: *The dog wagged its tail.*

<u>it's</u> is a contraction of <u>it is</u>: *It's cold outside.*

<u>their</u> is a plural pronoun: *The dogs wagged their tails.*

<u>there</u> is used to point something out: *The spoon is over there.*

<u>they're</u> is a contraction of <u>they are</u>: *They're going to the store later.*

<u>than</u> is used for comparisons: *This soup is hotter than the chicken.*

<u>then</u> is used for time: *I did my homework, then I went outside.*

The Twists

There are a lot of these rules! The rest of this guide is filled with short exercises that test a lot of them. There are probably a lot more that aren't in this guide. And each individual rule is unlikely to come up on any particular SAT, but as a whole, you should expect 1-3 FCW questions per exam. Like Writing Vocab and Diction, a lot of this comes down to luck. You're better off spending your time learning the Punctuation and Consistency grammar rules, but if you're approaching a perfect score, FCWs are a great place to lock in some difficult points.

Example 3

Choice D would create a run-on sentence, so it's wrong. Choice C is wrong because <u>that's</u> is a contraction of <u>that is</u>. Choice B sounds good, but <u>who's</u> is a contraction of <u>who is</u>. **Similar to Example 1, we want a possessive pronoun, which will not have an apostrophe, so Choice A is correct.**

Example 4

This is one of those rules that the SAT likes to test. <u>Affect</u> is used as a verb (think <u>affect</u> and <u>action</u> both start with A). Here, we need <u>effect</u> because the word is a noun. Notice that they say <u>a significant effect</u>, which makes it sound like we're talking about a thing.

After we've sorted through the Frequently Confused Words, we still need to decide the appropriate diction. You can probably hear that we're talking about <u>an effect on the disease</u>. **Choice A is correct.**

Frequently Confused Words — The Twists

<u>whose</u> is a possessive pronoun: *Whose book is this?*

<u>who's</u> is a contraction of <u>who is</u>: *Who's going to the movies later?*

<u>affect</u> is a verb: *The winter storm affected the remaining corn plants.*

<u>effect</u> is a noun: *The ice had an effect on the plants' roots.*

Answers: Frequently Confused Words

#1 — Answer = D

We saw <u>just as... so too</u> in the Fragments & Run-ons packet. <u>Too</u> is correct because we're emphasizing that the second part of the sentence is <u>also</u> true.

too	to
adds emphasis; means <u>also</u>	used for everything else
You're being too loud. My friend is hungry, and I am too.	*I need to go to the store to buy food.*
Hint: <u>too</u> has an extra O, so it means <u>extra</u>	

#2 — Answer = A

Since <u>pastures</u> is plural, we need the plural pronoun <u>these</u>. The correct word is <u>past</u> because we don't want a verb, which is what <u>passed</u> is.

passed	past
past tense of <u>pass</u> The car passed the house. The quarterback passed the ball. The student passed the exam.	the time before the present; beyond; by History is the study of past events. He drove past the house.
Hint: if you can turn the sentence into the present tense with <u>pass</u>, then <u>passed</u> is probably correct The car passes the house. (<u>passed</u> correct) He drove pass the house. (<u>passed</u> incorrect)	

#3 — Answer = D

Eliminate Choices B and C because <u>for</u> sounds bad. Choice D is correct because <u>lose</u> is the opposite of <u>find</u>.

lose	loose
the opposite of <u>win</u> or <u>find</u> Without its best player, the team will probably lose the game. Did you lose your keys?	the opposite of <u>tight</u> My pants are a little loose.
Hint: <u>loose</u> has an extra O, just like loose clothes have some extra room	

#4 — Answer = D

We need the plural verb <u>live</u> to match with the plural noun <u>people</u>, so Choices B and C are wrong. Choice D is correct because <u>who</u> is almost always correct. <u>The people</u> are doing the living, so we need the subject pronoun <u>who</u>.

whom	who
object pronoun, used when the person is "receiving" the action To whom did he give the present?	subject pronoun, used when the person is "doing" the action Who gave you the present?
Hint: <u>who</u> is almost always right	

#5 — Answer = B

<u>Might</u> sounds wrong. <u>Could of</u> is always wrong. You always mean <u>could have</u>.

could of would of should of	could have would have should have
always wrong	always right He could have used proper grammar, but he didn't care enough to check his work.

#6 — Answer = C

Choice B sounds bad. Choice A creates a run-on sentence. Choice C is correct because <u>who</u> is used for people, and the sentence is referring to <u>archaeologists</u>.

who	which
used for people The student, who hadn't studied, failed the exam.	used for things The university, which was very expensive, put the student on probation.
Hint: you should know this rule just by instinct; the answer choices will make it obvious that they're testing this rule, but be careful of run-on sentences	

Answers: FCW 2

#7 — Answer = C

Choices B and D should sound wrong. <u>Arise</u> is an old-timey word that won't come up often. Try to separate the phrase from the rest of the sentence. Which sounds better: <u>rising expectations</u> or <u>raising expectations</u>?

raise	rise
used with two things	used with one thing
He raised the book above his head.	*The balloon rises into the air.*
Hint: Make a simple sentence to see which one sounds better. (*He rises the book.* sounds bad)	

#8 — Answer = B

<u>By</u> and <u>for</u> sound bad, so you can eliminate Choices A and D. They are <u>agreeing to</u> a proposal, so Choice B is correct.

accept	except
to agree to	to leave out
This store accepts cash and credit cards.	*They take all credit cards except American Express.*

#9 — Answer = C

We need a plural verb to match the plural subject <u>visitors</u>. You can eliminate the singular verbs in Choices B and D. Choice C is correct because two things are involved in the action.

lay	lie
used for two things	used for one thing
He lays the blanket across the bed.	*He lies down on the bed.*

#10 — Answer = C

Eliminate Choices A and D because <u>to</u> sounds bad. Choice C is correct because we're talking about an idea or belief.

principle	principal
a belief, rule, or idea	the main thing; a leader
The principles of physics say that every action has an opposite reaction.	*The principal issue with the proposal is the cost.*
Hint: the first letter of the alphabet is A, so a <u>principal</u> (with an A) is the first, or most important, thing	

#11 — Answer = D

We need the plural pronoun <u>their</u> to match with the plural noun <u>students</u>. Eliminate Choices B and C because they have the singular pronoun <u>his or her</u>. Choice D is correct because the sentence is about spending time, not the body part.

waste	waist
to spend or use unwisely	the hips
Stop wasting time. Don't waste your money.	*Wrap the towel around your waist.*

#12 — Answer = A

You should be able to hear that <u>in</u> is wrong, so you can eliminate Choices C and D. Choice A is correct because the sentence is about the <u>path</u> of history.

course	coarse
path, route, track, program	rough, not smooth
I have to take a course on algebra. *The course of the river winds through the canyon.*	*The coarse sweater made me itchy.*
Hint: <u>coarse</u> has a very narrow meaning, so if you're not talking about something being <u>rough</u>, then you probably want to use <u>course</u>	

Answers: FCW 3

#13 — Answer = C

Choice B is wrong because we do not want to say <u>it</u> <u>is</u>. Choice C is correct because we're talking about moving a liquid.

pour	poor	pore
to move liquid; to flow	not rich; unfortunate	small opening in the skin
Please, pour me some tea.	*That poor boy has no shoes.*	*Use this cream to unclog your pores.*

#14 — Answer = A

Choice B is wrong because <u>that</u> doesn't get a comma. Choice D is wrong because <u>was featured ice cream</u> sounds bad. Choice A is correct because the sentence is about food, not sand.

desert	dessert
a dry, sandy place	a sweet food
Bring plenty of water when you camp in the desert.	*I'm so stuffed I have barely any room for dessert.*
Hint: <u>desert</u> has one S for <u>sand</u>; <u>dessert</u> has two S's for <u>sugar</u> and <u>sweet</u>	

#15— Answer = A

Choices C and D shouldn't sound great. You might also be able to hear that Choice B isn't quite right either. Choice A is correct because we're talking about one <u>instance</u>.

instance	instants
one event	multiple events (but the singular <u>instant</u> is used much more often)
In this instance, I don't think Bill knows what he's talking about.	*In only an instant, the fire had gotten out of control.*
Hint: if the sentence uses a singular pronoun, like <u>this</u>, then you need the singular <u>instance</u> or <u>instant</u>. The plural <u>instants</u> is unlikely.	

#16 — Answer = D

The rest of the sentence suggests the past tense because of <u>waved</u>. Only Choice D is in the past tense.

led	lead
the past tense of <u>lead</u>	to be in front (rhymes with <u>seed</u>); the hard metal (rhymes with <u>bed</u>)
The mayor led the parade down the wrong street.	*The opposition candidates lead in the polls.* *Ouch! You just hit me with a lead pipe!*
Hint: if you read all of the answer choices, you shouldn't make the mistake of confusing these two words; once you see <u>led</u> is an option, you should remember that <u>lead</u> rhymes with <u>seed</u>	

#17 — Answer = B

Choices A and D are wrong because <u>for</u> doesn't sound right. Choice B is correct because the sentence is talking about getting onto the beach.

access	excess
admission, entry	extra
The pass gave visitors access to a backstage tour.	*I need to go on a diet and lose some of this excess fat.*

#18 — Answer = C

Choices A and D are wrong because we're talking about <u>reading</u> words. Choice C is correct because we're talking about doing something <u>out loud</u>.

read	reed
turning letters into words and sentences	a piece of grass or small thin strip
I have so many pages to read for homework.	*Be careful of animals hiding in the reeds.*

allowed	aloud
able to; having permission	out loud
I'm not allowed to go out tonight.	*The charges were read aloud in front of the court.*
Hint: <u>aloud</u> includes the word <u>loud</u>, which is how you should read if asked to read <u>aloud</u>	

Answers: FCW 4

#19 — Answer = D

The first sentence is clearly negative, and the second sentence is clearly positive. We need a <u>but</u> word. Choice A is an <u>and</u> word, so you can eliminate it. Choice B is weird, but it doesn't sound like a contrast, so you can eliminate it. Choice D is correct because <u>irregardless</u> is not a word.

irregardless	regardless
not a word	showing a lack of concern; nevertheless
	Regardless of the weather, I'm going camping this weekend.

#20 — Answer = D

Choice B is wrong because <u>for</u> is wrong. Choice D is correct because the sentence is talking about a location.

cite	sight	site
to reference	having to do with seeing	location
Make sure you cite all of your sources in your research paper.	*I can't stand the sight of this giant mess.*	*This field was the site of a major battle during the war.*
Hint: you should link <u>cite</u> with <u>citation</u>, and it's called a <u>website</u> because it's a location (<u>site</u>) on the web. <u>Sight</u> is the other one.		

#21 — Answer = B

Choices C and D are wrong because a <u>record</u> doesn't have a size. Choice B is correct because the sentence is about <u>two boxers</u>.

better	best
used for 2 things	used for 3 or more things
I was always better at board games than my sister.	*But my dad was the best in our family. He'd always win.*
Hint: if the sentence is making a big point about telling you the number, then pay attention	

#22 — Answer = C

Hopefully Choice D looks bad because it's not a word. Neither is Choice A, but some people use it when they mean Choice C.

a lot	allot	alot
many	to give out, assign, distribute	not a word
I like candy a lot.	*To be fair, the teacher will allot each student three pieces of candy.*	
Hint: if you can replace the word with <u>a bunch</u> or <u>a ton</u>, then you can use <u>a lot</u>.		

#23 — Answer = C

Choice B hopefully sounds ridiculous. Choice D is the contraction <u>we will</u>. Choice C is correct because it's being used as an adverb to describe the action <u>did</u>. It also maybe sounds a bit better than <u>good</u> if you're used to more formal writing.

good	well
adjective (mostly); describes a condition	adverb (mostly); describes an action
The pitcher has a good fastball.	*He pitches well under pressure.*
Hint: this rule is a mess; trust your instincts — you get it right most of the time without thinking	

#24 — Answer = A

Choices B and C are wrong because <u>too</u> doesn't really sound good. Choice A is correct because the comedian is trying to <u>cause</u> laughter.

elicit	illicit
to cause, bring about	illegal
The professor used pop culture references to make his point, hoping to elicit a response from his bored students.	*The police chief promised to crack down on illicit activities within his jurisdiction.*
Hint: <u>illicit</u> contains the word <u>ill</u>, which suggests that it's something bad	

Answers: FCW 5

#25 — Answer = D

Choices B and C are wrong because the tense is incorrect. Choice D is correct because the <u>mythology</u> might <u>come before</u> the <u>settlement</u>.

proceed	precede
to go forward; continue	come before
Sorry I interrupted you. Please proceed with your argument.	*Thunder is typically preceded by a flash of lightning.*
Hint: the prefix <u>pre-</u> usually means <u>before</u>, so it makes sense that <u>precede</u> means <u>come before</u>	

#26 — Answer = C

Choice D hopefully sounds wrong. If you know the difference between the remaining words, you can also probably hear that Choice C is correct. Plus, the sentence is about disagreement.

decent	descent	dissent
good, kind	going down	disagreement
He's a decent man who always puts others first.	*The submarine's descent into the deep was slow and quiet.*	*The dictator deployed his army to stop all public dissent.*
Hint: <u>dissent</u> and <u>disagree</u> both start the same; <u>descent</u> is spelled like the similar word <u>descend</u>		

#27 — Answer = D

Choices B and C are wrong because <u>for</u> doesn't fit. Choice D is right because that's what we say. <u>Visual</u> should sound strange.

visible	visual
seeable, obvious	relating to sight
His anger was visible to everyone nearby.	*A graph is a visual representation of an algebraic equation.*
Hint: trust your instincts — you should be able to hear the correct word in most cases	

#28 — Answer = B

Choices C and D are wrong because <u>to</u> sounds bad. Since they're talking about time, <u>formerly</u> is the better fit.

formerly	formally
in the past	not informal
The president was formerly a reality TV show host… somehow.	*I'm formally withdrawing my application for this job.*
Hint: just drop the <u>-ly</u> and this becomes easier; <u>former</u> has to do with the past, and <u>formal</u> has to do with prom	

#29 — Answer = A

Choices B and C are wrong because the tense doesn't fit. Choice A is correct because the sentence is talking about making something less intense.

defuse	diffuse
to make less dangerous	spread out
Quick! Cut the blue wire and defuse the bomb!	*The candidate's diffuse support prevented him from winning a single precinct.*
Hint: <u>defuse</u> looks like what it means — you remove (<u>de-</u>) the <u>fuse</u>, which makes a bomb less dangerous	

#30 — Answer = C

Choices A and B sound bad. Choice C is the answer because Bertha is around a lot of people.

between	among
used with 2 things	used with 3 or more things
The rivalry between the two players is heating up.	*The consensus among their teammates is that both players are taking the rivalry too far.*

toward	towards
there is no difference between these words!	

Answers: FCW 6

#31 — Answer = B

Choices C and D should sound like they don't apply to this situation. You've probably heard former and latter used in academic writing before. Choice D is correct because the sentence is talking about agriculture, which is a reference to the farmers, the second of the two things listed.

former	latter
the first in a list of 2	the second in a list of 2
We can either go to the movies or stay in. I prefer the former because that new Brad Pitt comedy looks good.	*I'd rather do the latter. It's been a long week and we can just watch a movie on TV instead.*

Hint: the F in former stands for first; the L in latter stands for last

#32 — Answer = C

Choice C is correct because it's symmetrical to practical. The other choices don't sound as good.

desirable	desirous
pleasing	feeling desire
The fuel efficiency and standard luxury features make this a desirable car to own.	*Dennis is pretty ambitious and desirous of the boss's chair.*

Hint: desirous is a weird word and it's unlikely to be correct; trust your instincts

#33 — Answer = D

Choices B and C are the wrong tense. Choice D is correct because the sentence is talking about snow declining.

decline	recline
to go down	to lean back
The stock price has declined sharply over the past few months.	*Recline in this chair and enjoy the show!*

#34 — Answer = A

It's understandable if you have absolutely no idea on this question. Both words might be unfamiliar enough that even the prepositions don't seem wrong. Choice A is correct because organic foods would be good for farmers who don't use pesticides.

boon	bane
a beneficial thing	a harmful thing
The option to work from home has been a boon to families with small children.	*The increased rate of spam phone calls has been the bane of cell phone owners everywhere.*

Hint: you can think of Bane, who is a villain in Batman

#35 — Answer = A

We say this rule wrong all the time, so none of these choices might sound better or worse than the others. Choice A is correct because we're talking about <u>cookies</u>, which are countable.

fewer many	less much
used for countable things (number) *How many items do you have? 13? Okay, then you can't use the "10 items or fewer" line.*	used for uncountable things (amount) *She has much less patience than he does.*
Hint: some things can be divided into distinct pieces that could be counted (cookies, people, glasses of water); but other things can't get a number attached as easily (courage, time, water as an amount) — if you can put a number to something, then you should probably use <u>fewer</u>	

#36 — Answer = D

Choices B and C are wrong because <u>to</u> doesn't make sense. Choice D is correct because the sentence is about a direction.

forward	foreword
not backward *Move the desk forward a few inches, and then a little to the left.*	the intro to a book *The book's foreword explained how the author decided upon his subject.*
Hint: <u>foreword</u> includes <u>word</u>, which is what books are composed of	

Answers: FCW 7

#37 — Answer = A

Choice D should sound wrong because of <u>from</u>. Choice B should sound wrong because of the tense. Choice A is correct because the sentence is about referencing something.

allude	elude
refer to *The candidate managed to allude to her opponent's marital problems without directly insulting him.*	escape from *The criminals eluded capture by hiding out in an abandoned barn.*
Hint: try to link this rule with the similar one for the next question	

#38 — Answer = B

Choices C and D should sound wrong because of <u>with</u>. Choice B is correct because the sentence is about seeing something that isn't there.

allusion	illusion
a reference *The novel is filled with allusions to Shakespeare, but most readers won't recognize them.*	a false image *The intense heat created the illusion that there was a large puddle on the road ahead.*
Hint: you should be more familiar with the word <u>illusion</u> from daily life, so trust your instincts — if <u>illusion</u> doesn't make sense, then go with <u>allusion</u>	

#39— Answer = D

Choices B and C are wrong because they confuse president and precedent. Hopefully you know that Washington was a president who set precedents. Choice D is correct because Washington is being compared to a group that he's part of — the presidents.

any	any other
used to compare to a group the item or person is not part of	used to compare to a group the item or person is a part of
The coach is faster than any player on the baseball team.	The shortstop is faster than any other player on the baseball team.
Hint: this is a tricky rule; maybe remember that when what you're comparing is another member of the group, you have to use any other?	

president	precedent
a leader or head	a prior example
The president of the company stepped down because of the scandal.	The court had no choice but to follow precedent, even though the judges believed the earlier case had been wrongly decided.

#40 — Answer = A

Choices B and C are the wrong tense. Choice A is correct because the sentence is about things that go well together.

compliment	complement
praise	a good pairing
My new shoes have been getting a lot of compliments.	Complementary angles add to 90 degrees.
Hint: compliment has an I, and I love compliments!	

#41 — Answer = C

Choice B sounds the worst, then probably Choice D. You might be able to hear that Choice C is the only possible answer, but some people mispronounce Choice A. The last syllable rhymes with ate.

dominant	dominate
commanding, ruling	to be dominant
The dominant male made sure that no other moose came close to his territory.	A few big tech companies continue to dominate the market, pushing out competitors.
Hint: just take a second to actually pronounce these words in your head before answering	

#42 — Answer = D

Choices B and C are wrong because there should be no comma before and since it's only a list of two things. The sentence is hinting that we should pick a word that means the same thing as oppressed. Choice D is correct because persecuted means oppressed.

persecute	prosecute
to oppress	to sue in court
The dictator ruthlessly persecuted his opponents with threats and imprisonment.	The district attorney decided not to prosecute the CEO for misleading investors.
Hint: hopefully you've seen enough *Law and Order* to be comfortable with prosecute. The tricky thing is that tyrants often persecute their opponents by prosecuting them for fake crimes.	

Answers: FCW 8

#43 — Answer = B

Choice D sounds bad. From here, it's tricky. The sentence is about persuading the citizens, so assure is best.

assure	ensure	insure
to state confidently	to guarantee	to protect with insurance
I can assure you that I'm telling the truth.	Not even a 1600 on the SAT can ensure you admission to top schools.	The painting was insured in case it was stolen or damaged.

Hint: insure is probably the easiest to remember because it almost always has to do with insurance; assure is also easy because you're already comfortable with the similar word reassure, which basically means the same thing

#44 — Answer = D

Choices B and C are wrong because there's no need for apostrophes. Don't be tricked. Just because the sentence is about a doctor doesn't mean that we're talking about the people the doctor treats. The sentence is about the doctor's state of mind, so Choice D is correct.

patience	patients
ability to deal with annoying situations	people treated by a doctor
I have no patience for students who don't turn in assignments on time.	The patients were given an experimental treatment.

Hint: patients is clearly a plural of the word patient; if you're talking about multiple people, use patients; if you're not, then use patience

#45 — Answer = D

For once, it might be easier to focus on the Frequently Confused Words first. The sentence is saying that Shelby is at the high point of her career, so we should use peak, which refers to the top of a mountain. But she's not literally on top of anything, so on isn't the right preposition.

peak	peek	pique
high point	look at	annoy or excite
It took several hours, but we finally climbed the peak at sunset.	Can you take a peek at my essay to make sure I didn't make any mistakes?	His curiosity was piqued by the movie trailer, so he bought a ticket.

#46 — Answer = D

This looks like a Transitions question. You should be able to get rid of Choices B and C because but and yet mean the same thing. Choice D is the answer because neither must be paired with nor.

or	nor
pairs with either	pairs with nor
I'll either go to the movies or stay home.	I have neither the time nor the money to go shopping.

Hint: both neither and nor have Ns

#47 — Answer = A

We can mostly use the tenses to get this. Choices C and D could make sense based on the definition of reduce, but the tenses don't fit with the sentence. Choice A is correct because we're still talking about limiting the expenses.

deduct	deduce	reduce
to take away	to conclude	to make smaller
After I deduct the money you spent on gas, you'll owe $32 for the trip.	*Sherlock deduced that the murderer must have escaped through the window.*	*Many politicians want to cut spending as a way to reduce the national debt.*

#48 — Answer = B

Choices C and D are wrong because greater doesn't make sense. Choice B is correct because it's being used as a verb.

fair	fare
adjective — unbiased; light; clear noun — an exhibition or carnival	verb — to do well or poorly noun — ticket price; food
Everyone accused of a crime hopes for a fair trial. *I won a huge stuffed bear at the county fair.*	*The candidate did not fare well in the latest election.* *The restaurant provides ample fare and a cozy atmosphere.*
Hint: in your own life, you are far more likely to use fair in normal conversations; if you need a verb or you see the word used in a situation you aren't familiar with, then use fare	

Answers: FCW 9

#49 — Answer = D

Choices A and B are the wrong tense. Choice D is correct because affect is a verb.

#50 — Answer = B

Choices A and D are wrong because from is wrong. Choice B is correct because then is used when talking about time.

#51 — Answer = C

Choice D is wrong because it doesn't make a complete sentence if you keep reading. Choice B is wrong because the which is for things, but this sentence is about people. Choice C is right because the many people are doing the action, which is receiving cards. Also, whom sounds wrong.

#52 — Answer = A

Choice D is wrong because it's the past tense of paste. Choice C is wrong because the tense doesn't work. Choice B is wrong because we can't change the word to different tenses of pass. It is long pass time and long passes time sound terrible. That's a good sign that past is correct.

#53 — Answer = C

Choices A and D are wrong because this is a comparison, which means than is correct. Choice C is correct because penguins are countable, so we need to use fewer.

#54 — Answer = B

Choice A is wrong because no way they are team makes no sense. Choice C is wrong because we need the pronoun their to show that the team belongs to Jackson and DeAngelo. Choice B is correct because we do not want the pronoun their at the beginning.

Made in the USA
Monee, IL
21 February 2020